W9-BHI-476

# AT&T RELIABILITY MANUAL

# AT&T RELIABILITY MANUAL

Edited by

**David J. Klinger**
**AT&T Bell Laboratories**

**Yoshinao Nakada**
**AT&T Bell Laboratories**

**Maria A. Menendez**
**AT&T Bell Laboratories**

**VNR** VAN NOSTRAND REINHOLD
_____ New York

Library of Congress Catalog Card Number 89-24887
ISBN 0-442-31848-0

Printed in the United States of America

Van Nostrand Reinhold
115 Fifth Avenue
New York, New York 10003

Chapman and Hall
2-6 Boundary Row
London  SE1 8HN, England

Thomas Nelson Australia
102 Dodds Street
South Melbourne, Victoria 3205, Australia

Nelson Canada
1120 Birchmount Road
Scarborough, Ontario M1K 5G4, Canada

16  15  14  13  12  11  10  9  8  7  6  5  4  3  2

**Library of Congress Cataloging-in-Publication Data**

AT & T reliability manual/[edited by] David J. Klinger, Yoshinao
    Nakada, Maria A. Menendez.
        p.  cm.
    Rev. ed. of: Reliability information notebook. 5th ed.
    ISBN 0-442-31848-0
    1. Telecommunication—Apparatus and supplies—Reliability.
I. Klinger, David J.   II. Nakada, Yoshinao.   III. Menendez, Maria A.
IV. AT & T Bell Laboratories.    V. Reliability information notebook.
TK5103.A74   1989                              89-24887
621.382—dc20                                   CIP

# Preface

To meet the challenge of today's telecommunications market, new designs must do more than their basic system functions. They must also offer novel and increasingly sophisticated features to users. Custom very large scale integrated (VLSI) circuits and microprocessors are bringing about increases in system complexity and flexibility.

One result of the accelerating pace of technological innovation is the tightening of design schedules on new products. In this environment, lengthy field trials and user appraisals, common with telecommunications equipment in the past, often are not feasible. The concepts of good reliability engineering are, therefore, of paramount importance now. Before any systems are built, designers must have realistic estimates of the reliability that is expected of systems in the field. If the projected level of reliability is not adequate, designers must know what they can do to improve the design.

Once a system has been built, design and quality organizations must begin a monitoring process to ensure that reliability predictions are met in the actual performance. Many new systems *do not* initially perform as well as expected because of unanticipated device, design, or manufacturing problems. It is only through careful monitoring, comparison with expectations, and corrective feedback that these difficulties can be quickly identified and corrected. Subsequent improvement in system performance is often called "reliability growth."

The purpose of this *AT&T Reliability Manual* is to collect reliability concepts, methods, and currently available data into a single volume for telecommunications and electronics systems designers. The manual contains:

1. methods of estimating the *intrinsic reliability** of a system before its actual manufacture and use,

---

\* Intrinsic reliability is the reliability a system can achieve based on the types of devices and manufacturing processes used. Reliability estimation cannot predict device or equipment design errors or unanticipated defects induced in manufacturing. Such problems must be eliminated before the reliability estimates can be reached.

2. suggestions for improving system reliability, and

3. guidelines to help design organizations monitor system reliability through manufacturing tests and field appraisal programs.

Chapter 1 presents the fundamental concepts of reliability engineering. It describes the basic hazard rate model for electronic devices, emphasizing the practical aspects of electronic device reliability.

Chapter 2 expands on the device hazard rate model introduced in Chapter 1 and presents an introduction to device reliability. It gives details on the types of testing (such as accelerated life testing) and screening used by device organizations to ensure or improve device reliability. With a better understanding of these testing and screening techniques and their capabilities, system designers should be able to work more effectively with device engineers and reliability organizations. The effects of different application environments and burn-in are discussed also.

Chapter 3 presents an introduction to system reliability. It describes the procedure necessary for estimating system reliability based on the reliability of the devices used in manufacture. In addition to forming the basis for such procedures as life-cycle-cost analyses, these reliability estimates are essential for setting standards of reliability against which performance can be judged.

Chapter 4 tabulates estimates of device hazard rates obtained by AT&T Bell Laboratories. It contains a discussion of how the device application environment is taken into account in developing reliability estimates.

Chapter 5 discusses reliability monitoring programs—an integral part of the reliability feedback loop—and describes the steps that design organizations take to ensure that the reliability of AT&T manufactured systems meets customer expectations. This chapter describes how designers can implement these programs by using device burn-in, Operational Life Tests (OLT), and other reliability tests to correct problems during manufacture; by analyzing data from field quality appraisals; and by monitoring repairs of systems returned from the field to identify and correct potential system problems.

Chapter 6 contains reliability information on specific types of devices such as capacitors, inductors, integrated circuits, relays, and resistors. This section describes some of the known modes of failure and how system designers can overcome some of these potential problems to develop a more reliable design.

To keep up with the pace of today's telecommunications market and satisfy customer expectations of product reliability, sound reliability engineering practices must be implemented at all phases of the product life cycle. The reliability concepts and methods presented in this manual have proven useful toward advancing the reliability of AT&T products. The device information included here reflects years of research and experience by AT&T engineers and designers. It is hoped that this manual will serve as a valuable resource for estimating, improving, and monitoring reliability.

# Acknowledgments

The *AT&T Reliability Manual* is a revised, edited version of an AT&T Bell Laboratories document, the *Reliability Information Notebook*, that is currently in its fifth edition, and can be traced to origins in 1958. The *Reliability Information Notebook* has been produced as a cooperative project between the Integrated Circuit Reliability and Qualification Department and the Quality and Reliability Engineering Department of AT&T Bell Laboratories. Over the years, many people have contributed to the *Reliability Information Notebook*. Contributors to the chapter on reliability concepts have included F. W. Glenn, D. J. Klinger, M. A. Menendez, and R. C. Winans. Contributors to the sections on device reliability have included J. A. Augis, C. M. Bailey, W. A. Baker, C. W. Berthoud, R. M. Brownell, A. P. Broyer, L. DeChairo, J. G. Gribbons, F. C. Griese, E. Guancial, J. T. Hanlon, D. H. Hensler, D. J. Klinger, D. R. Kressler, H. A. Longfellow, M. A. Menendez, P. Miller, G. W. Mills, J. P. Mitchell, Y. Nakada, W. P. Simon, E. S. Sproles, and C. L. Winings. Contributors to the sections on system reliability and monitoring include H. D. Helms, D. P. Holcomb, D. J. Klinger, N. K. Kester, and G. T. Shaw. Contributors to the chapter on device hazard rates include C. M. Bailey, J. Gills, J. G. Gribbons, D. H. Hensler, D. J. Klinger, T. M. Porzuczek, and R. C. Winans. E. A. Elsayed, J. Gills, J. G. Gribbons, and A. Johnson were involved in the early stages of the manual project.

Many reviewers within AT&T must be thanked for their constructive comments. These include L. C. Alchesky, B. E. Aldridge, S. J. Amster, W. A. Baker, J. M. Balog, R. J. Berman, C. W. Berthoud, W. J. Bertram, C. K. Chan, L. C. Chan, L. H. Crow, H. Fickenscher, T. G. Ehrets, P. J. Gerondeau, P. Gillette, J. Gills, J. G. Gribbons, E. Guancial, H. D. Helms, D. H. Hensler, J. H. Hooper, M. Iannuzzi-Glogovsky, D. C. Lazar, A. M. R. Lin, M. C. Lin, M. J. LuValle, P. Miller, J. P. Mitchell, J. N. McGinn, L. S. Musolino, F. R. Nash, V. N. Nair, J. C. North, T. M. Porzuczek, J. J. Poukish, A. Reibman, T. F. Retajczyk, C. S. Sherrerd, E. S. Sproles, C. O. Thelen, M. Tortorella, T. L. Welsher, C. J. Uhl, and M. Youssef.

During the first stage of review, the comments of W. J. Bertram and W. A. Baker were particularly helpful, as were the comments of S. J. Amster, W. A. Baker, and

J. J. Poukish during the second stage of review, while the comments of W. A. Baker, M. Iannuzzi-Glogovsky and F. R. Nash were found to be particularly helpful during the final stages of review. The editors would like to thank these individuals especially, and Bill Baker in particular, for their comments.

The editors would also like to thank the copy editors, M. Hankinson and R. K. Wright, for their efforts during the production period. In the same vein, we should also like to thank M. Bace and M. Spencer of Van Nostrand Reinhold for their encouragement and continued support.

Finally, the editors would like to thank their management within AT&T Bell Laboratories, J. C. North, R. E. Kerwin, Y. S. Chen, and E. Fuchs, for their continued support.

# Contents

# AT&T RELIABILITY MANUAL

# 1

## RELIABILITY CONCEPTS

### INTRODUCTION

Electronic systems are designed to operate for a specified period of time, which is determined by customer requirements, as well as cost and performance. The ability of electronic systems to operate within this time frame is referred to generally as *reliability*.

Since electronic systems largely consist of electronic components (devices), system reliability is strongly dependent on the reliability of the individual components in the application environment. Currently, it is not feasible to predict the lifetime or degradation rate for any individual electronic component. It is, however, possible to treat large populations of components probabilistically, and thereby predict average lifetimes. The results obtained from measuring and then predicting component survivability are used as input to a probabilistic analysis of the reliability of an entire system.

Statistical measures of system reliability, based on such probabilistic analyses, form the basis for engineering decisions. The available reliability tools permit the systems designer to secure, in general, a system reliability *figure of merit** that meets the customer's requirements, provided the associated costs are acceptable.

The remaining sections in this chapter discuss the fundamentals of reliability concepts. The *Reliability Definitions* section lists the terms and their definitions that are used throughout this manual.

The *Mathematical Terminology: Measures of Reliability* section introduces the mathematical terminology used in reliability. It also discusses measures of reliability appropriate to nonmaintained systems.

---

\* A figure of merit is a numerical measure of performance, in this case, system reliability.

The *Maintained and Nonmaintained Systems* section describes the basic differences between maintained and nonmaintained systems. It also points out other distinctions that are relevant for systems which are maintained.

The *Measures of Reliability: Maintained Systems* section discusses measures of reliability for maintained systems. These measures include time to failure, failure rate, mean time between failure, mean operating time, mean repair time, and availability.

The *Electronic Device Hazard Rate Model* section discusses the common reliability model for electronic devices, the hazard rate model.

The *Failure Time Distributions* section introduces three statistical distributions for analyzing time-to-failure data. It also describes the principal properties of these frequently used failure-time distributions, including both their advantages and limitations.

The *AT&T Reliability Model* section describes the specific hazard rate model used by AT&T to characterize the reliability of electronic components.

The *Units and More Examples* section presents common units for electronic device hazard rate. It also gives supporting examples.

The *Considerations in the Infant Mortality Period* section discusses failures during the infant mortality period.

The *Considerations of Wearout During Service Life* section discusses points concerning the notion of wearout during the service life of components.


## RELIABILITY DEFINITIONS

*Reliability* is the ability of an item to perform a required function under stated conditions for a stated period of time.[1] The *required function* includes the specification of satisfactory operation as well as unsatisfactory operation. For a complex system, unsatisfactory operation may not be the same as failure. The *stated conditions* are the total physical environment including mechanical, thermal, and electrical conditions. The *stated period of time* is the time during which satisfactory operation is desired, commonly referred to as service life. In some cases, the stated period of time is relatively short. This is often true for military equipment. In a missile, for example, repairing a failure during flight is not considered. Consequently, the probability that failure does not occur during a mission is a completely adequate measure of reliability.

Depending on the application, different measures of reliability may be more appropriate than others. In particular, for applications in which the repair of failures is not considered, such as in a missile, *survivability* (given by the survivor function) may be an appropriate measure of reliability. *Survivability* is the probability that an item will perform a required function under stated conditions for a stated period of time, without failure. The differences between survivability and reliability are:

- Reliability, as previously defined, may only be described qualitatively while survivability may be described quantitatively. Reliability is an "ability" rather than a "probability;" this is appropriate if reliability is to describe an entire area of engineering.

- Reliability is defined broadly enough to include the possibility of repair, whereas survivability applies only to applications in which failures are not routinely repaired.

Most telecommunications equipment is designed for applications requiring continuous operation. As such, there is no well-defined mission time during which the equipment must operate properly. Consequently, other measures of reliability, more general than survivability, must be considered. These measures must include the possibility of repair as well as failure.

One such measure of reliability is *availability*, which applies to situations in which failures are routinely repaired. *Availability* is a measure of the degree to which an item is in an operable state when called upon to perform.[2] Throughout this book, availability is expressed as a probability. A more precise specification of availability is given in the *Mathematical Terminology: Measures of Reliability* section.

Another general measure of reliability, *maintainability*, refers to the maintenance process associated with system reliability. *Maintainability* is the degree to which an item is able to be retained in, or restored to, a specified operating condition.

The next section discusses these and other reliability concepts in more detail and introduces the mathematical relationships that form the basis for reliability assessment and prediction.

## MATHEMATICAL TERMINOLOGY: MEASURES OF RELIABILITY

This section introduces the mathematical terminology used in reliability. It introduces and gives examples in the use of reliability measures appropriate to nonmaintained systems.* Subsequent sections describe the terminology associated with maintained systems.

This section also defines and gives examples in the use of: the cumulative distribution function, the survivor function, the probability density function, the hazard rate, and the mean time to failure. The examples illustrate how the reliability engineer uses these measures of nonmaintained system reliability.

> *Note*: Those notions of probability and statistics that form the basis for a mathematical treatment of reliability will not be reviewed in this manual. To review background material, the reader is referred to texts on probability, statistics, and reliability.[3,4,5,6,7,8] For the most part, however, the mathematical material presented in this chapter is sufficiently basic so that, with some knowledge of calculus, the reader will be able to follow all discussions.

### Cumulative Distribution Function

The *cumulative distribution function* is one of the central concepts in reliability. If a system starts to operate at time $t = 0$, the probability that the system first fails at or before time $t$ is given by the cumulative distribution function and represented by

---

* A nonmaintained system is not repaired upon failure, nor does it receive preventive maintenance. See the *Maintained and Nonmaintained Systems* section for more information.

the function $F(t)$. If the failure time is denoted $X$, then

$$F(t) = \text{Prob} \ (X \leq t) \ . \tag{1.1}$$

The cumulative distribution function has the following properties:

$$F(t) = 0 \ \text{ for } \ t < 0 \ ,$$

$$0 \leq F(t) \leq F(t') \ \text{ for } \ 0 \leq t \leq t' \ ,$$

$$F(t) \to 1 \text{ as } t \to \infty \ . \tag{1.2}$$

## Survivor Function

The *survivor function* $S(t)$ gives the probability of surviving to time $t$ without failure.*    It is closely related to $F(t)$ by

$$S(t) = 1 - F(t) \ . \tag{1.3}$$

## Probability Density Function

What about the probability of failure within some time interval $\Delta t$, rather than the cumulative failure probability as represented by $F(t)$? The probability that the failure time $X$ lies between $t$ and $t + \Delta t$ is given by

$$Prob(t < X \leq t + \Delta t) = F(t + \Delta t) - F(t). \tag{1.4a}$$

Upon dividing by $\Delta t$ and taking the limit $\Delta t \to 0$, we get

$$\lim_{\Delta t \to 0} \frac{Prob(t < X \leq t + \Delta t)}{\Delta t} = \lim_{\Delta t \to 0} \frac{F(t + \Delta t) - F(t)}{\Delta t}$$

$$= F'(t) \tag{1.4b}$$

which we define to be the probability (of failure) density function; that is, the derivative of $F(t)$ is a *probability density function* represented by $f(t)$.

---

\*   Also commonly referred to as the reliability function, $R(t)$, in the field of electronic system reliability. In this manual, the biomedical terminology is used to avoid confusion with the broad definition of reliability given in the *Reliability Definitions* section.

That is,

$$f(t) = \frac{d}{dt} F(t) \quad \text{or} \quad F(t) = \int_0^t f(t') \, dt' \quad . \tag{1.4c}$$

So that

$$Prob \, (t < X \le t + t') = \int_t^{t+t'} f(u) \, du \quad . \tag{1.4d}$$

Similarly,

$$S(t) = \int_t^\infty f(t') \, dt' \quad \text{or} \quad f(t) = -\frac{d}{dt} S(t) \quad . \tag{1.4e}$$

Unlike $F(t)$ and $S(t)$, which are dimensionless, $f(t)$ has dimensions [time$^{-1}$]. As $f(t)$ is a probability density function, its integral must be finite. From the properties of $F(t)$ given in Equation (1.2), it is clear that

$$\int_0^\infty f(t) \, dt = \int_0^\infty \frac{dF(t)}{dt} \, dt = F(\infty) - F(0) = 1 - 0 = 1 \quad . \tag{1.5}$$

## Hazard Rate

For practical applications to nonmaintained systems, such as electronic components, the *instantaneous hazard rate* (or, simply, the hazard rate) is one of the more commonly used measures of reliability. The hazard rate $\lambda(t)$ represents the instantaneous rate of failure for units of a population *that have survived to time t.*

It is not surprising, therefore, that $\lambda(t)$ should be related to the survivor function $S(t)$. The relation of the hazard rate $\lambda(t)$ to the survivor function may be demonstrated as follows.

For a population of $N$ devices (units), the fraction of the original $N$ units that fail during a short time interval of length $\Delta t$ starting at time $t$ is

$$F(t+\Delta t) - F(t) \quad \text{or} \quad S(t) - S(t+\Delta t) \quad . \tag{1.6}$$

The average hazard rate $\Lambda(t)$, during the interval $\Delta t$, is the *fraction* of units that are operational at time $t$ *and* fail in the interval $\Delta t$. That is,

$$\Lambda(t) = \frac{S(t) - S(t+\Delta t)}{S(t) \cdot \Delta t} \quad . \tag{1.7}$$

Taking the limit $\Delta t \to 0$ gives the hazard rate.

$$\lambda(t) \equiv \lim_{\Delta t \to 0} \Lambda(t) = \lim_{\Delta t \to 0} \frac{S(t) - S(t+\Delta t)}{S(t) \cdot \Delta t}$$

$$= -\frac{1}{S(t)} \frac{dS(t)}{dt} = \frac{f(t)}{S(t)}$$

$$= \frac{f(t)}{1 - F(t)} = \frac{f(t)}{\int_t^\infty f(t')dt'} \quad . \tag{1.8}$$

As a result,

$$\lambda(t) = -\frac{d}{dt} \ln[S(t)] \quad , \tag{1.9}$$

which may be integrated to yield

$$S(t) = e^{-\int_0^t \lambda(t')dt'} \quad . \tag{1.10}$$

This is the form most commonly used to compute the survivor function when the integral of the hazard rate in the exponent can be easily evaluated. The hazard rate, like the probability density function, has dimensions $[\text{time}^{-1}]$. It is important to remember that the hazard rate is a rate of failure *relative* to the surviving population of units.

### Example 1.1

To better understand the reliability of some complex units, an engineer tests 1,000 units for 1,000 hours. When a unit fails, it is removed from the test; there is no repair. The engineer plots the probability density function for the observed results as a bar plot and fits a curve $f(t) = 0.001e^{-0.001t}$ to the data (see Figure 1-1).

**Question.** What can the engineer report about the hazard rate, cumulative distribution function, and survivability of these units?

Given the probability density function,

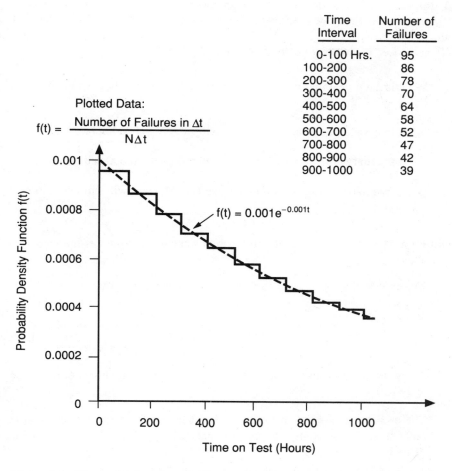

| Time Interval | Number of Failures |
|---|---|
| 0-100 Hrs. | 95 |
| 100-200 | 86 |
| 200-300 | 78 |
| 300-400 | 70 |
| 400-500 | 64 |
| 500-600 | 58 |
| 600-700 | 52 |
| 700-800 | 47 |
| 800-900 | 42 |
| 900-1000 | 39 |

Plotted Data:

$$f(t) = \frac{\text{Number of Failures in } \Delta t}{N \Delta t}$$

$f(t) = 0.001 e^{-0.001t}$

**Figure 1-1.** Observed failure time distribution for equipment with $N = 1,000$ units on test.

$$f(t) = 0.001 e^{-0.001t} \,, \tag{1.11}$$

then $F(t)$ and $S(t)$ may be readily calculated:

$$F(t) = \int_0^t f(x)dx = 1 - e^{-0.001t} \tag{1.12a}$$

$$S(t) = 1 - F(t) = e^{-0.001t} \tag{1.12b}$$

$$\lambda(t) = \frac{f(t)}{S(t)} = 0.001 \,. \tag{1.12c}$$

From the last Equation (1.12), the engineer concludes that the pattern of equipment failures may be described by a constant hazard rate of 0.1 percent per hour.

The engineer also wants to answer the following questions:

1.  What is the probability that a unit will operate without failure for the first 200 hours?

2.  What fraction of the initial 1,000 units will survive to 600 hours?

3.  What fraction of the initial 1,000 units will fail between 600 and 800 hours?

4.  What fraction of those units that survive to 600 hours will fail between 600 and 800 hours?

**Solution.**   The engineer makes the following calculations to answer the questions listed above.

1.  The probability of survival to time $t$ is given by $S(t)$. That is, for $t = 200$ hours,

$$S(t) = e^{-0.001t} = e^{-0.2} = 0.82 \ . \tag{1.13}$$

Therefore, the probability that a unit survives the first 200 hours of operation is 0.82 .

2.  The probability of survival to time $t_1$ is given by $S(t_1)$, where $t_1$ is equal to 600 hours. Consequently, the fraction that may be expected to survive to 600 hours is given by

$$S(600) = e^{-0.001(600)} = 0.55 \ . \tag{1.14}$$

That is, approximately 55 percent of the population on test may be expected to survive to 600 hours.

3.  The probability of failure between $t_1$ and $t_2$, where $t_2 > t_1$, is given by $S(t_1) - S(t_2)$. The probability of failure between 600 and 800 hours is then $[S(600) - S(800)] = e^{-0.001(600)} - e^{-0.001(800)} = 0.10$ . That is, there is approximately a 10 percent chance of failing in this interval.

4.  To determine the probability of failure between 600 and 800 hours, given survival to hour 600, the previous two results are combined; namely,

$$\text{probability of failure between 600 and 800 hours given survival to 600 hours} = \frac{S(600) - S(800)}{S(600)} = \frac{e^{-0.6} - e^{-0.8}}{e^{-0.6}}$$

$$= 1 - e^{-0.2} = 0.18 \ . \tag{1.15}$$

Therefore, the probability of failing between 600 and 800 hours, given survival to 600 hours, is about 18 percent.

### Mean Time To Failure

Another measure of reliability is the *mean time to failure* (MTTF). The MTTF is the expected time to failure. It is computed with the probability (of failure) density function:

$$\text{MTTF} = \overline{t} \equiv \int_0^\infty tf(t)dt \quad . \tag{1.16}$$

More precisely, $\overline{t}$ is the mean time to (first) failure.

### Example 1.2

The reliability engineer, introduced in Example 1.1, has been asked for the mean time to (first) failure (MTTF) of the complex units previously tested.

**Question.**   Based on the data displayed in Figure 1-1, what is the MTTF of these units?

**Solution.**   The probability (of failure) density function was found to be well described by $f(t) = \lambda e^{-\lambda t}$, where $\lambda = 0.001$. The MTTF then is given by

$$\text{MTTF} = \overline{t} = \int_0^\infty tf(t)dt = \int_0^\infty t\lambda e^{-\lambda t}dt ,$$

$$= \frac{1}{\lambda} \quad . \tag{1.17}$$

This result is both interesting and well known. Namely, the MTTF is equal to the reciprocal of the hazard rate *when the hazard rate is constant*, that is, when $\lambda(t) = \lambda$ or, equivalently, when the probability density function is of the form $\lambda e^{-\lambda t}$ and $\lambda$ is constant. Note that the MTTF, in general, is *not* equal to the reciprocal of the hazard rate. This is seen by comparing the definition given by Equations (1.8) and (1.16). For a general probability density function $f(t)$,

$$\int_0^\infty tf(t)dt \neq \frac{\displaystyle\int_t^\infty f(t')dt'}{f(t)} \quad . \tag{1.18}$$

The inequality may be replaced by an equality only if $f(t) = \lambda e^{-\lambda t}$ with $\lambda$ constant.

For maintained systems, other measures of reliability are needed to characterize system reliability. However, before introducing these quantities, some distinctions between nonmaintained systems (such as, electronic components) and maintained systems (such as, electronic switching systems) are discussed.

## MAINTAINED AND NONMAINTAINED SYSTEMS

Maintained systems are subject to repair and/or preventive maintenance. The reliability engineering of maintained systems differs from that of nonmaintained systems in two fundamental ways.* The first difference is obvious but, too often, not emphasized.

- If a system is repaired upon failure, *it may fail more than once*. Consequently, the reliability of a maintained system is not characterized by a single failure time, but by a *sequence of failure times*. Using the terminology introduced in the *Mathematical Terminology: Measure of Reliability* section, a maintained system may be characterized by the mean time to first failure, mean time to second failure, mean time to third failure, and so on.

- Maintenance *must be characterized probabilistically*, just as failure is characterized.

These basic differences between maintained and nonmaintained systems lead to the following additional distinctions, which should be kept in mind as the subject of maintained system reliability is introduced.

If repairs are performed when failure occurs, the number of systems being considered does not change; that is, when evaluating the rate of occurrence of failure, there is *no decreasing* population of systems. The rate of failure of maintained systems, therefore, is described somewhat differently than by a hazard rate, which is generally used to describe the rate of failure in nonmaintained systems. The term hazard rate is commonly used in actuarial calculations to describe the rate at which failure (death) events occur in a diminishing (aging and dying) population.

The rate of occurrence of failure in maintained systems is *not* necessarily relative to a diminishing population. The failure rate is defined to be the time rate of change of the expected number of failures. A more precise definition of failure rate is given in the next section.

Similarly, the MTTF, is most appropriate for nonmaintained systems. If a system undergoes repeated cycles of failure and repair, then it is the *times between failure* that are most important because these times characterize the reliability of a maintained system over its service life. The next section discusses this and other measures of maintained system reliability.

---

* Chapter 3 gives a more detailed discussion of maintained system reliability.

## MEASURES OF RELIABILITY: MAINTAINED SYSTEMS

Maintained systems undergo repeated cycles of failure and repair. Figure 1-2 shows several such cycles for an unspecified, single system.

In discussing maintained system reliability, the *sequence* of times to failure and the *sequence* of times to repair must be characterized *probabilistically*, just as the *single* time to failure of a nonmaintained system was characterized in previous sections.

As shown in Figure 1-2, the time between startup (or turn on) of a system and first failure, is called $X_1$. This is the *time of first failure* of the maintained system. (In the discussion of nonmaintained systems it was called $X$, with no subscript.) The time between startup and second failure is denoted $X_2$. This is the *time of second failure* of the maintained system. Times of third, fourth, and subsequent failure are defined similarly and are denoted $X_3, X_4$, etc. The $R_i$ represent the times at which the repair of the $i^{th}$ failure are completed. Similarly to the $X_i$, the $R_i$ are referred to as times of repair; that is, $R_1$ is the time of first repair (completion), $R_2$ is the time of second repair, etc.

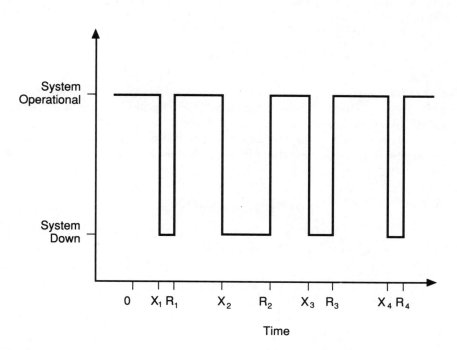

**Figure 1-2.** Failure and repair cycle for a maintained system. The $X_i$ are times of failure and the $R_i$ are times at which repair was completed. Note that $X_1$ was previously referred to in Equation (1.1) as $X$, the time to failure.

It is more convenient, however, to focus on the *operating times between completion of repair* (or startup) *and failure*, more commonly referred to as *operating times* or *up times* defined as

$$Y_i \equiv \begin{cases} X_i & i=1 \\ \\ X_i - R_{i-1} & i>1 \ . \end{cases} \qquad (1.19)$$

The partial sums of the $Y_i$, denoted $Z_i$, are defined as

$$Z_i \equiv Y_1 + Y_2 + \cdots + Y_i \ . \qquad (1.20)$$

That is, $Z_i$ represents the total operating time up to the $i^{\text{th}}$ failure. Similar definitions can be made for the repair process. However, to keep subsequent expressions simple, repair times are considered negligible in this section unless explicitly mentioned. With the repair times negligible, $Z_i$ represents the total time up to the $i^{\text{th}}$ failure and is equal to $X_i$ for all $i$. Note that now, with repair times negligible, the times of completion of repair coincide with the times of failure, that is, $R_i=X_i$ for all $i$. A cumulative distribution function for each $Z_i$ may now be defined:

$$F_i(t) = \text{Prob} \ (Z_i \leq t) \ . \qquad (1.21)$$

The $F_i$ must satisfy the properties of a cumulative distribution function given in Equation (1.1). Given a cumulative distribution function for each $Z_i(t)$, the sequence of failure times is fully characterized.

The $N(t)$ is defined as the number of failures that have occurred as of time $t$. This number of failures is less than $i$, if and only if the $i^{\text{th}}$ failure time $X_i$ is greater than $t$.[9] That is,

$$N(t) < i \ \text{ if and only if } \ X_i > t \ . \qquad (1.22)$$

The probability of these two events then is equal:

$$\text{Prob} \ [N(t) < i] = \text{Prob} \ (X_i > t) \ ,$$

$$= \text{Prob} \ (Z_i > t) \ ,$$

$$= 1 - F_i(t) \ . \qquad (1.23)$$

The second equality in Equation (1.23) follows from our assumption that repair time is negligible. Recall that, in this case, $X_i = Z_i$ for all $i$. The third equality in Equation (1.23) follows from the definition of a cumulative distribution function.

The probability of $N(t)$ being *equal* to $i$, with repair times negligible, is constructed by using Equation (1.23),

$$\text{Prob } [N(t) < i+1] - \text{Prob } [N(t) < i] = [1-F_{i+1}(t)] - [1-F_i(t)] , \qquad (1.24)$$

which may be rewritten,

$$\text{Prob } [N(t) = i] = F_i(t) - F_{i+1}(t) . \qquad (1.25)$$

The expression for the average value of $N(t)$ follows from Equation (1.25):

$$\overline{N(t)} = \sum_{i=1}^{\infty} i \text{ Prob } [N(t) = i]$$

$$= \sum_{i=1}^{\infty} i\{F_i(t) - F_{i+1}(t)\} = \sum_{i=1}^{\infty} iF_i(t) - \sum_{i=1}^{\infty} iF_{i+1}(t)$$

$$= \sum_{i=1}^{\infty} (i-1+1) F_i(t) - \sum_{i=1}^{\infty} i F_{i+1}(t)$$

$$= \sum_{i=1}^{\infty} (i-1) F_i(t) + \sum_{i=1}^{\infty} F_i(t) - \sum_{i=1}^{\infty} i F_{i+1}(t)$$

$$= \sum_{i=1}^{\infty} i F_{i+1}(t) + \sum_{i=1}^{\infty} F_i(t) - \sum_{i=1}^{\infty} i F_{i+1}(t)$$

$$= \sum_{i=1}^{\infty} F_i(t) . \qquad (1.26)$$

## Failure Rate

A *failure process* is a mathematical description of the *sequence*[3,10] of failure times. The *failure rate* of a failure process is given by [11]

$$v(t) = \frac{d}{dt} \overline{N(t)} . \qquad (1.27)$$

Given a failure process defined by the $F_i(t)$, the rate of occurrence of failure is the time derivative of the average value of $N(t)$. Note again that the failure rate is *not* conditional on the surviving population, as is the hazard rate. If the repair times are considered to be negligible, for example, repair is effected instantaneously, then

$$v(t) = \sum_{i=1}^{\infty} \frac{d}{dt} F_i(t) = \sum_{i=1}^{\infty} f_i(t) . \qquad (1.28)$$

This formalism leads to a definition of the mean operating time.

### Mean Operating Time and Mean Time Between Failure

The *mean operating time* (MOT) is the average time of system operation during which all functions are performed within specified limits.   Use caution in interpreting this definition. In general, the average time of system operation (the average value of $Y_i$) between failures is not constant. Unless the system reliability model in use is of a rather restrictive nature, the average operating time will be a *function of time*.

If, however, the model of system reliability is such that after a failed system is repaired the system is as good (or as bad) as new, then

$$MOT = a \text{ constant } \quad and$$

$$MOT = MTTF \tag{1.29}$$

> *Note:* In general, Equation (1.29) *does not hold*. For a discussion of when Equation (1.29) does hold, refer to Chapter 3. It is worth pointing out here, without proof, that when the failure rate is constant, it is numerically equal to the hazard rate.[11]

In this introductory section, other measures of system reliability are suggested for use. For example, the reciprocal of the failure rate $1/v(t)$ may be a useful measure of the times between failures, although $1/v(t)$ is *not* the mean times between failures (MTBF) nor the mean operating time. The mean time between failures* is given by the average of $X_i-X_{i-1}$. Again, this is not the mean operating time, which is given by the average of $X_i-R_{i-1}$. The MOT is equal to the MTBF only when repair times are negligible.

System reliability, however, is often quoted in terms of an MTBF that is constant. Note that a constant system failure rate is implied by any reference to a constant MTBF. Because equipment failure rates in early life typically decrease with time, it is difficult to relate reliability performance to the objective MTBF. By using a plot, such as Figure 1-3, a designer can state that after four months of operation the equipment is meeting its design objective and will continue to do so even if the improving (declining) failure rate levels off and approaches a constant failure rate. Barring some unforeseen wearout condition (that might start failure rates rising again), failure-rate improvement beyond the level attained by the fourth month of operation will reflect better performance than that required by the design objective.

The next section discusses *availability*, a commonly used measure of maintained system reliability. Note that repair times may no longer be neglected. It will become clear that if repair times are neglected, the system is always "available."

---

* Also called mean cycle (of failure and repair) time.

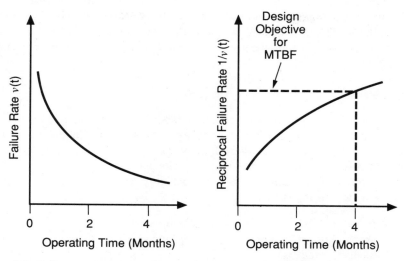

**Figure 1-3.** Failure rate and reciprocal failure rate versus time for time-dependent failure rate.

To model system availability, the time required to repair a system must be quantified. Until now, the assumption has been made that the time to repair is negligible, that is, effectively zero. The process of repair can be modeled in the same manner as failure. Then, the *downtime between occurrence of failure and completion of repair* or the *time to effect repair*, or the *repair time*, (see Figure 1-2) is given by

$$B_i = R_i - X_i \ , \quad i > 1 \ . \tag{1.30}$$

Similarly, cumulative distribution functions for the various repair times may be introduced, $G_i\,(t)$, and an average number of repairs $\overline{N_r(t)}$ may be defined as for failure. However, unless the *operating times* are negligible, the expression for the average, or expected number of repairs is not as simple as Equation (1.26) is for failure. More generally, the expected number of repairs is,

$$\overline{N_r}\,(t) = \sum_{i=1}^{\infty} Prob\ (R_i \le t) \tag{1.31}$$

where the $R_i$ are the various times of completion of repair. See Figure 1-2.

The time derivative of $\overline{N_r(t)}$ is the repair rate $v_r(t)$. That is,

$$v_r(t) = \frac{d}{dt}\ \overline{N_r(t)} \ . \tag{1.32}$$

## Mean Repair Time

The *mean repair time* is the average time that a system is "down" or inoperable. The same caution that applied to MOT also applies to MRT: the MRT (the average value of the $B_i$) is *not*, in general, a constant. Unless the system model of repair is of a rather restrictive nature, the average time to effect a repair will be a function of time.

## Availability

As mentioned in the *Introduction* section, reliability of maintained systems is often expressed in terms of availability. Strictly speaking, there are a number of different availabilities. This section describes three types: the instantaneous availability, the interval availability, and the steady-state or limiting availability.

The *instantaneous availability* is the probability that a system is operating at time $t$. For systems that have

- failure times that are independent and identically distributed (iid),[3] and probability (of failure) density functions given by $f(t) = \lambda e^{-\lambda t}$ where $\lambda$, the hazard rate, is constant and

- repair times that are iid and probability (of repair) distribution functions given by $g(t) = \mu e^{-\mu t}$, where $\mu$, the equivalent of hazard rate for repair, is constant,

then the instantaneous availability is given by[8,9,11]

$$A(t) = \frac{\mu}{\lambda + \mu} + \frac{\lambda}{\lambda + \mu} e^{-[(\lambda + \mu)t]} \quad . \tag{1.33}$$

The *interval availability* is the average of the instantaneous availability over some interval of time. Interval availability is the definite integral of $A(t)$ over an interval of time, divided by that interval of time, so that

$$A(t_1, t_2) \equiv \frac{1}{t_2 - t_1} \int_{t_1}^{t_2} A(t)dt \quad . \tag{1.34}$$

The *limiting or steady-state availability* is the availability of a system in the limit of large operating times. More precisely, the limiting availability is given by the limit of the instantaneous availability as $t \to \infty$. In the case that Equation (1.33) holds (discussed above), the limiting availability is given by

$$A = A_L = \lim_{t \to \infty} A(t) = \frac{\mu}{\lambda + \mu} \quad . \tag{1.35}$$

As this notation implies, an unqualified use of the term availability will refer to the limiting availability.

## ELECTRONIC DEVICE HAZARD RATE MODEL

Any of the functions $F(t)$, $f(t)$, or $\lambda(t)$ can be used to describe a reliability model for electronic devices. The definitions given in the *Mathematical Terminology: Measures of Reliability* section show that any one of these functions is sufficient to specify a probability of failure distribution uniquely. From any of the three functions, the other two may be obtained: see Equations (1.4), (1.8), and (1.9). Furthermore, these functions provide a measure of the probability of the first and only failure occurring in a nonmaintained system. Electronic components experience failure only once—when integrated circuits, transistors, and capacitors fail, they are *replaced* rather than *restored* to working condition. In this manual, reliability models for nonmaintained systems, such as electronic components, are presented in terms of the hazard rate.

Historically, hazard rates have been modeled in terms of the traditional bathtub curve shown in Figure 1-4. Patterned on actuarial tables for human mortality, such a curve has three regions, each with distinct characteristics. The regions are associated with infant mortality, steady-state operation, and wearout.

*Infant mortality* is characterized by an initially high, but rapidly decreasing hazard rate. The early failures come from a small fraction of the population that can be considered "weak." These weak units have defects that are not immediately fatal, but cause failure within a short period of time.

After the bulk of the weak units fail, operation moves into the *steady-state region*, in which failures occur at a much lower rate, characterized by a constant or slowly changing hazard rate.

*Wearout* occurs when the hazard rate rises and the remaining units fail. Wearout, strictly speaking, is defined to occur when the hazard rate increases monotonically with time. The notion of a wearout period dates back to the first observations of the performance of mechanical equipment in which physical wear occurs and eventually leads to failure. Severe reliability problems occur when equipment in service reaches this wearout region.

In most cases, nonmechanical electronic devices do not exhibit wearout during the intended device life.* Their failures are observed predominantly in the infant mortality and steady-state hazard rate periods. Sometimes, however, low-quality devices of unproven reliability exhibit wearout failures. Designers of high-reliability equipment avoid using these devices. Electronic devices from reputable suppliers should not be expected to exhibit wearout during the intended device life. This should be contrasted with interconnections[13] where an *increasing* hazard rate, a characteristic of wearout, has been observed.

Figure 1-5 shows the conceptual reliability model for electronic devices used within AT&T.[14] Wearout is not included because it is not expected to occur for most devices during service life.† The failures that occur *during* operation are called

---

\* There are a few types of nonmechanical devices for which failures corresponding to wearout can occur. Examples are light bulbs in which the filament can degrade and electrolytic capacitors in which the electrolyte can dry out.

† This is not to say that wearout is not studied at AT&T, merely that the experience of reliability engineers at AT&T does not point to a need to model wearout as a feature of most electronic devices. By studying wearout failure mechanisms, devices may be designed not to display such failure mechanisms during the intended service life.

*device operating failures* (DOFs). Failures that occur during first tests are called *dead-on-arrivals* (DOAs). DOAs are another aspect of infant mortality and are represented by the vertical box in Figure 1-5. DOAs can occur during tests after a new level of assembly or after shipment, even though the devices might have worked properly before. For example, DOAs can be found during the first circuit pack test after circuit pack assembly or during a system test after the circuit packs are assembled into a system. Some DOAs appear later when the system is first tested after shipment to the field. In addition, DOAs cannot be related to operating time. A component can test as satisfactory, be assembled into equipment, and then fail to work before the system has been in operation. The rate of such failures may be event-dependent rather than time-dependent. Handling during manufacture may damage a component or induce failure of a previously damaged component. Also, DOAs are not reflected in the reliability model. Although their existence is recognized, an accurate quantitative estimate of failure due to DOAs is not currently possible.

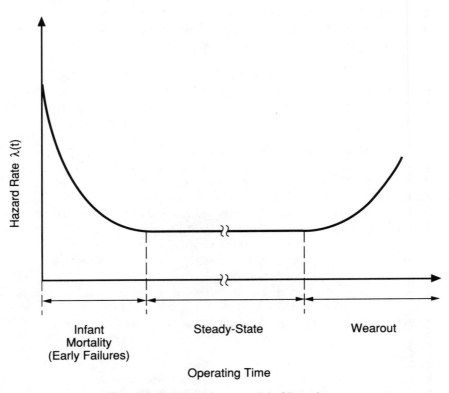

**Figure 1-4.** Bathtub curve model of hazard rate.

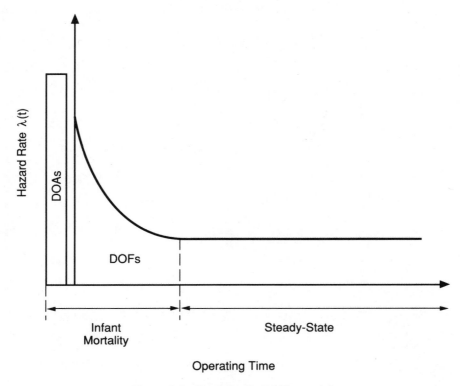

**Figure 1-5.** Conceptual reliability model.

## FAILURE TIME DISTRIBUTIONS

Previous sections discussed probability density functions and hazard rates in general terms. This section introduces three statistical distributions that are useful in analyzing time-to-failure data and presents the principal properties of the most commonly used failure-time distributions, their applications, and their limitations.

### The Exponential Distribution

The *exponential distribution* is widely used in reliability analysis. It is the simplest distribution, characterized by a constant hazard rate. The exponential distribution is often used to describe a steady-state hazard rate and has historically been used to model the performance of equipment that is beyond the infant mortality period.

Pertinent functions for the exponential distribution are listed below and illustrated in Figure 1-6:

- The probability density function is:

$$f(t) = \lambda e^{-\lambda t} \quad (t \geq 0 \ \lambda > 0) \ . \tag{1.36}$$

- The cumulative distribution function is:

$$F(t) = \int_0^t f(x)dx = 1 - e^{-\lambda t} \ . \tag{1.37}$$

- The survivor function is:

$$S(t) = 1 - F(t) = e^{-\lambda t} \ . \tag{1.38}$$

- The hazard rate is constant:

$$\lambda(t) = \frac{f(t)}{S(t)} = \lambda \ . \tag{1.39}$$

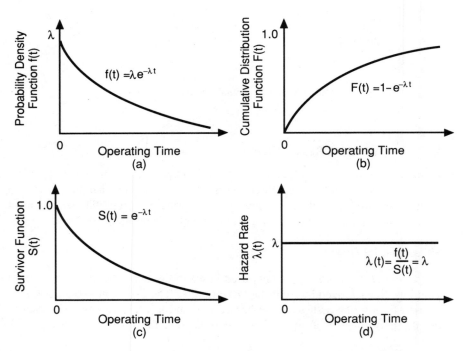

**Figure 1-6.** Plots of $f(t)$, $F(t)$, $S(t)$ and $\lambda(t)$ for the exponential distribution. The exponential distribution is extremely convenient. With a single number, the hazard rate and, hence, the reliability of a nonmaintained system may be characterized.

## The Lognormal Distribution

The *lognormal distribution* has often been used to describe failure time data obtained from accelerated testing of semiconductor devices (see Chapter 2). It is closely related to the normal distribution. For the lognormal distribution, the natural logarithm of the failure time is distributed normally; see Equation (1.40). Pertinent functions for the lognormal distribution are listed below:

- The probability density function is:

$$f(t) = \frac{1}{\sigma t \sqrt{2\pi}} \, e^{-\frac{1}{2}\left[\frac{ln(t)-\mu}{\sigma}\right]^2} \quad (\sigma > 0) \; . \tag{1.40}$$

- The cumulative distribution function is:

$$F(t) = \frac{1}{\sigma \sqrt{2\pi}} \int_0^t \frac{1}{t} \, e^{-\frac{1}{2}\left[\frac{ln(t')-\mu}{\sigma}\right]^2} \, dt' \; . \tag{1.41}$$

- The survivor function is:

$$S(t) = 1 - F(t). \tag{1.42}$$

- The hazard rate is:

$$\lambda(t) = \frac{f(t)}{S(t)} \; . \tag{1.43}$$

In Figure 1-7, the lognormal distribution is plotted for several values of $\sigma$, where $\sigma$ is the standard deviation of the natural logarithm of the failure time. The location parameter $\mu$ is equal to the mean of the natural logarithm of the failure time. Note that regardless of the value of the two lognormal parameters, $\sigma$ and $\mu$, the hazard rate associated with the lognormal distribution always decreases at sufficiently large times.

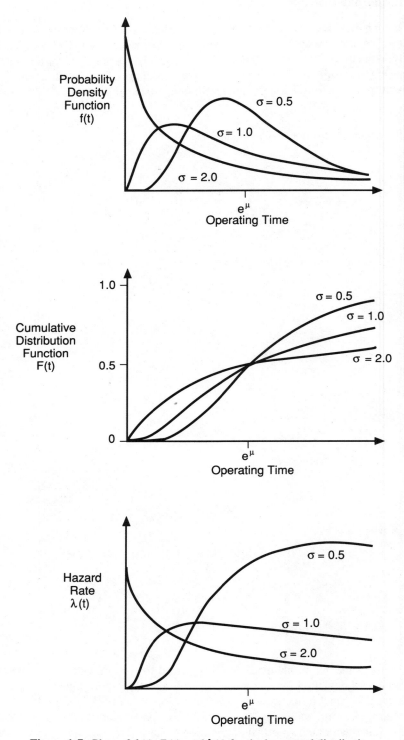

**Figure 1-7.** Plots of $f(t)$, $F(t)$, and $\lambda(t)$ for the lognormal distribution.

## The Weibull Distribution

The *Weibull distribution* is one of the most widely used life distributions, especially in modeling infant mortality failures.*  For a Weibull distribution, the hazard rate varies as a power of device age.  The principal properties of the Weibull distribution are listed below:

- The probability density function is:

$$f(t) = \lambda_1 t^{-\alpha} e^{\frac{-\lambda_1 t^{1-\alpha}}{1-\alpha}} , \qquad (1.44)$$

  where $\lambda_1 > 0$ is the scale parameter of the distribution hazard rate, and $\alpha$ is the shape parameter of the distribution.

- The cumulative distribution function is:

$$F(t) = \int_0^t f(x)dx = 1 - e^{\frac{-\lambda_1 t^{1-\alpha}}{1-\alpha}} . \qquad (1.45)$$

- The hazard rate is:

$$\lambda(t) = \lambda_1 t^{-\alpha} , \quad \alpha < 1 , \quad t > 0 . \qquad (1.46)$$

- The survivor function is:

$$S(t) = 1 - F(t) = e^{\frac{-\lambda_1 t^{1-\alpha}}{1-\alpha}} . \qquad (1.47)$$

When $0 < \alpha < 1$, the hazard rate, $\lambda(t)$, decreases with time: See Equation (1.46). Therefore, a positive $\alpha$ is used to model infant mortality.  Note that if $\alpha < 0$, the Weibull hazard rate increases with device age.  Device wearout may be modeled for this range of the Weibull shape parameter.  If $\alpha = 0$, the hazard rate is constant and the exponential distribution is recovered.  This shows that the exponential distribution is a special case of the Weibull distribution.

The "shape" of the Weibull distribution changes with $\alpha$; therefore, $\alpha$ is called the shape parameter.*  The variation of the shape of the distribution, as displayed by the probability density function, is shown in Figure 1-8.

---

\*    It is important to note that the parametrization of the Weibull presented herein is different from those commonly found in the reliability or statistics literature.  This form has been chosen for use within AT&T so that the function most commonly used by AT&T reliability engineers, the hazard rate, is simple.  Care must be used in comparing this parametrization to one of those used in the literature.

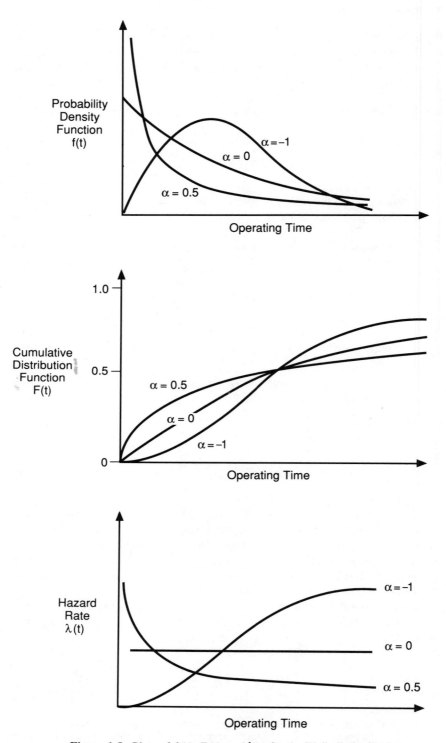

**Figure 1-8.** Plots of $f(t)$, $F(t)$, and $\lambda(t)$ for the Weibull distribution.

## AT&T RELIABILITY MODEL

This section describes a specific hazard rate model. In particular, this is the hazard model used within AT&T to characterize electronic component reliability. The hazard rate in the infant mortality region is modeled by a Weibull hazard rate that decreases with time.[14] That is,

$$\lambda(t) = \lambda_1 t^{-\alpha} , \qquad 0 \leq \alpha < 1 , \quad 0 < t < t_c, \qquad (1.48)$$

where $t_c$, the crossover time, is taken to be equal to $10^4$ hours. One feature of this distribution is that the hazard rate is a straight line when plotted on a log-log paper as in Figure 1-9. In such a plot, the slope is $-\alpha$, with $0 \leq \alpha < 1$, and the intercept at $t = 1$ hour is $\lambda_1$. Beyond some time $t_c$, taken to be $10^4$ hours (slightly over 1 year), the hazard rate is assumed to remain constant; that is, $\lambda(t) = \lambda_L$, for $t \geq t_c = 10^4$ hours. A constant hazard rate is a characteristic of the exponential distribution. Therefore, the exponential is the appropriate distribution for the steady-state region of the model.

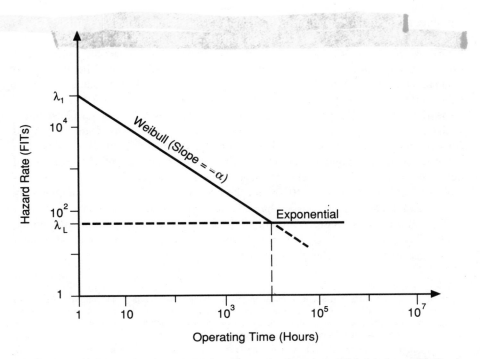

**Figure 1-9.** AT&T hazard rate model for electronic components (shown by solid lines). The model is a combination of a Weibull and an exponential distribution. The hazard rate unit is a FIT ($10^{-9}$ hour$^{-1}$). The hazard rates are typical but do not correspond to any particular device.

Modeling of device reliability is discussed in detail in Chapter 2. The basis for this model is described here as background.

There are two distinct sources of information on device reliability: accelerated life tests* and monitored performance in the factory or field. These provide two quite different measures of reliability. Accelerated life tests are meant to provide information about reliability in the very long term, that is, several to scores of years.[†] Factory and field data give a measure of actual device reliability in the short term, that is, less than a few years.

Because most devices are quite reliable, only a small fraction of those put into service have failed even after many years. Therefore, accelerated test conditions are *required* to observe the lifetime distribution of the main population of devices. For semiconductor devices, the main lifetime distribution in accelerated tests usually is well described by a lognormal failure distribution. Based on such measurements, the distribution of lifetimes at normal use conditions can be estimated.

Furthermore, the general *level* of the hazard rate in the long term can be estimated from experiments performed under accelerated test conditions. Specifically, the maximum hazard rate, at use conditions, can be determined from accelerated life test data. This hazard rate may be used to obtain a *bound* on the hazard rate during the service life of the component (see Figure 1-10). The discussion of accelerated testing in Chapter 2 describes how this is done. In the plot shown in Figure 1-10, the hazard rate estimate obtained for long-term (> 1 year) operating times is of the order of the Weibull hazard rate, evaluated at $t = 10^4$ hours.

In contrast to the long-term behavior, short-term hazard rates can be directly measured. These are based on field tracking studies that usually continue for no more than 2 to 3 years where, primarily, only infant mortality is observed. In such studies, a plot of the logarithm of the observed hazard rate versus the logarithm of time is usually found to be reasonably well fit by a straight line. Therefore, such data can be adequately modeled by a Weibull distribution. These data are the basis for the infant mortality portion of the hazard rate model in Figure 1-10.

Beyond the infant mortality period these field studies have not provided much statistically significant information about the hazard rate. The commonly used constant hazard rate model associated with the exponential distribution is then adopted for times beyond $10^4$ hours. This is a conservative approach if the hazard rate continues to fall or levels off. The chosen crossover time of $10^4$ hours is arbitrary but reasonable. By $10^4$ hours the observed hazard rate is changing very slowly, and, therefore, the constant hazard rate model should be adequate.

Figure 1-11 shows Figure 1-9 replotted on linear scales rather than on logarithmic scales. The plots in Figure 1-11 might provide a more intuitive depiction of how the various distributions change with time.

---

\* In an accelerated test, environmental conditions such as temperature, voltage, and humidity are altered to place a greater degree of stress on the device than there would be in the application environment. This increased level of stress is applied to *accelerate* whatever reaction is believed to lead to failure, hence the term accelerated stress testing, or simply accelerated testing.

† An assumption implicit in accelerated testing is that whatever causes failure at the more stressful conditions also causes failure at use conditions. This need not be, and often is not, true. See Chapter 2 for a discussion of accelerated life testing.

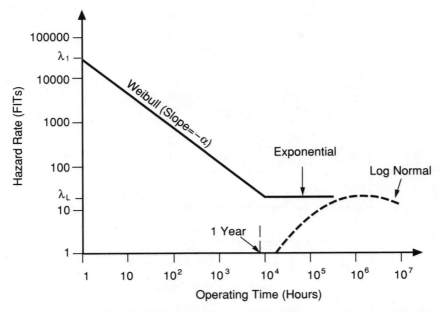

**Figure 1-10.** Possible relationship between accelerated stress test results and the AT&T device hazard rate model is shown by the dashed curves. The hazard rate unit is a FIT ($10^{-9}$ hour $^{-1}$). The hazard rates are typical but do not correspond to any particular device.

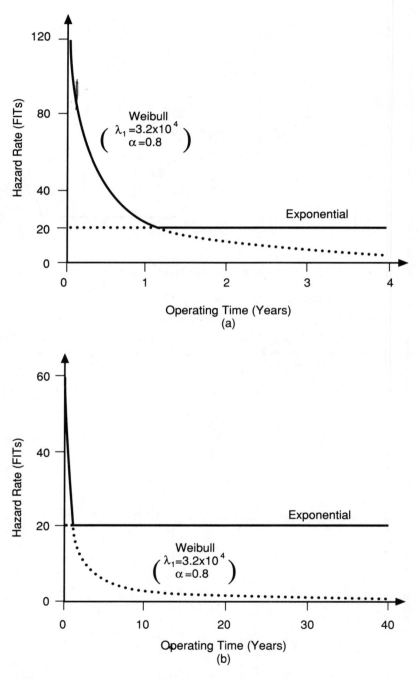

**Figure 1-11.** AT&T hazard rate model for electronic components (linear scales).

## UNITS AND MORE EXAMPLES

Frequently, device reliability is expressed in terms of the device hazard rate, and device hazard rate is expressed in units of percent of failures per unit time. Other common units for hazard rate include:

- FITs: 1 FIT is a unit of hazard rate equal to $10^{-9}$ hour$^{-1}$. This may be interpreted to mean a failure probability of $10^{-9}$ in the next hour given survival up to the time in question. The unit of hazard rate called a FIT was developed to characterize constant hazard rates but may also be used to characterize nonconstant hazard rates;

- Percent failing per 1,000 hours of operation (common in military work).

Note that system availability $A(t)$ and survivability $S(t)$ are probabilities and, therefore, are dimensionless. As previously mentioned, the hazard rate has dimensions [time$^{-1}$].

## Example 1.3

The hazard rate of a piece of equipment is constant and estimated at 325,000 FITs.

**Question 1.** What is the probability that this equipment will first fail in the interval of:

- 0 to 6 months of operation?

- 6 to 12 months?

- 6 to 12 months if it has survived the first 6 months?

**Solution.** The constant hazard rate, $\lambda = 325,000$ FITs, may be rewritten

$$325{,}000 \text{ FITs } \frac{10^{-9}/\text{hour}}{1 \text{ FIT}} = \frac{325{,}000}{10^9 \text{ hour}} = 3.25 \times 10^{-4}/\text{hour} \quad . \qquad (1.49)$$

The probability of failing in the first 6 months (6 months = 4,380 hours) is

$$F(6 \text{ months}) = 1 - S(6 \text{ months}) \qquad (1.50)$$

for the exponential model, $S(t) = e^{-\lambda t}$, so that

$$S(4{,}380 \text{ hours}) = e^{-1.4} = 0.24 \quad . \qquad (1.51)$$

The probability of failure in the first 6 months is 0.76. The probability of failing in the interval from 6 to 12 months is

$$S\,(6\text{ months}) - S\,(12\text{ months}) = 0.241 - 0.058$$

$$= 0.18\,. \qquad (1.52)$$

The probability of failing in the interval from 6 to 12 months, given the system survives the first 6 months, is

$$\frac{S\,(6\text{ months}) - S\,(12\text{ months})}{S\,(6\text{ months})} = 0.76\,. \qquad (1.53)$$

*Note:*   This is. the same result as in the first part of the problem.  This is not surprising, since the following is always true for the exponential failure distribution: if a system is operating at any time $t$, the probability that it will fail in the next $X$ months will be the same as the probability of its failure in the first $X$ months.

**Question 2.**   If 100 of these systems are installed in the field, but are not repaired when they fail, how many will still be expected to be working after 12 months?

**Solution.**   If the systems are *not* repaired as troubles occur, $S\,(12\text{ months}) = 0.06$. Therefore, 6 of the original 100 systems are expected to survive 12 months of operation.

**Question 3.**   What is the equipment MTTF?  Assuming an average repair time of 4 hours, what would the steady-state availability be?  How would this change if the average repair time were 50 hours?  Assume a constant repair rate (and constant hazard rate for repair[12]).

**Solution.**   If the hazard rate is constant,

$$\text{MTTF} = 1/\lambda$$

$$= \frac{1}{3.25 \times 10^{-4}/\text{hour}} = 3{,}077\text{ hours.} \qquad (1.54)$$

Since the repair rate is constant, it is numerically equal to the hazard rate for repair, which is given by

$$\frac{1}{\text{MTTR}} = 0.25/\text{hour.} \qquad (1.55)$$

With constant $\mu$ and $\lambda$, the steady-state availability $A$ equals $\dfrac{\mu}{\lambda+\mu}$, where

$\lambda = 3.25 \times 10^{-2}$ percent of surviving population failing per hour and $\mu = 25$ percent of failed population being repaired per hour. In this case,

$$A = \frac{25}{25 + 0.0325} = 0.999 . \tag{1.56}$$

Thus, the probability that a system will be available when needed is greater than 99 percent. For an average repair time of 50 hours,

$$A = \frac{2}{2 + 0.0325} = 0.98 . \tag{1.57}$$

The availability would be reduced but, on the average, such a system is expected to be operational more than 98 percent of the time.

## CONSIDERATIONS IN THE INFANT MORTALITY PERIOD

The AT&T hazard rate model for electronic components shown in Figure 1-9 is not constant during the early life. This is true for the devices used in equipment and, thus, for the equipment as a whole.

Failures due to "early life weakness" or infant mortality can appear in two different ways: Device Operating Failures (DOFs) and Dead on Arrivals (DOAs). With DOFs, failures occur during operation after some time. The rate of occurrence of failure is time-dependent. The infant mortality part of the reliability model describes DOFs during early life. As previously discussed, the reliability model does not apply to DOAs.

Costs due to infant mortality failures are incurred in the equipment factory as well as in the field. These include costs due to failures during incoming tests, circuit pack tests, system tests and burn-in, field installation and prove-in, and in service. The lowest costs are associated with drop-outs at incoming device tests. Equipment repair costs increase at each stage. The lowest cost for equipment repair is after failure at the first circuit pack tests, and the highest cost is after failure of in-service units.

Since the probability of infant mortality failures, which are DOFs, diminishes rapidly with operating time, equipment is often operated, or "burned-in," until performance levels are acceptable. Chapters 3 and 4 contain procedures and data that can be used to estimate equipment infant mortality levels. Chapter 2 describes the effect of burn-in on device hazard rates. When this burn-in model is combined with the information of Chapters 3 and 4, the effect of burn-in on equipment reliability can be modeled.

Although the existence of DOAs is recognized, little quantitative data about their occurrence exists. Therefore, DOA data and methods for dealing with DOAs are not included in this manual. Nevertheless, the predicted number of failures in the field is greater when DOAs are considered. These added failures are associated mainly with first equipment turn-on.

## Example 1.4

Assume the following for an integrated circuit: The long-term hazard rate, $\lambda_L = 10$ FITs and $\alpha = 0.8$.

**Question.**   For a population of such devices, what percentage might be expected to fail

- in the first month of operation,

- in the first 6 months of operation,

- in 10 years of operation?

**Solution.**   The first month of operation is within the infant mortality period. We first need, therefore, to calculate $\lambda_1$ from $\lambda_L$. Recall Equation (1.48),

$$\lambda_{IM}(t) = \lambda_1 t^{-\alpha} \tag{1.58}$$

and that at $t=10^4$ hours

$$\lambda_{IM}(t) = \lambda_{L,} \tag{1.59}$$

so that

$$\lambda_L = \lambda_1 (10^4)^{-\alpha} \tag{1.60}$$

or

$$\lambda_1 = \lambda_L 10^{4\alpha}. \tag{1.61}$$

Inserting the values of $\lambda_1$ and $\alpha$ that are given, we find,

$$\lambda_1 = (10)\ 10^{(4)(.8)} = 15849 \text{ FITs} \tag{1.62}$$

and

$$\lambda_1 = 15849 \text{ FITs } \frac{10^{-9} \text{ hour}^{-1}}{1 \text{ FIT}}$$
$$\approx 1.58 \times 10^{-5}/\text{hour}\ . \tag{1.63}$$

The number of hours in a month is obtained as follows:

$$\frac{\text{\# hours}}{\text{month}} = \frac{365 \dfrac{\text{days}}{\text{year}} \left[ 24 \dfrac{\text{hours}}{\text{day}} \right]}{12 \dfrac{\text{months}}{\text{year}}}$$

$$= \frac{365(24)}{12} \frac{\text{hours}}{\text{month}} = 730 \frac{\text{hours}}{\text{month}} \qquad (1.64)$$

We may now use Equation (1.45) for the cumulative distribution function of a Weibull distribution:

$$F(t) = 1 - e^{\frac{-\lambda_1 t^{1-\alpha}}{1-\alpha}} . \qquad (1.65)$$

Substituting the appropriate values for $\lambda_1$, $\alpha$, and $t$, we find

$$F(730 \text{ hours}) = 1 - e^{\left[ \frac{-(1.58 \times 10^{-5})(730)^{1-0.8}}{1-0.8} \right]} = 1 - e^{-0.0003} ,$$

$$= 0.0003 \quad \text{or} \quad 0.03\%. \qquad (1.66)$$

This is the expected percentage failing in the first month of operation, excluding DOAs.

In the first 6 months of operation (730 x 6 = 4380 hours), again using Equation (1.45),

$$F(t) = 1 - e^{\left[ \frac{-(1.58 \times 10^{-5})(4380)^{1-0.8}}{1-0.8} \right]} = 1 - e^{-0.00042} ,$$

$$= 0.0004 \quad \text{or} \quad 0.04\%. \qquad (1.67)$$

In 10 years of operation (87,600 hours):

The first $10^4$ hours is infant mortality:

$$F_{IM} = 1 - e^{\left[\dfrac{-(1.58 \times 10^{-5})(10^4)^{1-0.8}}{1-0.8}\right]} = 1 - e^{-0.0005},$$

$$= 0.0005 \quad \text{or} \quad 0.05\% \text{ (first } 10^4 \text{ hours)}. \tag{1.68}$$

Beyond $10^4$ hours, $\lambda(t) = \text{constant} = \lambda_L = 10$ FITs $= 10^{-8}$ hour$^{-1}$ or $10^{-6}$ expected percentage of surviving population failing per hour and:

$$\int_{t_1}^{t_2} \lambda(t)dt = \lambda_L(t_2 - t_1) = 10^{-8} \, (77,600) = 0.00078$$

$$F(t) = 1 - e^{-0.00078} = 0.08\% \text{ (from } 10^4 \text{ hours to } 87,600 \text{ hours)}. \tag{1.69}$$

Therefore, the total expected drop-out over 10 years due to (1) the infant mortality for $10^4$ hours and (2) the constant failure rate from 10,000 to 87,600 hours is 0.13 percent $[(0.0005 + 0.0008)100]$ of the original population.

## CONSIDERATIONS OF WEAROUT DURING SERVICE LIFE

All devices will eventually fail. However, current designs and processes can produce devices that will last well beyond system service life before failing, while operating in any normal telecommunications environment. Device life testing and product qualifications intend to ensure that devices will show no wearout during the normal equipment design life when used within the design ratings.

It is assumed throughout this manual that wearout does not need to be considered, providing that

- devices are protected by appropriate specifications for life testing and qualifications;

- devices are not stored or used in conditions beyond the allowable ratings;

- devices are not used in products whose field life is longer than the device design life.

Therefore, it becomes the responsibility of device designers (or specification engineers) to ensure that their devices, when used within the normal ratings, will not begin to wear out in any normally anticipated equipment life and environment. As mentioned earlier, wearout is, strictly speaking, the monotonic increase of the hazard rate as time tends to infinity. This type of variation of the hazard rate is believed to be reasonable for, say, biological species or nonmaintained mechanical devices. However, this behavior is not typical of electronic components. The usage of the term *wearout* is, therefore, somewhat different when referring to electronic components.

> In this manual, we follow the standard practice in electronic device reliability engineering and refer to wearout as a monotonically increasing hazard rate <u>during</u> service life.

What this means is that, for example, if a lognormal hazard rate is fit to some electronic device failure time data, and if the *increasing* part of the lognormal hazard rate curve occurs during the intended service life of the device, and *persists* until at least the end of the intended service life, then we shall refer to this as wearout. Others may, quite correctly, point out that eventually the lognormal hazard rate curve levels off, and then begins to decrease regardless of lognormal distribution parameter values, and so the lognormal distribution *cannot*, strictly speaking, describe wearout.[12] We have taken a somewhat simpler approach and only consider the variation of the hazard rate during the intended service life of an electronic device.

## REFERENCES

1.  British Standards Institution, *Quality Vocabulary*, Part 1, *International Terms*, BS 4778, ISO 8402-1986, United Kingdom, 1987.

2.  Department of Defense, *Definitions of Terms for Reliability and Maintainability*, MIL-STD-721C, U.S. Government Printing Office, Washington, D.C., 1981.

3.  W. Feller, *An Introduction to Probability Theory and its Applications*, Volume I, 3d ed., 1968 and Volume II, 2d ed., 1970, Wiley, New York.

4.  W. Mendenhall, R. L. Schaeffer, D. D. Wackerly, *Mathematical Statistics with Applications*, 3d ed., Duxbury Press, Boston, 1986.

5.  H. F. Martz and R. A. Waller, *Bayesian Reliability Analysis*, Wiley, New York, 1982.

6.  M. L. Shooman, *Probabilistic Reliability: An Engineering Approach*, McGraw-Hill, New York, 1968.

7.  R. Billinton and R. N. Allan, *Reliability Evaluation of Engineering Systems: Concepts and Techniques*, Pitman, Hanshfield, Mass., 1983.

8.  P. D. T. O'Connor, *Practical Reliability Engineering*, 2d ed., Wiley, New York, 1985.

9.  D. R. Cox, *Renewal Theory*, Methuen, London, 1962.

10. E. Parzen, *Stochastic Processes*, Holden Day, San Francisco, 1962.

11. W.A. Thompson, Jr., "On the Foundations of Reliability," *Technometrics* **23**, 1 (1981): p. 1.

12.  H. E. Ascher, "Reliability Models for Repairable Systems," in *Reliability Technology — Theory and Applications*, edited by J. Moltoft and F. Jensen, Elsevier Science, Amsterdam, 1986. For more details see: H. E. Ascher, and H. Feingold, *Repairable Systems Reliability: Modeling, Inference, Misconceptions and their Causes*, Marcel Dekker, New York, 1984.

13.  J. P. Clech, W. Engelmaier, R. W. Kotlowitz, J. A. Augis, "Surface Mount Solder Attachments Reliability Figures of Merit—'Design for Reliability' Tools," *Proceedings of the SMART V (Surface Mount Advanced Related Technologies) Conference*, January 9-12, 1989, New Orleans, Louisiana, technical paper SMT V-48.

14.  D. P. Holcomb, and J. C. North, "An Infant Mortality and Long-Term Failure Rate Model for Electronic Equipment," *AT&T Technical Journal* **64**, 1 (1985): p. 15.

# 2

---

# DEVICE RELIABILITY

---

## INTRODUCTION

Reliability analysis of a complex system often entails representing a system as a collection of subsystems whose reliability may be estimated. This representation is then decomposed, to as fine a detail as is necessary to characterize the reliability of each part of the whole system. In electronic systems, such a decomposition results in a collection of block diagrams containing integrated circuits, discrete components,* interconnections, etc. Consequently, an understanding of reliability at the component (or device) level is essential to develop accurate estimates of system reliability.

Details of the aforementioned decomposition and how device reliability information is used to estimate overall system reliability are discussed in the next chapter. This chapter deals with device reliability. More specifically, device reliability is discussed in terms of the AT&T hazard rate model for electronic devices introduced in the previous chapter. But to use this model as a framework for the characterization of electronic device reliability, we must first understand some aspects of accelerated failure time models. This type of model forms the basis for accelerated life testing,† an essential ingredient of a comprehensive electronic device reliability program. Next, we discuss electronic device reliability during the infant mortality period of the life of an electronic component. The infant mortality period is characterized by a *decreasing* hazard rate. Then we consider the reliability

---

\* Discrete semiconductor electronic components whose operation involves the activity associated with a junction, such as diodes and transistors, are referred to as *active devices*. Discrete non-semiconductor electronic components, such as resistors and electrolytic capacitors, are referred to as *passive devices*. Monolithic microelectronic devices, or integrated circuits, are the third type of electrical component in this scheme.

† Also referred to as accelerated stress testing.

of electronic devices in the "long-term" or "steady-state" period of device life. The long-term period of device life is characterized within the framework of the AT&T hazard rate model for electronic components by a *constant* hazard rate.* Emphasis is placed on how the reliability engineer estimates the hazard rate of electronic components *in the application environment*, during both of the aforementioned periods of device life. The chapter ends with a discussion of two phenomena which may have a significant effect on device survivability: electrostatic discharge (ESD) and electrical overstress (EOS), followed by a discussion of latch-up. The reader should note that although most of the discussion in this chapter focuses on semiconductor devices, the techniques are general and may be used to evaluate the reliability of other devices as well. It should be noted that throughout this book we are concerned with three reliability classifications: Level I, Level II, and Level III, in increasing order of reliability. They are based on the degree of AT&T control of the product quality. They correspond roughly to the Quality Levels I, II, and III of the Bell Communications Research document *Reliability Prediction Procedure for Electronic Equipment*,[1] formerly (before divestiture by AT&T of the Bell Operating Companies) the *AT&T Reliability Prediction Procedure for Electronic Equipment*. All AT&T devices are designed and manufactured to achieve the highest reliability level, that is, Level III.

## ACCELERATED LIFE TESTING

Modern electronic devices are, generally speaking, very reliable—so reliable, in fact, that it is very difficult to assess the reliability of modern VLSI devices by monitoring the operation, in a laboratory, of some number of devices in the hopes of observing the failure times. The difficulty stems from a number of factors, only some of which are directly related to characteristics of the actual devices. For example, if the market window of the particular product that an electronic device is used in is small, for example, one or two years, then the time allowed for reliability evaluation of that device may be days (or weeks at best), not months (or years). Furthermore, if this kind of testing is performed at normal use conditions, it is unlikely to yield a statistically significant number of failures, unless an enormous number of devices are tested (tens of thousands). For most modern devices this type of test is not practical because the cost is too high. Consequently, a methodology has to be used that allows for the evaluation of the reliability of electronic devices, especially during the post-infant mortality period, even when reliability testing must be performed in a few weeks and perhaps with only a limited number of devices.

One such method is accelerated life testing. In an accelerated life test, a number of devices are subjected to failure-causing stresses that are at levels above what

---

* Again, it is worthwhile mentioning that the constant hazard rate part of this model is an approximation, to the post-infant mortality (taken to be post $10^4$ hours) hazard rate. This approximation is conservative so long as wearout has been designed *out* of the device during service life. For a discussion of alternative approaches used within AT&T for specialized applications, see, for example, the *AT&T Technical Journal*, March 1985, a special issue on submarine lightwave system reliability.

these devices would experience in the application environment, for example, the inside of an electronic switching system in an air-conditioned central office. This type of accelerated aging test allows a distribution of failure times to be obtained, albeit at more stressful conditions than ordinary operating conditions.

To use such a method, however, we must be able to relate the distribution of failure times at accelerated aging conditions to the distribution of failure times that would be expected under conditions encountered by devices in service. Such a relationship is provided by the accelerated life model.

## Accelerated Life Model

An accelerated life model[2] is usually taken to be characterized by a linear relationship between failure times at different sets of conditions. In particular,

$$t_1 = At_2 \tag{2.1}$$

where $t_1$ is the failure time of a device at, for example, use conditions, while $t_2$ is the failure time of that same device if it were operated at the more stressful conditions,* and $A$ is an acceleration factor.† It follows from Equation (2.1) that the *same* distribution of failure times holds at different stress levels. It follows from Equation (2.1) that (see Appendix A for a derivation)

$$\lambda_1(t) = \frac{1}{A} \lambda_2(t/A) , \tag{2.2}$$

where $\lambda_1(t)$ is the hazard rate at use conditions and $\lambda_2(t)$ is the hazard rate at the more stressful conditions. Recall that the hazard rate is the probability (of failure) density at time $t$, *given* survival up to time $t$ (see Chapter 1). Relationships analogous to Equation (2.2) are easily obtained for the cumulative distribution function,‡ the survivor function, and the probability (of failure) density function (see Table 2.1). Based on the first relationship in the table, given by Equation (2.1), the other relationships follow.

Until now no mention has been made of the type of accelerating stress, the form of the acceleration factor, or of any particular distribution of failure times. These expressions are completely general, given the assumption that the distributions of failure time at two different sets of conditions are strictly proportional to each other.

---

* Also known as accelerated stress conditions.

† It is worthwhile noting that Equation (2.1) holds for every device under consideration and, therefore, it holds quantile by quantile;[1] very often texts on component reliability write Equation (2.1) for one particular time, typically the median time to failure, $t_{50}$. Although this may be convenient, it avoids an important issue, namely does data support the use of an accelerated life model in the first place.

‡ A probabilistic and, therefore, weaker form of the accelerated life model is given by assuming the relationship for the cumulative distribution function in Table 2.1, rather than Equation (2.1).

**TABLE 2.1.**  Accelerated Life Model

| | |
|---|---|
| Failure time | $t_1 = A\, t_2$ |
| Cumulative distribution function | $F_1(t) = F_2(t/A)$ |
| Probability density function | $f_1(t) = (1/A)f_2(t/A)$ |
| Hazard rate | $\lambda_1(t) = (1/A)\lambda_2(t/A)$ |

It is worthwhile noting that the adequacy of the accelerated life model is easily tested.  It follows from Equation (2.1) that

$$\ln t_1 = \ln t_2 + \ln A \quad .\tag{2.3}$$

Quantile-Quantile plots[3] of the log of the failure times for different environmental conditions should have slope 1, with $y$-intercept equal to $\ln A$ (see Figure 2-1).

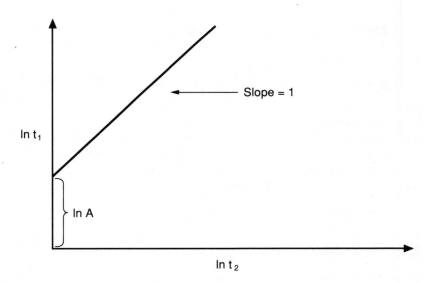

**Figure 2-1.** A quantile-quantile plot of the log of the failure times at two different conditions is a straight line with a slope of 1 and $y$-intercept of $\ln A$, when the accelerated life model holds.

Note that this form is used to estimate the hazard rate at use conditions based on data obtained at the more stressful conditions.  An important application is the estimation of hazard rates at use conditions from those hazard rates reported at a reference temperature of 40°C ambient.*  The basis for the use of this reference temperature is discussed in Chapter 4.

The acceleration factor in Equation (2.1) may depend on a number of variables, often called stress variables, which characterize the conditions at which the different failure times were recorded.  The stress variable of greatest interest in reliability engineering has traditionally been temperature.  One of the reasons for this, no doubt, is that through kinetic theory, we may obtain a sound physical basis for the functional form of $A = A(T)$.

### The Arrhenius Model

In his experimental study of the inversion of sucrose, Svante Arrhenius[4] fit the temperature dependence of the rate constant of the reaction to a particular form which now bears his name.†  The equations that follow provide background needed for our discussion of Arrhenius's work within the context of reliability.

One of the simplest chemical reactions is one in which some substance, $A$, is transformed into another substance, $B$.  This reaction process may be symbolically described by

$$A \rightarrow B .$$ (2.4)

In this simple example, the rate of change of the concentration of reactant $A$ is described by

$$\frac{d[A]}{dt} = -k[A] ,$$ (2.5)

where $[A]$ may be thought of as representing the concentration of $A$, and $k$ is the rate constant.  The rate constant is independent of time.  Arrhenius fit the temperature dependence of a rate constant to a form such as

$$k = k_0 e^{-E_a/k_B T} ,$$ (2.6)

where $T$ is the absolute temperature (degrees Kelvin), $E_a$ is called the activation energy, $k_B$ is the Boltzmann constant, and $k_0$, the pre-exponential factor, is constant.  The notation used is modern, as are the following interpretations.

---

\* Ambient temperature in AT&T, within the context of component reliability, is defined as the temperature at the midpoint between circuit packs (boards), averaged over frame locations, inside a frame in a central office environment.

† Arrhenius noticed that plots of the natural logarithm of the reaction rate versus $1/T$ was often a straight line.  This is now commonly referred to as an Arrhenius plot.

The pre-exponential factor $k_0$, represents different things for different reaction mechanisms. For a bimolecular reaction,[5] it is called the *frequency factor* and represents the probability of collision of the two reacting species. We will not discuss this last point further, or other interpretations of $k_0$, but refer the interested reader to any of the indicated references on reaction kinetics.[5,6] The activation energy has come, through the development of the kinetic theory of Boltzmann,[6,7] to be understood as a physically significant quantity, not just a curve-fitting parameter. It may be thought of as an energy barrier that separates reactants from products in some chemical or physical process. This is to be distinguished from a Boltzmann factor, which relates the relative populations of two states of a system in equilibrium, to the energy *difference* between the states of a system.[8] Still these two very different factors have common origins, but that is beyond the scope of this manual.[6]

If the equation that describes the reaction does not contain time explicitly on the right side of Equation (2.5)—regardless of the dependence on other quantities, for example, the various concentrations—then[9] it follows that the time to failure $t_f$ (see Appendix B) is inversely proportional to the rate constant, $k$. That is,

$$t_f = D/k \ , \tag{2.7}$$

where $D$ is a proportionality constant, independent of the time and temperature. It is worth emphasizing that Equation (2.7) is deterministic. If we consider a distribution of failure times then for most cases [10], the randomness on the right side of Equation (2.7) is manifest through the distribution of the proportionality constant $D$. It follows from Equations (2.6) and (2.7) that

$$t_f = \frac{D}{k_0} e^{E_a/k_B T} \ . \tag{2.8}$$

For two different temperatures, $T_1$ and $T_2$, the ratio of the times to failure, $t_1$ and $t_2$, can be expressed as

$$\frac{t_1}{t_2} = \frac{k_2}{k_1} = e^{\frac{E_a}{k_B}[\frac{1}{T_1} - \frac{1}{T_2}]} = A_T \ , \tag{2.9}$$

where $A_T$ is the *Arrhenius* temperature acceleration factor, which relates the failure times at two different temperatures. This is the Arrhenius Model or equation of reliability engineering. The acceleration factor for comparing reliability at two different temperatures can now be calculated with Equation (2.9) if the activation energy for the process leading to failure is known.

## Other Models of Acceleration

As mentioned previously, the Arrhenius form is phenomenological; it continues to be used because it fits data well. Even for the simple reaction

$$A \rightarrow B \ , \qquad\qquad (2.10)$$

the rate constant turns out to have a somewhat more complicated temperature dependence than that in Equation (2.6). That is, rather than $k = k_0 e^{-E_a/k_B T}$, the reaction rate is given by

$$k = k_0' T^n e^{-E_a/k_B T} \ , \qquad\qquad (2.11)$$

where $n$ depends on the specifics of the reaction dynamics[5,6] and $k_0'$, the pre-exponential factor, is constant. For the simplest case of hard spheres,* $n=1/2$. This form should be associated with the work of Wigner,[11] Polanyi,[12] and Eyring,[13] among others.[5,6] In the reliability community, it is usually referred to as the Eyring Model.

Because the exponential temperature dependence usually dominates the $T^n$ factor, the phenomenological Arrhenius form is almost always adequate, given the uncertainty associated with kinetics data.[5]

What about the dependence of a reaction rate or an acceleration factor on other stress variables such as voltage or relative humidity? There is no generally accepted answer to this question. Except in particular cases in which the failure mechanism is well understood,[14] most approaches are hybrids; that is, the reliability engineer uses whatever information and data are available, in the absence of theoretical underpinning. Some recent work[15] in this area suggests that a consistent thermodynamic approach to the problem is possible, but this approach has yet to be shown useful in practical applications.

For completeness, we mention the proportional hazards or Cox Model.[2] For the proportional hazards model, it is the hazard rate, rather than the failure time, which is scaled by a stress-dependent multiplication factor. This model is believed to be inapplicable to the field of reliability of electronic components,[16] although it is found often in the biomedical literature.[17]


## EARLY LIFE RELIABILITY (INFANT MORTALITY PERIOD)

As discussed in Chapter 1, the two parts of device life that are of concern from a reliability perspective are the infant mortality period and the steady-state period since wearout is not expected to occur during the period of time for which the device is designed to operate (see Chapter 1, the *Electronic Device Hazard Rate Model* section). The reliability of devices during the infant mortality period is the

---

\* Hard spheres are ideal particles that, at the atomic level, are incompressible and do not attract each other. We say ideal because neither of these properties is strictly correct, even though this idealization is often useful.

main topic of this section, especially semiconductor devices, hazard rate models, and hazard rate mechanisms. Effects of screening and burn-in on device reliability are also discussed.

## Device Infant Mortality Defects

Infant mortality defects in semiconductor devices stem from a variety of device design, manufacturing, handling, and application-related causes.[18] The device failure mechanisms causing infant mortality may change in type and degree from product to product and from lot to lot within the same product. It should be emphasized that, despite its variability, infant mortality can still be modeled adequately. The hazard rate parameters for infant mortality may not necessarily describe the performance of individual device lots accurately. They will, however, give a reasonable estimate of the performance of a number of lots averaged together.

Infant mortality failures are generally caused by manufacturing defects. Examples of such defects include oxide pinholes, photoresist or etching defects resulting in near opens or shorts, conductive debris on the chip, contaminants, scratches, weak bonds, and partially cracked chips or ceramics.[18] Complex MOS devices are subject to early oxide-defect failures. Some infant mortality failures result from surface inversion problems, probably due to gross contamination or gross passivation defects. Figures 2-2 through 2-4 show examples of common infant mortality defects.

Some of the defects are attributed to the workmanship and manufacturing variations which can produce devices with infant mortality characteristics significantly different from their target values. Such variations can be reduced by changes in design or fabrication techniques, or in handling of the devices during manufacture. Other infant mortality defects are inherent in design rules and constraints or in the practical limitations of the manufacturing process and material control.

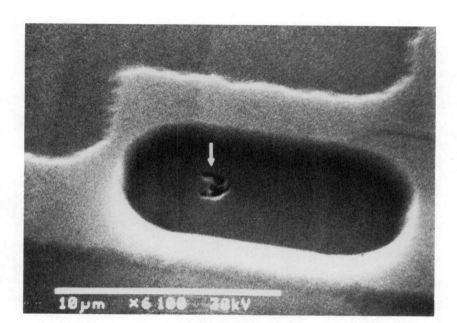

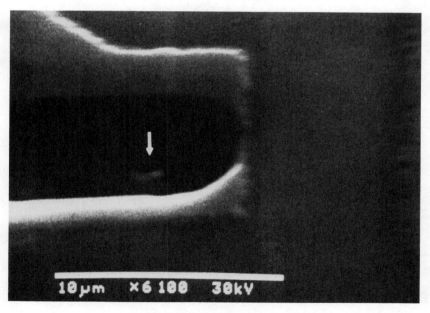

**Figure 2-2.** Gate oxide defects.

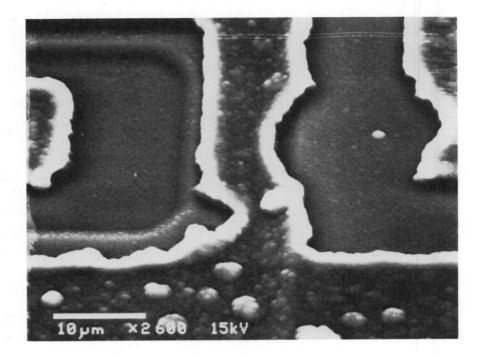

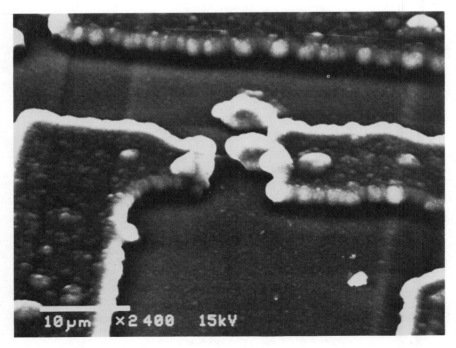

**Figure 2-3.** Infant mortality failure of an integrated circuit due to a mask defect during processing.

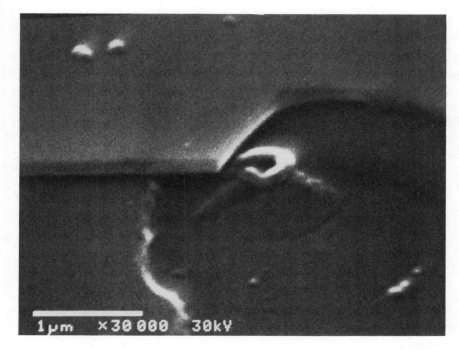

**Figure 2-4.** An oxide pinhole (center of photograph) caused the infant mortality failure in this memory device. The pinhole is the source of a short-circuit through the oxide layer.

## Infant Mortality Modeling

The model of infant mortality, discussed in Chapter 1, is described by a Weibull distribution. The hazard rate is written as

$$\lambda(t) = \lambda_1 t^{-\alpha}, \tag{2.12}$$

where $t$ is the time in hours, $\lambda_1$ is the hazard rate at 1 hour, and $\alpha$ is the infant mortality shape parameter. This gives the hazard rate of the entire population due to infant mortality. Two of the features of this representation are that it is both mathematically and graphically simple, as discussed in Chapter 1, the *Mathematical Terminology: Measures of Reliability* section.

In many cases, either the lognormal or the Weibull distribution can be used to describe the distribution of failure times during the infant mortality region. However, the Weibull is often used because it is analytically simpler than the lognormal. The method of maximum likelihood is often used to calculate the Weibull parameters that yield the best fit to the time-to-failure data. These parameters are then used to express the hazard rate as a function of time.

Large sample sizes are generally required to provide enough data to characterize infant mortality because of the small percentages of devices failing. However, it is often impractical during the device qualification to obtain large enough samples to determine infant mortality hazard rate estimates. In many cases, field data is necessary. Reasonable hazard rate estimates, however, can often be made based on similarities to other technology, knowledge of the failure mechanisms, and limited accelerated stress test data.

## Effects of Temperature on Infant Mortality Hazard Rates

Studies of the infant mortality period indicate a rather low activation energy for these failure mechanisms. Figure 2-5 shows the temperature acceleration of infant mortality failures.[19] The infant mortality data points, collected from many sources, are shown to indicate rather distinct ranges for SSI/MSI bipolar devices and for MOS/LSI devices (largely dynamic RAMs). The uniformity of the "effective activation energy" (represented by the slope of the lines surrounding the data) is significant, considering the mix of potential failure mechanisms involved.* All failure data indicate an effective activation energy of 0.37 to 0.42 electron volts (eV). The data shown here suggests, therefore, that for these device types, a single activation energy of 0.4 eV is a reasonable estimate for establishing time-temperature trade-offs in screens for infant mortality.[19] *In this manual, the infant mortality activation energy will be assumed to be 0.4 eV for all devices.* Based on the assumed 0.4 eV activation energy, the temperature acceleration factor can be easily calculated from Equation (2.9).

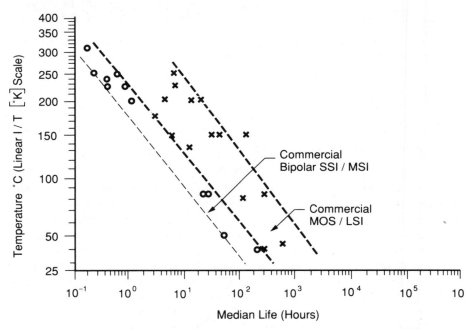

**Figure 2-5.** An Arrhenius plot of bipolar and MOS infant mortality data.[19]

---

*   We say effective activation energy precisely because there is a mix of mechanisms and, hence, reactions that are responsible for the temperature dependence of the hazard rates.

It cannot, however, be used directly as a multiplier to obtain the hazard rate at the desired operating temperature. That simple procedure is only proper when the hazard rate is constant. When the hazard rate has a Weibull form, as in Equation (2.12), the multiplier for the hazard rate is $(A_{IM,})^{1-\alpha}$ where $\alpha$ is the Weibull slope parameter and $A_{IM}$ is given by Equation (2.9). The hazard rate $\lambda(t)$ is then given by*

$$\lambda(t) = (A_{IM})^{1-\alpha}\lambda_1 t^{-\alpha} \ . \tag{2.13}$$

### Effect of Operating Voltage on Infant Mortality Hazard Rates

The dielectric breakdown of an oxide film can be accelerated by an applied field. The failure mode analyses of burn-in dropouts from MOS device lots indicate that a sizable fraction (about 30 percent) of the infant mortality failures is due to oxide-related failures. One would, therefore, expect applied voltage to have a large influence on infant mortality. Crook[20] found that the electric field acceleration factor for oxide breakdown is $10^7$/MV/cm, where MV is the unit of applied voltage and cm is the unit of oxide thickness. These findings were confirmed by an investigation of gate oxide breakdown failures in 64K DRAMs made within AT&T. Crook's early findings have led to extensive investigations to establish a voltage-dependent acceleration factor that could be applied to MOS device burn-in, where a voltage stress in excess of operating voltage is applied. The investigations resulted in the following relationship:

$$A_V = e^{\left[\frac{C}{t_{ox}}(V_1 - V_2)\right]} \tag{2.14}$$

where $C$ is the voltage acceleration constant in angstroms/volt, $t_{ox}$ is the oxide thickness in angstroms, $V_1$ is the stress voltage in volts, and $V_2$ is the operating voltage in volts.

The value of the constant $C$ has been the subject of considerable investigation. Hokari, et al.,[21] Baglee,[22] and Eachus, et al.,[23] reported $C$ values of 400, 438, and 600 Å/V, respectively. This acceleration factor can be used only when device failure can be attributed to oxide breakdown. Therefore, the FIT rate of a group of devices cannot be calculated by a simple multiplication by this acceleration factor. One must determine what fraction of the failures is related to oxide breakdown. Eachus, et al.,[23] measured a composite voltage acceleration constant from a study of the burn-in of 64K DRAMs.

The AT&T investigation resulted in a conservative estimate of $C = 290$ Å/V. As an example for MOS devices in which gate oxides are 250 Å thick and to which a voltage of 2 volts in excess of the operating voltage is applied, use of Equation

---

* See Appendix C for a derivation of the Weibull hazard rate multiplier $(A_{IM})^{1-\alpha}$.

(2.14) yields a voltage acceleration factor $A_V = 10.2$. Recently, forms other than Equation (2.14) have been reported.[24]

### Effect of Temperature Cycling on Infant Mortality Hazard Rates

Mechanical defects constitute a significant fraction of the failures in the infant mortality period. These mechanical defects include such defects as weak wire bonds, poor bond pad adhesion, and partially cracked chips on ceramics. These failure mechanisms involve either plastic deformation or crack propagation, which can be caused by repeated application of stress in alternate directions and can result in fatigue failure. The speed of fatigue failure[25] can be directly accelerated by increasing the amplitude of deformation or indirectly by increasing the range of temperature excursion $\Delta T$. However, the form for an acceleration factor is currently unknown. The literature[26,27] indicates that temperature cycling of devices results in decreasing hazard rates as the number of cycles increases. Figure 2-6 and Figure 2-7 show such examples.

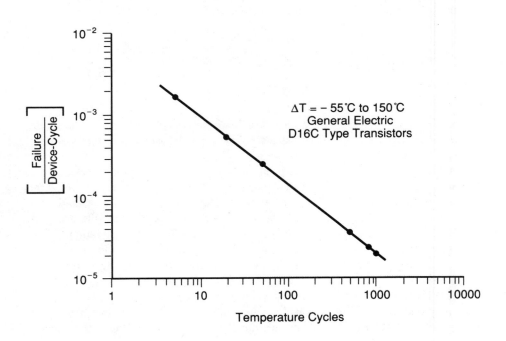

$$\frac{\text{Failure}}{\text{Device-Cycle}} \text{ vs. Number of Temperature Cycles}$$

**Figure 2-6.** Effect of temperature cycling on infant mortality hazard rates.[26]

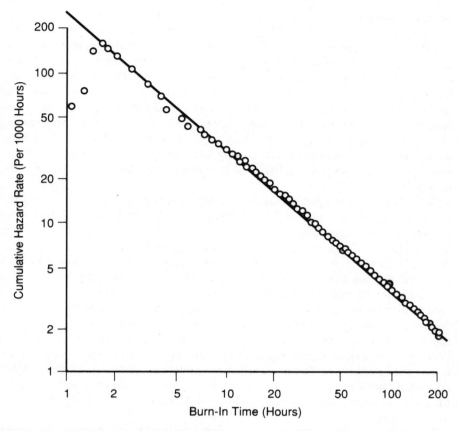

**Figure 2-7.** Cumulative hazard rate of IBM computer 4 Π versus screening time. The screen consisted of one temperature cycle (−65°F to +160°F) per 4 hours.[27]

### Infant Mortality Screening

The term "screening" describes the application of some stress to 100 percent of the product to remove (or reduce the number of) defective or potentially defective units. In the broad sense, electrical, parametric or functional testing is a screen. However, the focus here is on the use of accelerated stresses as screens for reducing or eliminating infant mortality defects. The conditions used for screens are typical of accelerated testing of semiconductor devices, involving such stresses as temperature, temperature cycling, and combined temperature and bias. The selection of the proper accelerated-stress condition for the screen depends largely on the nature and degree of the failure mechanisms contributing to the infant mortality defects and the way they are accelerated by the particular stress.

AT&T does not tolerate defects in any of its products or services, including electronic components, and is working toward the elimination of all defects. Until this goal is reached, screens continue to be a useful, albeit costly, way to reduce the number of defects that a customer will encounter.

The use of screens is reduced or even eliminated entirely as sufficient process control in manufacturing is achieved (so as to make the screen unnecessary). Screens which consistently yield 0% dropout (failure) are of no value.

Temperature cycling followed by a gross functional and continuity test proved to be effective in screening out many mechanical defects. Temperature cycling will screen out poor wirebonds, inadequate die attach, and other mechanical problems. It accelerates failures caused by the formation of intermetallics in gold-aluminum wirebond systems if temperature cycling follows a high-temperature bake. For those systems, it is usually followed by a centrifuge test to detect those bonds that have been weakened by intermetallics. When followed by leak tests, temperature cycling is an effective screen for poor seals of hermetic devices. In plastic encapsulated devices, temperature cycling accelerates defects caused by fatigue stressing of wire bonds due to the plastic materials surrounding the lead and the bond area.

The modeling of temperature cycling effects on infant mortality defects and the determination of the optimum test conditions is a difficult problem. The failure mechanisms in temperature cycling are likely to reflect the peculiarities of the specific device or structure, and several competing mechanisms might exist in one device. This makes analysis complicated and generally requires consideration of each failure mechanism separately. This, however, does not reduce the effectiveness of temperature cycling as a screen.

Screening with temperature alone (usually called "stabilization bake" or "temperature storage") involves storing devices at an elevated temperature for a specified period of time. It can be used to test for diffusion and chemical effects, material decomposition, etc. For example, the thermal stress applied during the bake accelerates failures caused by oxide and gross contamination defects. For the gold-aluminum wirebond systems, screening at elevated temperature accelerates the formation of intermetallics; if followed by temperature cycling, bond failures will occur sooner.

The discussion above describes some of the screening methods used for infant mortality defects. There are others, such as power-aging of transistors, high temperature-voltage-stressing of MOS devices and voltage-stressing of on-chip capacitors in linear integrated circuits. As with temperature and temperature-cycling, they are designed to accelerate the predominant infant mortality failure mechanisms of specific device types. One effective screening method, called *burn-in,* uses two types of stresses (temperature and electric field) and is discussed in detail in the following section.

## Burn-in

Burn-in is an effective means for screening out defects contributing to infant mortality. This screening typically combines electrical stresses with temperature over a period of time in order to activate the temperature- and voltage-dependent failure mechanisms in a relatively short time.

There are two distinct types of burn-in: static and dynamic. In static burn-in, a dc bias is applied to the device at an elevated temperature. The bias is applied in such a way so as to reverse-bias as many junctions as possible in the device. In dynamic burn-in, the devices are operated so as to exercise the entire circuit by simulating actual system operation. A model for the effect of dynamic burn-in is discussed later in this section.

Static burn-in is only performed at the device level, that is, before the devices are assembled into equipment. For dynamic burn-in, however, there are two options: (1) device level burn-in, and (2) burn-in of the system after assembly of devices (called system burn-in). System burn-in is generally limited to lower temperatures than device burn-in (even if the operation takes place at normal operating temperature, it is still called burn-in). System burn-in does, however, eliminate the need for special burn-in equipment as the system itself provides all the biases and signals to the devices.

The choices of the type of burn-in (static or dynamic, device or system level) and the specific stress conditions depend on the device technologies and the reliability requirement (as with any screen or life test, there are also cost trade-offs, which are not considered here). Dynamic burn-in appears to be the more effective technique for complex VLSI circuits.

A burn-in model based on the assumption of the Weibull distribution for infant mortality assumes that the hazard rates of electronic devices are monotonically decreasing. Operation during device or system burn-in produces a certain amount of aging and will result in a reduced hazard rate during subsequent system operation. Subsequent operation begins at the reduced hazard rate and continues to decrease with additional operating time.

The direct data supporting the Weibull model come from the results of device-level and system-level burn-in testing. The burn-in of devices will lead to reduced device replacement rates during the operational life of the equipment. The effect of temperature during device burn-in is described by the Arrhenius equation within the context of the accelerated life model with a characteristic activation energy[19] of 0.4 eV.

The modeled effect of burn-in depends on both the burn-in temperature and the subsequent operating temperature. The effective operation time due to burn-in, $t_{eff}$, is determined by multiplying the actual burn-in time by the temperature acceleration factor, $A_T$, and the voltage acceleration factor $A_V$.

$$t_{eff} = A_T A_V t_{bi} \qquad (2.15)$$

where $t_{bi}$ is the burn-in time at $T_{bi}$, the ambient burn-in temperature. The Arrhenius equation [see Equation (2.9)] can be used to find the acceleration factor, $A_{bi}$, for burn-in compared to normal operation at the device hazard rate reference temperature,* 40°C ambient, assuming an infant mortality activation energy of 0.4 eV. This acceleration factor can also be found from Figure 4-1 (curve A8).

---

* See Chapter 4 for a discussion of this reference temperature.

The hazard rate at $T_r$, the reference ambient temperature, 40°C, is

$$\lambda(t) = \lambda_1 (t_{eff} + t)^{-\alpha}, \tag{2.16}$$

where $t = 0$ corresponds to the start of device aging *after* the burn-in.

As illustrated in Figure 2-8, the effect of the burn-in is a decrease in the early life hazard rate. It should be noted that once $t_{eff} + t$ are greater than $10^4$ hours, the IM period is taken to be over and the hazard rate is taken to then be given by $\lambda_L$. This expression, Equation (2.16), applies only to the IM period of device life.

This characterization of burn-in assumes that burn-in will eliminate all the failures that would appear in an equivalent time of operation. This is an oversimplification. Since the burn-in stress is typically temperature, failures that might result from temperature cycling, mechanical shock, etc., may not be eliminated. Actual experience may, therefore, show a higher initial hazard rate after burn-in than predicted by Equation (2.16), followed by a more dramatic decrease in hazard rate after burn-in than shown in Figure 2-8.

If the temperature of subsequent operation is not at the device hazard rate reference temperature, then the situation is slightly more complicated. If $A_{op}$ is the acceleration factor for the operating temperature relative to the reference temperature, then the hazard rate without burn-in [see Equation (2.13)] is

$$\lambda(t) = (A_{op})^{1-\alpha} \lambda_1 \, t^{-\alpha}. \tag{2.17}$$

To calculate the effect of the burn-in, $t_{eff}$ must be known. In this case, however, $t_{eff}$ is relative to operating temperature, which is different from the reference temperature. It is computed as follows:

$$t_{eff} = t_{bi} \left[ \frac{A_{bi}}{A_{op}} \right]. \tag{2.18}$$

where the operating temperature is taken to be in between $T_{bi}$ and $T_{ref}$.

The hazard rate, $\lambda(t)$, after burn-in is then

$$\lambda_\alpha(t) = (A_{op})^{1-\alpha} \lambda_1 \; [t + t_{bi} (A_{bi} / A_{op})]^{-\alpha} \tag{2.19}$$

where

$$A_{bi} = A_T A_V. \tag{2.20}$$

## Example 2.1

The purpose of this example is to compare the early-life reliabilities of a burned-in device to that of a nonburned-in device. The device burn-in is performed at 150°C for 10 hours. The subsequent operation of the devices is at a temperature of 40°C, the reference (ambient) temperature.

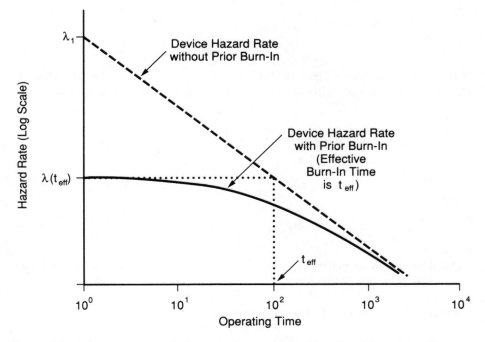

**Figure 2-8.** Effect of dynamic device screening on initial device hazard rate, according to Equation (2.16).

**Question 1.** If the device has an early-life hazard rate characterized by $\lambda_1 = 2 \times 10^4$ FITS, and $\alpha = 0.8$, and if no burn-in is performed, what percentage of the devices will fail during the first month (730 hours) of operation?

**Solution.** The expected number of failures, $\overline{N}$, for independent devices (with no replacement) is given by

$$\overline{N} = n \, F(t) \, , \tag{2.21a}$$

where $n$ is the number of devices and $F(t)$ is the cumulative distribution function, given by

$$F(t) = 1 - e^{-\int_0^t \lambda(t') dt'} \tag{2.21b}$$

The *percent* of failure is given by

$$\frac{\overline{N}}{n} = F(t) = 1 - e^{\frac{\lambda_1}{1-\alpha}t^{1-\alpha}} \tag{2.21c}$$

where we have used Equation 1.42 for the cumulative distribution function associated with the Weibull distribution. Evaluating this expression, we find

$$F(t) = 1 - e^{-\frac{10^{-9}2\times10^4}{1-0.8}(730)^{1-0.8}} = 1 - e^{-0.00037}$$

$$\approx 0.0004 \tag{2.21d}$$

$$= 0.04\% \tag{2.21e}$$

**Question 2.**  What percentage of devices will fail during the first month if they have been burned in for 10 hours at 150°C?

**Solution.**  The hazard rate after burn-in is

$$\lambda(t) = \lambda_1(t_{eff} + t)^{-\alpha}. \tag{2.22a}$$

If $\int_0^t \lambda(t')dt' \ll 1$, then we may use the approximate formula for dropout (see Appendix D):

$$\% \text{ failing} = 10^{-7} \int_0^{730} \lambda_1(t_{eff} + t')^{-\alpha}dt' = 10^{-7}\lambda_1 \int_{t_{eff}}^{t_{eff}+730} t^{-\alpha}dt \tag{2.22b}$$

$$= 10^{-7}\frac{2\times10^4}{1-0.8}\left[(t_{eff}+730)^{1-0.8} - (t_{eff})^{1-0.8}\right] \tag{2.22c}$$

so that

$$\% \text{ failing} = 10^{-2}\left[(t_{eff} + 730)^{0.2} - (t_{eff})^{0.2}\right]$$

Using $E_a = 0.4\ eV$, $k_B = 8.6\times10^{-5}\ eV/°K$, $T_2 = 423°K$ (the burn-in temperature), and $T_1 = 313°K$ (reference temperature), Equation (2.9) gives

$$A_T = e^{\left[\frac{0.4}{8.6\times10^{-5}}\left[\frac{1}{313}-\frac{1}{423}\right]\right]} , \tag{2.23a}$$

$$\approx 48. \tag{2.23b}$$

Here, $A_{op} = 1$ since the operating temperature is the reference temperature. If, in addition, the device in question is an MOS device with gate oxide thicknesses of 250Å and is nominally operated at 5.5 volts but is burned in at 7.5 volts, Equation (2.14) gives

$$A_V = e^{\left[\frac{290}{250}(7.5-5.5)\right]} , \tag{2.24a}$$

$$\approx 10. \tag{2.24b}$$

So $A_{bi} = A_T A_V = (48)(10) = 480$, $A_{op} = 1$, for $t_{bi} = 10$ hours so that $t_{eff} = 4800$ hours. The percentage failing is then, using (2.22c),

$$\% \text{ failing} = 10^{-\alpha}\left[(4800+730)^{0.2}-(4800)^{0.2}\right] , \tag{2.25a}$$

$$= 0.0015\% . \tag{2.25b}$$

This burn-in clearly produces a very significant reduction in the number of failures during the first month of operation. These dropout figures may be expressed in terms of an average hazard rate. This is not to say that the exponential model is used to determine dropout. Once $\bar{N}/n$ is determined with the Weibull, the average hazard rate is computed as follows:

$$\lambda_{ave} = \frac{\bar{N}}{n} \times \frac{10^9}{time} \quad \text{(FITs)} \tag{2.25c}$$

where time is in hours. Here, the time is one month, or 730 hours. The average hazard rate for the first month drops from 548 FITs with no burn-in, to 21 FITs with burn-in. This large reduction is due principally to the large temperature acceleration being modeled.

We next consider aspects of the reliability of electronic devices in the long-term or steady-state period of device life.

## LONG-TERM (STEADY-STATE) DEVICE RELIABILITY

Perhaps the most important objective of a device reliability program is to ensure that long-term reliability is adequate, primarily by ensuring that wearout does not occur during the service life of a device. Long-term device reliability refers to device reliability in the post-infant mortality period of device life, also referred to as the steady-state period of life. Typically, device reliability during this period of device life is described by a constant hazard rate. As discussed in the last chapter, this description is used for convenience, and may be a reasonable approximation to a slowly changing hazard rate. The AT&T hazard rate model for electronic components represents the hazard rate of an electronic device to be constant in the post-infant mortality of device life. It is important to note that whenever a hazard rate is cited that is not further qualified by specifying the age of a device, for example, a "10 FIT device," that rate refers to a constant hazard rate model. In this manual, whenever the AT&T hazard rate model for electronic components is referred to in such a way, that reference would necessarily refer to the post-infant mortality portion of the model, that is, times after the crossover time, $t_c = 10^4$ hours (see Chapter 1, the *AT&T Reliability Model* section). A knowledge of the contributing failure modes and failure mechanisms* and of how to control them is necessary to interpret long-term hazard rates properly. Accelerated stress testing is used to assess, and thereby ensure, the long-term reliability of commercial devices procured under Level III specifications.

The reliability of AT&T devices is ensured by design and process control programs, which are supplemented by an accelerated stress testing program. Though the design and process control program has a direct effect on device reliability, it is a product-dependent program, and discussion of it is beyond the scope of this manual. Therefore, our discussion of reliability of electronic devices in the steady-state period of device life begins with a discussion of accelerated life testing as it pertains to this period of device life.

### Accelerated Stress Testing during the Steady State

The motivation for performing accelerated life testing (ALT) was presented in the *Early Life Reliability (Infant Mortality Period)* section. These reasons pertain to the steady-state part of device life as well. There is, however, an even more important, very simple consideration that leads us to use ALT to assess steady-state reliability. Without ALT, we would have to test devices for over a year before even entering the steady-state period of device life! And, of course, the accelerating effect of some stress must be well characterized, if we are to interpret accelerated life testing with this stress.

The relationship between stress and time to failure for a given device is completely characterized by the activation energies of the failure mechanisms which are dominant in that device within the context of: (1) the accelerated life model and (2) the Arrhenius model for the acceleration factor. The activation energies are

---

* A failure mode is defined as the manifestation of a failure, such as an open or short circuit. A failure mechanism is the physical, chemical, or other type process resulting in a failure mode.

determined from extensive accelerated life testing, usually done at the time the failure mechanism is first discovered. A tabulation of failure mechanisms and their associated activation energies, as found in the literature, are listed in Table 2.2.

**TABLE 2.2.** Time-Dependent Failure Mechanisms in Silicon Devices[28,29]

| Device Association | Failure Mechanism | Relevant Factors | Accelerating Factors | Acceleration ($E_a$ = Apparent Activation Energy for Temp.) |
|---|---|---|---|---|
| Silicon Oxide and Silicon-Silicon Oxide Interface | Surface charge accumulation | mobile ions, V,T | T | $E_a$ = 1.0–1.05 eV |
| | Dielectric breakdown | E,T | E | |
| | Charge injection | $E,T,Q_{ss}$ | E,T | $E_a$ = 1.3 eV (slow trapping) |
| Metallization | Electromigration | T, j, A, gradients of T and j, grain size | T, j | $E_a$ = 0.5–1.2 eV j to $j^4$ dependence |
| | Corrosion (chemical, galvanic, electrolytic | contamination, H,V,T | H,V,T | strong H effect $E_a \approx$ 0.3–0.6 eV (for electrolysis) V may have thresholds |
| | Contact degradation | T, metals, impurities | varied | |
| Bonds and Other Mechanical Interfaces | Intermetallic growth | T, impurities, bond strength | T | Al-Au: $E_a$ = 1.0-1.05 eV |
| | Fatigue | bond strength, temperature cycling | T extremes in cycling | |
| Metal Penetration | Aluminum Penetration into Silicon | T, j, A | T, j | $E_a$ = 1.4–1.6 $eV$ |
| Hermeticity | Seal leaks | pressure differential, atmosphere | pressure | |

V – voltage    E – electric field    A – area    $Q_{ss}$ – interfacial fixed charge
T – temperature    j – current density    H – humidity

To determine the relation between stress and time to failure for a given device, the most likely failure mechanisms are assumed, based on a knowledge of device technology, design rules, and function. Based on known activation energies for device failure mechanisms, high temperature experiments can be undertaken to determine the effects of the accelerating stress on device lifetime. The stress is applied to a sample of the devices, and the failures are analyzed. Since we assume an activation energy, hazard rates at lower temperature can be extrapolated from the high temperature data.

It is important to treat the different failure mechanisms that may occur within a sample independently, because they may be accelerated differently, and extrapolations from combined data can be very misleading. (This emphasizes the need for failure analysis to identify the failure mechanism.)

With a knowledge of the number of failures of each failure mechanism and their corresponding activation energies, a lifetime distribution can be fit to the failure times and the device reliability can be predicted.

It is important to realize that stresses other than those listed in Table 2.2 might also give rise to end-of-life failure mechanisms, and that the effects of these stresses on the lifetime distribution of the device will also need to be investigated.

**Failure Distributions**

The use of failure data to predict the long-term reliability of a device assumes that a well-defined statistical distribution of failure times has been determined. The mathematical description of such a distribution should include formulas describing standard functions of reliability engineering, such as the mean time to failure. The Weibull and lognormal distributions have been found through experience to best describe semiconductor failure time data at different acceleration conditions. The Weibull distribution is useful in modeling the infant mortality portions of an electronic device hazard rate. The lognormal distribution has been successfully used to describe the failure times resulting from a single semiconductor failure mechanism or a closely related group of failure mechanisms which depend on contaminant concentrations and diffusion constants, current densities and temperature gradients, and temperature variations and voltage gradients. See Chapter 1, the *Mathematical Terminology: Measures of Reliability* section for a description of different distributions that are useful in analyzing data gathered for the purposes of assessing reliability.

If the accelerating stress is electrical (passive components only), then an additional acceleration factor* is given by[30]

$$A = A_E = e^{m(p_1 - p_0)} \ ,$$ (2.26)

where $m$ is a parameter determined[30] from expressions in MIL-HDBK-217D,[31] $p_1$ is the percent of maximum rated electrical stress, and $p_0$ is the reference percent of rated electrical stress (25 percent). Note that those expressions in MIL-HDBK-

---

* This type of hazard rate multiplier is sometimes referred to as a derating factor.

217D that formed the basis for Equation (2.26) remained the same in MIL-HDBK-217E,[32] the latest edition. For resistors, $p$ represents power dissipated; for capacitors, $p$ is voltage; while for relays and switches, $p$ is contact current.

Within AT&T, the reference electrical stress rating (power, voltage, or current) is 25 percent, as this had been common practice in the Bell System before divestiture. When percent of rated electrical stress above 25 percent is employed, we use Equation (2.26), along with the above discussion to estimate the hazard rates under these more stressful conditions. Equation (2.26) may also be used to estimate the *reduction* in hazard rate associated with electrical stress ratings (power, voltage, or current) *less* than 25 percent.

### Failure Mechanisms in Accelerated Testing

As previously mentioned, there are many accelerating stresses other than elevated temperature that can be used to activate different failure mechanisms. Some of the other common stresses of interest are temperature cycling, power cycling, humidity, voltage, and current density. In each case, an equation that relates stress to time-to-failure must be determined, and the distribution of failure times must be known or identifiable by test. Refer to Table 2.2 for a summary of many of the failure mechanisms in silicon devices.[28,29] This table lists the processes leading to failure, some relevant factors associated with failure, appropriate acceleration factors, and the associated activation energies.

Although it is difficult to list all failure mechanisms, it is possible to group some mechanisms together according to the type of accelerated conditions that affect them:

1.  Elevated temperature without applied electrical bias can test for diffusion effects, chemical reactions, and decomposition of materials, sometimes in combination with other environments, but sometimes alone. Two examples of using elevated temperature without electrical bias are: chemical reaction in contact areas, where contact metals can react with the semiconductor material, and growth of intermetallic materials at the bonds of dissimilar metals such as gold and aluminum.

2.  Elevated temperature and voltage can detect mechanisms such as surface inversion, surface charge movement, and dielectric breakdown.

3.  The cycling of temperature results in a fatigue stressing of materials. This can reveal conditions such as weak wire bonds, mismatches of seal materials in hermetic packages, and mismatch of the coefficients of thermal expansion of the silicon device chip and its package in the die attach region.

4.  Temperature, humidity, and voltage, aided by some contamination to provide an electrolyte, can cause particular problems with materials subject to corrosion. Electrolytic corrosion of aluminum, gold, or palladium exposed to humidity and normal circuit bias is a good example. Depending on the material, different failure modes may be observed. Electrolytic corrosion of aluminum typically produces open metal lines; on the other hand, electrolytic corrosion of gold or palladium leads to dendritic growths, resulting in shorts from one line to the next. External leads can corrode enough to fall off in

extreme conditions. Figures 2-9 and 2-10 are examples of corrosion of aluminum and palladium, respectively.

5.  Reduction of temperature is an unusual acceleration condition, but at least two failure mechanisms cause failures more rapidly at reduced temperature. In the first mechanism, moisture sealed within a package condenses at a temperature that depends on the amount of moisture present. When condensation occurs, surface conductivity and leakage increase. The possibility of corrosion also increases since a better electrolyte is produced when condensation occurs. The second mechanism involves hot-electron induced degradation of metal-oxide semiconductor (MOS) devices which causes a higher hazard rate at a lower temperature than at a higher temperature.

6.  High temperature and high current density can accelerate electromigration of metallization stripes on circuits. In this mechanism, metal ions are swept by the impact of current flow. This action produces hillocks of metal at one end of a line and voids at the other end until an open circuit develops.

7.  Naturally occurring $\alpha$-particles can cause soft errors in small-cell MOS dynamic memory devices. Existing ceramic packaging materials have trace, though significant, levels of materials such as thorium and uranium-containing isotopes which decay, emitting $\alpha$-particles. When an $\alpha$-particle penetrates the chip surface, it can create enough electron-hole pairs to cause discharging of a memory cell, resulting in a random, single-bit error. The errors are not permanent; that is, no physical defect is associated with the failed bit. This failure mechanism depends largely on the physical memory cell size (or on the amount of charge being stored). Accelerated testing is performed with a high flux $\alpha$-particle source.

8.  Where high electric field gradients exist through an insulator, voltage is an accelerating factor for dielectric failures in MOS circuits and in on-chip capacitors of linear circuits.

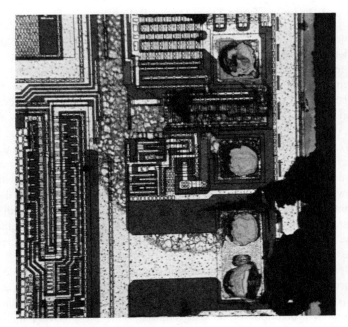

**Figure 2-9.** Photograph showing corroded aluminum metallization.

**Figure 2-10.** Example of palladium dendritic growth due to corrosion. The TiPdAu metallization system is used on the ceramic substrates of hybrid integrated circuits. The photograph was made using transmitted light; therefore, the metal appears dark. The dark tree-like structures are Pd dendrites that have grown out of the TiPdAu metal runners.

### Influence of Design on Long-Term Device Reliability

Device design features can influence the susceptibility of the device to given failure mechanisms. Since it is difficult, if not impossible, to develop general design rules that relate design features to the device reliability, the influence of design on the long-term device reliability is demonstrated through examples. One failure mechanism which often limits the reliability of semiconductor devices is surface inversion (see Figure 2-11). The failure mechanism of this figure is explained as follows: the presence of positive charge in (or on) the oxide inverts the P-type base material due to induced negative charge, making it an N-type material. Similarly, the presence of negative charges can invert the N-type collector material to P-type. These inversions result in increases in leakage current (shunt) paths, decreases in breakdown voltages, and, hence, failure of the device. The source of the charges is ionic contamination on the chip surface. The positively charged sodium ion is a particular problem since it is quite mobile and is a very common contaminant. To eliminate this failure mechanism, the chip surface must be protected from the presence of the ions.

In typical small- or medium-scale commercial chips, the deposition of phosphorous on the outer surface of the thermally grown silicon dioxide protects against contaminating ions. Some manufacturers also add phosphorous to the top layer (scratch protection) of deposited glass. This glass covers the whole chip, including the aluminum metallization, except at the bonding pads. Despite this protection, some chips are still susceptible to surface inversion.

In integrated circuit devices, an aluminum metallization system is commonly used. Gold or aluminum wires are bonded to aluminum pads on the chip and are connected to the package pins. The chip is mounted face-up in a hermetically sealed ceramic package or molded in a plastic material and a layer of silicon nitride covers the chip, except in the area of the bonding pads. This layer acts as a barrier against mobile ions. In addition, the phosphorous dopant acts as a sodium getter. This technology produces reliable devices if careful process control is exercised in manufacturing.

Very important device reliability considerations arise from the use of activated water soluble solder fluxes in the process of circuit pack assembly. Because of the presence of chloride ions in these fluxes, they are corrosive to integrated circuit lead metallization as well as the chip metallization. It is extremely important that these fluxes be completely removed by a thorough rinse. Any trace of flux allowed to remain on the circuit board or around the package leads will result in the corrosion of the metallization. The corrosive ions in these fluxes only damage the chip metallization if they are allowed to penetrate the package and interact with moisture at the surface of the chip. Plastic packaged devices made by AT&T, as well as those produced by other manufacturers under Level III or Level II specifications, are qualified to insure that there is no serious corrosive ion penetration.

Once the use of accelerated testing for reliability prediction of devices and the effect of design features on the device reliability are understood, one needs to develop methodologies for acceptance or qualification of devices supplied by different sources. Such methodologies are explained below.

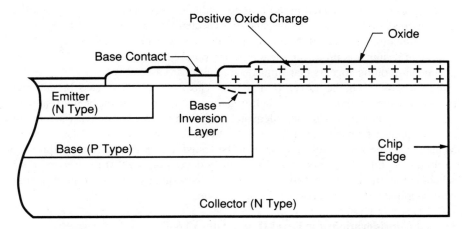

**Figure 2-11.** Illustration of surface inversion due to ionic contamination.

### Qualification and Reliability Monitoring of Devices

Qualification refers to the steps taken to demonstrate that the required reliability objectives of a new semiconductor device or technology can be met. Particular emphasis is placed on the use of accelerated stress testing for that purpose. Reliability monitoring testing refers to the tests and criteria established to ensure that the reliability and performance objectives for the device, once qualified, continue to be realized in production for a particular group (say, one lot) of devices.

Within AT&T, direct exchange of information among designers, manufacturing engineers, reliability engineers, and quality assurance engineers during the design phase results in optimization of design features and process techniques.

Qualification testing is typically conducted on samples of devices that incorporate the design features, materials, and processes to be used in production; that is, the technology is qualified. The purpose of this technology qualification is to identify or confirm the main failure mechanism and to provide data to predict or confirm the required long-term reliability and establish the lot-acceptance criteria. The sample sizes chosen are sufficiently large to give statistical confidence in the long-term hazard rate predictions. The accelerated stress tests used vary in nature and degree depending on the device technology, the expected failure mechanisms, and the reliability requirements. For example, a new device technology needs more extensive qualification than does an extension of an existing one.

An important aspect of qualification is testing of prototype units in circuit packs. This is frequently needed to prove the design and to ensure that the models used for qualification are correct from an applications standpoint.

For both Level II and Level III devices, long-term reliability is assured by the reliability monitoring program that is run by the manufacturer and monitored by AT&T. Level III devices are also subject to lot acceptance testing requirements.

Qualification of Level II and Level III devices also includes accelerated stress tests. The tests are selected based on knowledge of the specific device technology used by the supplier of the devices and on expected failure mechanisms. As part of the qualification, a physical examination of the device is performed to document the important design and processing features, and preceeding the accelerated stress tests a "preconditioning" occurs that simulates circuit board assembly.

Features of both the Level II and non-AT&T Level III device procurement procedures are an initial vendor facility survey to assure that the vendor standard quality assurance programs are adequate, along with the requirement for ongoing, on-site quality management programs by AT&T. For Level III, AT&T Quality Management personnel select samples to be tested, check the suppliers' equipment calibrations and testing procedures, and verify data. For Level II devices, regularly scheduled audits assure that the approved standard quality assurance programs are being applied to the production of Level II devices.

## Special Considerations for Level II and Non-AT&T Level III Devices

Before a non-AT&T manufactured semiconductor device can be purchased for use in AT&T equipment under a Level II or Level III specification, notification to use these devices must be made for each different application of the device in that equipment. An AT&T procedure, Notification-to-Use (NTU), has been established for this purpose. This procedure is intended to minimize the risk of poor performance, failure in service, or unavailability of AT&T systems on schedule due to semiconductor device problems.

In order to realize maximum benefit from the NTU procedures, the AT&T equipment designer must review the tentative semiconductor device selection as early as possible in the design cycle. This early interaction will allow time to consider alternate devices to minimize the risks mentioned previously.

Importantly, the NTU request sets into motion the preparation of a Level II or Level III specification or other appropriate action and qualification of the device and the supplier. Considerable time may be required to complete this activity. If the request is to add an additional code to an existing Level II or Level III specification and the supplier is one with which AT&T has had experience, then the effort required is minimal, and the specification can be issued in one or two months.

Level II and Level III specification devices are purchased through a central AT&T purchasing organization, which negotiates contracts in advance with the suppliers. Orders for specific needs can then be placed in accordance with the agreements.

## CROSSOVER TIME FROM INFANT MORTALITY TO STEADY-STATE HAZARD RATE

As discussed earlier in this chapter and the previous one, most electronic devices exhibit two different hazard rate regions: the infant mortality and the long-term regions. The crossover time is that time at which the infant mortality period ends and the long-term period starts. Under ordinary operating conditions, the infant mortality and steady-state hazard rates have the same value at $10^4$ hours at reference conditions. However, for increased electrical stress or temperature, the constant hazard rate part of the model typically increases more than the infant mortality hazard rate. This leads to an apparent discontinuity in the model at $10^4$ hours. But the infant mortality region of the model is only intended to model failures that occur at a rate greater than the long-term rate. Therefore, the transition time may be taken to be that time when the infant mortality hazard rate becomes equal to the steady-state hazard rate. For operation at accelerated conditions, the transition should then occur before $10^4$ hours. This shift is displayed in Figure 2-12.

There is an apparent paradox of this procedure. If the accelerating stress has more of an effect on the infant mortality hazard rate, in spite of the $1 - \alpha$ power to which the infant mortality acceleration factor is raised, then it is possible to have the infant mortality part of the hazard rate curve extend beyond the unaccelerated crossover time of $10^4$ hours. But this truly is no paradox. The form of the AT&T hazard rate model for electronic devices is based on there being different failure causing mechanisms at work in electronic components. The different mechanisms lead to different forms for the hazard rate of some device population, over different time periods.

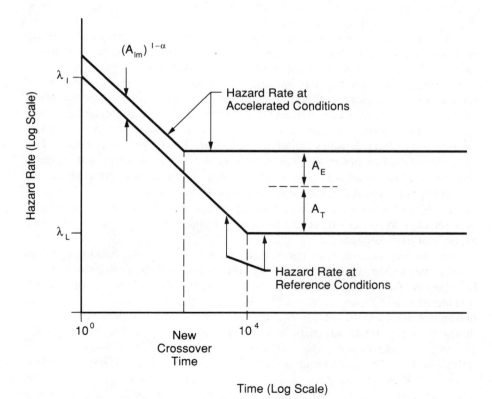

**Figure 2-12.** Shift in the transition point from an infant mortality to a constant hazard rate under accelerated conditions, that is, due to elevated temperature and increased electrical stress.

We may think of the infant mortality curve as continuing beyond the crossover time, but that any effect is negligible, similarly for any constant hazard rate during the infant mortality period. Such a constant hazard rate may be thought of as present, say due to the tail of a wearout mode, but negligible. And so, if the declining part of this composite hazard rate is more affected by some accelerating stress than the constant part, then it may take longer for the declining (with time) part of the curve to become dominated by the constant part.

For each device, the time where the transition occurs depends on the accelerating conditions. Therefore, a circuit pack hazard rate may be the sum of device hazard rates with different transition points occurring at various times. Computing such a system hazard rate is cumbersome. A reasonable approximation is to calculate the circuit pack infant mortality curve and make the transition where the pack infant mortality hazard rate meets the system steady-state hazard rate.

## ELECTROSTATIC DISCHARGE AND ELECTRICAL OVERSTRESS

An important aspect of overall device reliability is the capacity to survive extraordinary electrical stresses generated during manufacture, testing, handling, installation, and use. It is convenient to divide electrical stress into two general categories based on the electrical parameters of the source: electrical overstress (EOS) and electrostatic discharge (ESD).

ESD and EOS cause four failure mechanisms which can damage or weaken integrated circuit devices. These are metallization damage, oxide breakdown, junction damage, and stress-induced spiking of metal through junctions. High stress currents flowing through metallization stripes can cause excessive joule heating and subsequent melting, resulting in an open circuit. Electric fields produced by stress events can exceed the dielectric breakdown strength of gate and field oxides, usually causing a conductive short through the oxide. High instantaneous power densities can induce secondary breakdown in junctions. The resulting melt filaments in the silicon deform the lattice structure and produce junction leakage. In addition, the associated high temperatures accelerate metal-silicon interdiffusion and can drive a metal spike through a junction. The degree of vulnerability of silicon integrated circuit devices to each of these mechanisms is very sensitive to device layout and processing technology. Figure 2-13 shows an example of EOS damage.

EOS can be produced by or transmitted through a live system backplane and is usually minimized through careful system design. ESD protection can be incorporated in the chip design. If so, then testing of ESD protection can be considered a part of qualification. ESD has two main sources: contact with charged human operators and the rapid release of triboelectric charge acquired by the device during passage through automatic handlers or shipping tubes. The study of ESD effects is, therefore, based upon two circuit models: the Human Body Model[32] (HBM) and the Charged Device Model[32] (CDM). Figures 2-14 and 2-15 show schematics of circuits that have been developed to simulate each type of ESD in the laboratory and Table 2.3 summarizes the electrical conditions for EOS and ESD. ESD failure thresholds tend to decrease as device geometries shrink if designers do nothing to improve the situation. But because the ESD sensitivity of a specific device is an extremely sensitive function of input/output circuit layout, ESD failure thresholds are actually *increasing* with decreasing dimensions, because designers are more and more conscious of the importance of ESD and EOS issues. Optimum ESD performance is obtained when the I/O circuit geometries ensure a maximally uniform distribution of both voltage and current throughout the volume of the circuit under stress. This uniformity can be achieved through careful consideration by the integrated circuit designer of layout parameters, such as, metal linewidths and spacings, contact window distribution, and N+/P+ areas and perimeters. Design rules for a particular technology that have been implemented in computer aided design (CAD) tools greatly help the designer. Within a given integrated circuit technology, processing parameters, such as, junction depth and gate oxide thickness, largely determine which failure mode limits the ESD performance, while the layout largely determines the absolute failure threshold of the dominant mode. In addition, changes occur in the relative importance of the various failure modes as integrated circuit technologies continue to evolve. Thus, designing for ESD protection is a dynamic issue that must be re-evaluated with the introduction of each new device technology.

**Figure 2-13.** Failure due to electrical overstress on metal line of an integrated circuit.

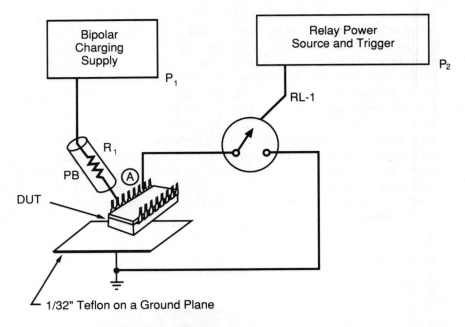

Component List

P₁    0 to 3KV DC Power Supply
P₂    12V DC Relay Power Supply
PB    Charging Probe
R₁    100 Megohm Resistor
RL-1  Vacuum Relay

**Figure 2-14.** Charged device ESD simulator. Power supply P1 is used to electrically charge the device through R1 while the relay RL-1 is open. Then the device is discharged to ground through pin A by closing RL-1.

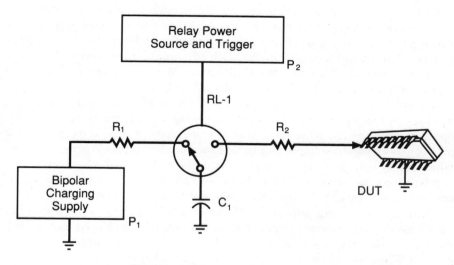

### Component List

| | |
|---|---|
| $P_1$ | 0 to 3KV DC Power Supply |
| $P_2$ | 12V DC Relay Power Supply |
| $R_1$ | Five 1 Megohm Resistors in Series, 1 Watt, Carbon Composition or Equivalent |
| $R_2$ | 1.5 Kilohms Resistor, 1 Watt, Carbon Composition 5% or Equivalent |
| $C_1$ | 100 pF, 5KV Capacitor |
| RL-1 | Mercury Relay |

**Figure 2-15.** Schematic of human body ESD simulator. Capacitor C1 first is charged through R1. It is then discharged through R2 and the device-under-test (DUT) to ground by switching the relay RL-1.

**TABLE 2.3.** Typical Parameters for Various Types of EOS/ESD

| Parameter | EOS | HBM ESD | CDM ESD |
|---|---|---|---|
| Energy (J) | $>1.0\times10^{-3}$ | $1.0\times10^{-5}$ | $1.0\times10^{-5}$ |
| Duration (s) | $>1.0\times10^{-6}$ | $1.0\times10^{-7}$ | $2.0\times10^{-9}$ |
| Source Impedance ($\Omega$) | $<10$ | $\sim1500$ | $\sim1$ |

## CMOS LATCH-UP

Latch-up is a failure mode associated with CMOS devices. If latch-up occurs, the CMOS device becomes nonfunctional and draws excessive power supply current which generally causes severe overheating and permanent device damage. Latch-up is initiated by various triggering events, such as power supply overvoltage or noise spikes on an output. A CMOS device will remain latched-up until either the power supply voltage is removed or the device self-destructs.

A CMOS device can be triggered into latch-up by many different means. Voltages appearing on any pin that exceed the manufacture's recommended operating limit can cause latch-up. This would include ringing on input or output pins or power supply voltages that exceed the specified limit. The rate at which power supply voltage is applied to the device can also induce latch-up, as well as improper sequencing of supplies. ESD induced latch-up can occur when an operating circuit pack or its associated equipment enclosure is subjected to ESD.

The many ways of triggering a CMOS device into latch-up are all related in that each triggering mechanism causes excessive amounts of charge to be injected into the device. The injected charges cause latch-up by altering the conduction state of parasitic SCR (silicon-controlled-rectifier) structures within the CMOS device. The parasitic SCRs are formed during IC manufacturing and are present in all CMOS devices. Normally, in the off state, the parasitic SCRs do not interfere with the operation of the device. However, if a parasitic SCR(s) is triggered into conduction, it develops a low impedance between VCC and ground, which can result in the high power supply current that is characteristic of latch-up. It is generally true that most devices will latch-up if the triggering event has sufficient charge to trigger an internal SCR(s) into conduction; however, the amount of charge needed to latch-up one device may significantly differ from the amount of charge needed to latch-up a similar device from a different supplier. Differences in IC design and processing account for the wide variation in the actual triggering levels needed to cause latch-up.

To determine the actual triggering level and, thus, identify potentially latch-up sensitive devices, AT&T has developed a latch-up test procedure. This procedure subjects a CMOS device to various triggering levels while monitoring the device for latch-up. AT&T's internal device qualification program requires that all CMOS devices meet a minimum triggering criteria for latch-up. Further, CMOS devices manufactured by outside suppliers and purchased according to a Level II or Level III specification for use in AT&T products are also tested for latch-up and must meet the same strict standards that are set for AT&T's CMOS devices.

In this chapter, we have introduced the concepts of electronic device reliability including the important topic of accelerated life testing. We have gone on to consider the central issues relevant to device reliability in both the infant mortality period as well as the steady-state period. And finally we have briefly considered the topics of ESD and EOS which are so important to the reliability of electronic devices.

## REFERENCES

1. *Reliability Prediction Procedure for Electronic Equipment* (TR-TSY-000332), Issue 2, Bell Communications Research, July 1988.

2. D. R. Cox and D. Oaks, *Analysis of Survival Data*, Chapman and Hall, London, 1984.

3. J. F. Lawless, *Statistical Models and Methods for Lifetime Data*, Wiley, New York, 1982.

4. S. Arrhenius, *Z. Physik. Chemie* **4** (1889): p. 226.

5. R. E. Wetson and H. A. Schwarz, *Chemical Kinetics*, Prentice Hall, Englewood Cliffs, 1972.

6. R. Stephen Berry, S. A. Rice, J. Ross, *Physical Chemistry*, Wiley, New York, 1980, and references contained therein.

7. L. Boltzmann, *Lectures on Gas Theory*, (translated by S. Brush), University of California Press, Berkeley, 1964.

8. F. Reif, *Fundamentals of Statistical and Thermal Physics*, McGraw-Hill, New York, 1965.

9. D. J. Klinger, "Failure Time and the Rate Constant of Degradation: An Argument for the Inverse Relationship," (submitted to *IEEE Transactions on Reliability*).

10. W. B. Joyce, K-Y Liou, F. R. Nash, P. R. Bossard, R. L. Hartman, "Assuring High-Reliability of Lasers and Photo-Detectors for Submarine Lightwave Cable Systems: Methodology of Accelerated Aging," *AT&T Technical Journal* **64**, 3 (1985): p. 717.

11. E. Wigner, "Transition State Method," *Faraday Soc. (London) Trans.* **34** (1938): p. 29, and references contained therein.

12. M. G. Evans and M. Polanyi, "Inertia and Driving Force of Chemical Reactions," *Faraday Soc. (London) Trans.* **34** (1938): p. 11, and references contained therein.

13. H. Eyring, S. H. Lin, S. M. Lin, *Basic Chemical Kinetics*, Wiley, New York, 1980.

14. M. J. LuValle, T. L. Welsher, J. P. Mitchell, "A New Approach to the Extrapolation of Accelerated Life Test Data," *Proceedings of the Fifth International Conference on Reliability and Maintainability*," European Space Agency, 1986: p. 630. See also M. J. LuValle, T. L. Welsher, S. W. Swoboda, "Acceleration Transforms and Statistical Kinetic Models," *J. Stat. Phys.* **52** (1988): p. 311 and references contained therein.

15. D. J. Klinger, "On the Notion of Activation Energy in Reliability: Arrhenius, Eyring, and Thermodynamics" (in preparation).

16. E. A. Elsayed and C. K. Chan, "Estimation of Thin Oxide Reliability Using Proportional Hazards Models," (to be published in *IEEE Transactions on Reliability*).

17. S. C. Darby and J. A. Riceland, "Low Levels of Ionizing Radiation and Cancer—Are We Underestimating the Risk," *J. Royal Stat. Soc.* **A144** (1981): p. 298.

18. W. A. Bertram, "Yield and Reliability," in *VLSI Technology*, 2nd Edition, edited by S. M. Sze, McGraw-Hill, New York, 1988. See also E. A. Amerasekera and D. S. Campbell, *Failure Mechanisms in Semiconductor Devices*, Wiley, New York, 1987, and references contained therein.

19. D. S. Peck, "New Concerns about Integrated Circuit Reliability," *Proceedings of the International Reliability Physics Symposium*, IEEE, 1978: p. 1.

20. D. Crook, "Method of Determining Reliability Screens for Time Dependent Dielectric Breakdown," *Proceedings of the International Reliability Physics Symposium*, IEEE, 1979: p. 1.

21. Y. Hokari, T. Baba, N. Kawamura, "Reliability of 6-10 nm Thermal $SiO_2$ Films Showing Intrinsic Dielectric Integrity," *IEEE Transactions on Electron Devices* **32** (1985): p. 2485.

22. D. A. Baglee, "Characteristics of 100 Å Oxides," *Proceedings of the International Reliability Physics Symposium*, IEEE, 1984: p. 132.

23. J. Eachus, J. Klema, S. Walker, "Monitored Burn-In of MOS 64K Dynamic RAMS," *Semiconductor International*, February, 1984: p. 104.

24. J. C. Lee, I. Chen, C. Hu, "Modeling and Characterization of Gate Oxide Reliability," *IEEE Transactions on Electron Devices* **35**, 12 (1988): p. 2268.

25. J. L. Dais and F. L. Howland, "Fatigue Failure of Encapsulated Gold-Beam Lead and TAB Devices," *IEEE Transactions on Components, Hybrids, and Manufacturing Technology* **1** (1978): p. 158.

26. R. E. Kuehn, "Results of Production Thermal Cycle Screening," *IEEE Transactions on Reliability* **23** (1974): p. 273.

27. E. A. Herr and A. Poe, "Transistor High-Reliability Program," *Proceedings of the Industry Application Society*, IEEE, 1977: p. 833.

28. J. Wood, "Reliability and Degradation of Silicon Devices and Integrated Circuits," in *Reliability and Degradation*, edited by M. H. Howes and D. V. Morgan, Wiley, New York, 1981.

29. D. S. Peck, "Practical Applications of Accelerated Testing—Introduction," *Proceedings of the International Reliability Physics Symposium*, IEEE, 1975: p. 253.

30. The hazard rates of MIL-HDBK-217 (beginning with version C and updated regularly, now with version E being current, see Reference 31, below) have been used to obtain steady-state hazard rates within the context of the AT&T hazard rate model for electronic devices. By comparing AT&T hazard rates (longterm) for composition resistors with those from MIL-HDBK-217, it was determined that Level III parts correspond to quality level I of MIL-HDBK-217. The early life data, in terms of the Weibull shape parameter $\alpha$, was determined for each device type based on experience with OLT, factory burn-in, and field tracking. With an $\alpha$ for each device type and knowledge of

the appropriate quality factor to be used, the MIL-HDBK data was recast in the form commonly used with AT&T for those device types without sufficient field or factory data upon which we might estimate hazard rates confidently. Similarly, the electrical stress factors were transcribed, but in a form appropriate for AT&T designers, i.e., with no "acceleration" when the electrical stress is 25 percent of maximum rating.

31. Department of Defense, *Reliability Prediction of Electronic Equipment*, MIL-HDBK-217D, U. S. Government Printing Office Washington, D.C., 1982.

32. Department of Defense, *Reliability Prediction of Electronic Equipment*, MIL-HDBK-217E, U. S. Government Printing Office, Washington, D.C., 1986.

33. T. S. Speakman, "A Model of the Failure of Bipolar Silicon Integrated Circuits Subjected to Electrostatic Discharge," *Proceedings of the International Reliability Physics Symposium*, IEEE, 1974: p. 60.

# 3

---

# SYSTEM RELIABILITY

---

## INTRODUCTION

An *integral* part of the design process is the evaluation of the reliability of each system or subsystem at each stage of design. This is a *necessary* part of the design process in order to comply with early life and steady-state reliability requirements, a part of all AT&T designs.

System reliability analysis is also important in the *establishment* of the reliability requirements for a particular design.

In the last chapter, we developed the framework and methodology for characterizing the reliability of electronic devices.

In this chapter, we discuss how to use this information to characterize subsystems, parts of subsystems or entire systems. In doing so, we make a careful distinction between maintained and nonmaintained systems, and the figures of merit appropriate in each case. The chapter concludes with a discussion of electrostatic discharge (ESD) in the context of system reliability.

## SYSTEM RELIABILITY MODELING

To assess the *inherent reliability** of a system, we must have a concrete design to analyze. And for a particular design we need a methodology for performing the analysis. Given the structure of modern telecommunications equipment, a natural scheme presents itself. Typically, systems or subsystems, however large or small,

---

* By *inherent reliability* we mean the maximum reliability for that system, not necessarily what is observed. Our discussion does not, for example, take into account the effect of *unusual* events, for example an earthquake. On the other hand, *common* external events that cause failure (referred to as *extrinsic failure modes*) are included in system reliability calculations if the inputs to those calculations are based on good quality field data, rather than laboratory tests.

contain a number of circuit packs* and a frame or a backplane into which the circuit packs are inserted. It is natural, therefore, to subdivide systems into a collection of blocks that represent circuit packs. These blocks are then organized into what is called a *reliability block diagram*.

### Reliability Block Diagram

The construction of the reliability block diagram is the first step in the analysis of system reliability. It is a way of capturing, or modeling, the *reliability structure* of a system. This structure, we shall see shortly, is independent of the *failure model* and, in the case of maintained systems, the *repair model*.

Structural models are formulated and the calculus of probability is used to calculate total system reliability figures of merit in terms of the block reliability figures of merit. The following example illustrates the construction of a reliability block diagram for a simple system.

**Example 3.1.**   Consider a simple system in which either of elements *A* or *B* must work, and element *C* must work for the system to function properly.

**Problem.**   Draw a reliability block diagram of the system.

**Solution.**   The reliability block diagram of the system is shown in Figure 3-1. The reliability block diagram provides a guide for combining the probabilities associated with each block. The following notation is used throughout this chapter:

$A$       —       state in which element $A$ is working,

$\bar{A}$       —       state in which element $A$ is not working,

$P_A$       —       probability that element $A$ is working, and

$P_{\bar{A}}$       —       probability that element $A$ is not working.

Note that $P_{\bar{A}} = 1 - P_A$.

If a collection of circuit packs exists such that the failure of any one of them leads to system failure, then we say that these circuit packs are "in series." We may say equally well that for a series system to be working, all elements must be working. The simplest example of a series system is shown in Figure 3-2.

In a series system, all elements must be operational for the system to be operational. Consequently, the event representing the system being in an

---

* Also called circuit boards.

operational state is represented by the intersection of those events representing the operational state of the two elements.  In other words,

$$W = A \cap B \tag{3.1}$$

where $\cap$ is the logical AND. *If the element probabilities are independent*, the probability of the system functioning is

$$P_W = P_A P_B \enspace . \tag{3.2}$$

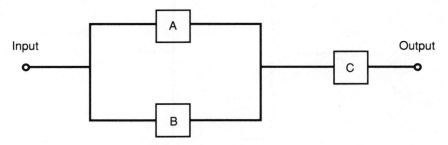

**Figure 3-1.** Reliability block diagram of Example 3.1.

**Figure 3-2.** The simplest example of a series system.  If either *A* or *B* fails then an input does not result in an output.

To increase reliability, a system designer may employ circuit packs redundantly. The simplest example of a redundant system is a two-block parallel system, illustrated in Figure 3-3.

In the system in Figure 3-3, if either $A$ or $B$ is functioning, an input results in output. A failure occurs *only* if $A$ and $B$ fail.* The description of the system working, being operational, is

$$W = A \cup B \tag{3.3}$$

where $\cup$ is the logical OR. For a parallel system, it is simpler to consider system failure (not working) which is represented by

$$\overline{W} = \overline{A} \cap \overline{B} \ . \tag{3.4}$$

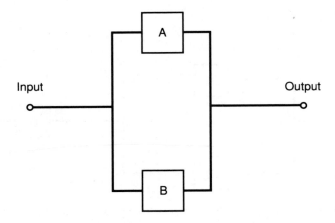

**Figure 3-3.** Simple parallel, two-block system.

---

* Note that we are assuming that if $A$ is operating and $B$ is standing by, then (1) perfect monitoring of the state of $A$ is in place and (2) perfect switching of the operational path through $A$ to one through $B$ occurs when $A$ fails. We also assume $B$ is a hot standby, that is, $B$ is powered up for the entire time $A$ is. We may wish to relax these assumptions when making more refined estimates of complex system reliability, but this is beyond the scope of the introductory material presented here.

Again, assuming independent probabilities,

$$P_{\overline{W}} = P_{\overline{A}}P_{\overline{B}} \ .\tag{3.5}$$

The probability of the system working is

$$P_W = 1 - P_{\overline{W}} = 1 - P_{\overline{A}}P_{\overline{B}} \ ,\tag{3.6}$$

so that the probability of the system working is given by one minus the probability that both $A$ and $B$ are not working. This type of reasoning can easily be extended to systems with $N$ elements in parallel, where system failure occurs only if all $N$ elements fail.

The probability of such a system functioning is

$$P_W = 1 - P_{\overline{W}} \ \text{or} \ P_W = 1 - P_{\overline{1}}P_{\overline{2}} \cdots P_{\overline{N}} \ .\tag{3.7}$$

## R-OUT-OF-N SYSTEMS

A variation of the simple parallel system is the r-out-of-n system in which at least $r$ out of $n$ elements must function for the system to function properly. If each of the $n$ elements is identical, then the probability of the system working is found by considering the binomial distribution and is given by[1]

$$P_W = \sum_{i=r}^{n} \begin{bmatrix} n \\ i \end{bmatrix} P^i \ (1-P)^{n-i} = \sum_{i=r}^{n} \frac{n!}{i!(n-i)!} \ P^i \ (1-P)^{n-i}\tag{3.8}$$

where $P$ is the probability that each (identical) element in the system is operational. It is assumed that each element of the system is independent. That is, the probability of one element failing is independent of all the other elements.

The following example shows how a reliability block diagram is used in a more realistic case and how the probability of a system working may be calculated.

## Example 3.2

A design engineer is developing a new Private Branch Exchange (PBX) system that consists of the following elements:

- an operator console,

- a system processor and memory,

- 20 trunk circuits,

- 200 line circuits and station sets.

The system can operate successfully (no customer complaint) with at least 18 out of 20 trunks working. A failure is defined as a customer complaint.

**Question.** What is the probability that the system is operating without failures?

**Solution.** For successful operation of the system, the console and processor/memory must function successfully. Eighteen out of the 20 trunks must be working and all 200 line circuits and station sets must work. The reliability block diagram is shown in Figure 3-4.

Let   $P_A$   =   Probability that the operator console is working

$P_B$   =   Probability that the processor and memory are working

$P_C$   =   Probability that at least 18 out of 20 trunks are working

$P_D$   =   Probability that all 200 line circuits and station sets are working

$P_l$   =   Probability that a line circuit and its station set are working

$P_t$   =   Probability that a trunk is working

$P_W$   =   Probability that the system is working.

The probability of the system working, $P_W$, is given by

$$P_W = P_A P_B P_C P_D \tag{3.9}$$

where again we have assumed A, B, C, and D to be independent, and with

$$P_C = \sum_{i=18}^{20} \binom{20}{i} P_t^i (1-P_t)^{20-i} . \tag{3.10}$$

In Equation (3.9), $P_D$ is given by

$$P_D = (P_l)^{200} . \tag{3.11}$$

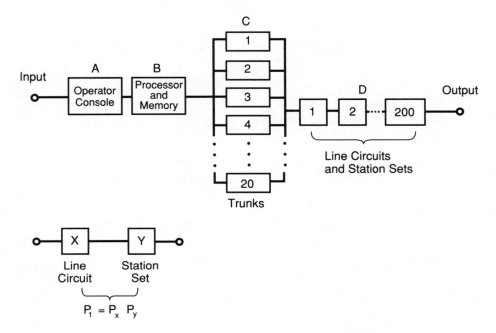

**Figure 3-4.** Reliability block diagram for the PBX.

## ANALYSIS OF COMPLEX RELIABILITY STRUCTURES

Complex reliability structures represent systems that cannot be decomposed into simple series, parallel, or r-out-of-n subsystems. Reliability analysis of such complex structures can be made using any of the following three methods (A, B, or C):

A. The first method makes use of the theorem of total probability.[2] If $A$ is an element of a system $S$, the probability of $S$ working given that $A$ is working is denoted by $P(S \mid A)$. The probability of $S$ working given that $A$ is not working is $P(S \mid \bar{A})$. Then the theorem states

$$P_W = P(S \mid A)\, P(A) + P(S \mid \bar{A})\, P(\bar{A}) \qquad (3.12)$$

where $P_W$ is the probability of system $S$ working and $P(A)$ is the probability of $A$ working.

This method can be easily used when a "key" element that binds together the reliability structure is properly selected. The following example illustrates the use of this method for determining the probability of the system working.

*Example 3.3*:    Consider the reliability block diagram shown in Figure 3-5.

*Problem*:    Determine the probability of the system being operational.

*Solution*:    In this case, it is convenient to select $B$ as the "key" element, and $P_W$ is expressed as

$$P_W = P(S \mid B) P(B) + P(S \mid \bar{B}) P(\bar{B}) . \tag{3.13}$$

If element $B$ is working, the block diagram is that shown in Figure 3-6.

Assuming independence between elements, then

$$P(S \mid B) = P_D + P_E - P_D P_E . \tag{3.14}$$

If $B$ is not working, the block diagram for the system is shown in Figure 3-7.

Thus, the probability of the system working, given that $B$ is not working, $P(S \mid \bar{B})$ is

$$P(S \mid \bar{B}) = P_A P_D + P_C P_E - P_A P_D P_C P_E . \tag{3.15}$$

Substituting Equations (3.14) and (3.15) into Equation (3.13), we obtain

$$P_W = (P_D + P_E - P_D P_E) P_B + (P_A P_D + P_C P_E - P_A P_D P_C P_E) (1 - P_B) . \tag{3.16}$$

B.    The second method is based on the idea of a "tie-set."[3] A tie-set (or path set) is a continuous line drawn from the beginning to the end of a reliability block diagram. A minimum tie-set is one that contains no others within it. Successful system operation is given by the union of all minimum tie-sets; that is, a system will operate if *all* of the blocks in *any* minimum tie-set operate. In the system shown in Figure 3-8, the tie-sets are $AE$, $DC$, $ABC$ (all are minimum tie-sets).

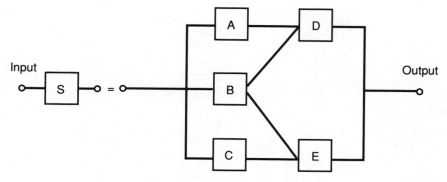

**Figure 3-5.**  A complex reliability block diagram.

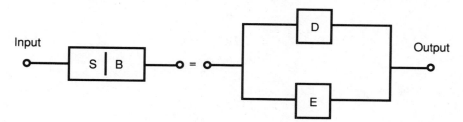

**Figure 3-6.**  The reliability block diagram when $B$ is working.

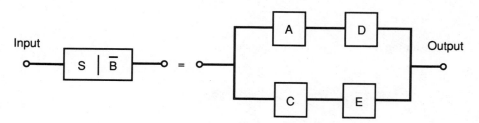

**Figure 3-7.**  The reliability block diagram when $B$ fails.

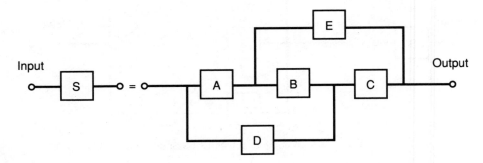

**Figure 3-8.** Reliability block diagram used in the tie-set method of paragraph B (above).

The state of the system being operational is given by

$$W = AE \cup DC \cup ABC. \tag{3.17}$$

Using the relation[2]

$$P(X \cup Y) = P(X) + P(Y) - P(X \cap Y), \tag{3.18}$$

we have

$$P_W = P(AE) + P(DC) + P(ABC)$$

$$- P(AE \cap DC) - P(AE \cap ABC) - P(DC \cap ABC)$$

$$+ P(AE \cap DC \cap ABC). \tag{3.19}$$

Assuming the units operate independently,

$$P_W = P_A P_E + P_D P_C + P_A P_B P_C$$

$$- P_A P_E P_D P_C - P_A P_E P_B P_C - P_D P_C P_A P_B$$

$$+ P_A P_E P_D P_C P_B . \tag{3.20}$$

One can also use the "cut-set" idea which is the complement of the "tie-set" in estimating the probability of the successful system operation. A cut-set is defined as a set of blocks (units) which interrupts all connections between the input and the output when removed from the system. All system failures can be represented by the removal of at least one minimal cut-set from the system. The probability of a system failure is, therefore, given by the probability that at least one minimal cut-set fails[1].

C.   The third method for evaluating system reliability is based on a Boolean truth table.[1,3] It is a tedious but straightforward method. A truth table contains a box for every possible state of the system. A state of the system refers to the operational state (working or not working) of all the blocks in the system (see Table 3.1). There is a column for each block; each row represents a different state. A "1" represents a working block and a "0" represents a nonworking block. Each row is examined to see whether it is a state in which the system will work. This is determined by using an equation such as Equation (3.17). For example, according to Equation (3.17) the system is "true" ("working" or "on" represented by a "1") if (A and E) or (D and C) or (A and B and C) is "true" ("working" or "on" represented by a "1"). Whether the state considered is a working state or not is indicated by a "1" or a "0" in the system column. Then the state probability is computed for each row that represents a working state. The sum of these state probabilities gives the probability that the overall system will work. Table 3.1 is a truth table for the block diagram from Figure 3-8. The right-hand column gives the probability for each working state. If these are added up and the expression simplified, the result is the same as Equation (3.20). Notice that there are $2^n$ rows in the table, where $n$ is the number of units in the block diagram. The method, therefore, becomes impractical for any but small diagrams.

Of the three methods of analysis described here, those based on (1) the conditional probability and (2) tie-sets may be the preferred methods, since these methods, unlike the third approach, do not require complete enumeration of the system states. All three will work, but in any individual case, one may be considerably more convenient; which one depends on the structure of the block diagram to be analyzed. In fact, it may be convenient to use different methods for different parts of the same block diagram.

**TABLE 3.1.** Boolean Truth Table

| A | B | C | D | E | System State | State Probability |
|---|---|---|---|---|---|---|
| \multicolumn{5}{Block States} | | |
| 1 | 1 | 1 | 1 | 1 | 1 | $P_A P_B P_C P_D P_E$ |
| 1 | 1 | 1 | 1 | 0 | 1 | $P_A P_B P_C P_D (1-P_E)$ |
| 1 | 1 | 1 | 0 | 1 | 1 | $P_A P_B P_C (1-P_D) P_E$ |

**TABLE 3.1.** Boolean Truth Table (cont.)

| A | B | C | D | E | System State | State Probability |
|---|---|---|---|---|---|---|
| 1 | 1 | 1 | 0 | 0 | 1 | $P_A P_B P_C (1-P_D)(1-P_E)$ |
| 1 | 1 | 0 | 1 | 1 | 1 | $P_A P_B (1-P_C) P_D P_E$ |
| 1 | 1 | 0 | 1 | 0 | 0 | |
| 1 | 1 | 0 | 0 | 1 | 1 | $P_A P_B (1-P_C)(1-P_D) P_E$ |
| 1 | 1 | 0 | 0 | 0 | 0 | |
| 1 | 0 | 1 | 1 | 1 | 1 | $P_A (1-P_B) P_C P_D P_E$ |
| 1 | 0 | 1 | 1 | 0 | 1 | $P_A (1-P_B) P_C P_D (1-P_E)$ |
| 1 | 0 | 1 | 0 | 1 | 1 | $P_A (1-P_B) P_C (1-P_D) P_E$ |
| 1 | 0 | 1 | 0 | 0 | 0 | |
| 1 | 0 | 0 | 1 | 1 | 1 | $P_A (1-P_B)(1-P_C) P_D P_E$ |
| 1 | 0 | 0 | 1 | 0 | 0 | |
| 1 | 0 | 0 | 0 | 1 | 1 | $P_A (1-P_B)(1-P_C)(1-P_D) P_E$ |
| 1 | 0 | 0 | 0 | 0 | 0 | |
| 0 | 1 | 1 | 1 | 1 | 1 | $(1-P_A) P_B P_C P_D P_E$ |
| 0 | 1 | 1 | 1 | 0 | 1 | $(1-P_A) P_B P_C P_D (1-P_E)$ |
| 0 | 1 | 1 | 0 | 1 | 0 | |
| 0 | 1 | 1 | 0 | 0 | 0 | |
| 0 | 1 | 0 | 1 | 1 | 0 | |
| 0 | 1 | 0 | 1 | 0 | 0 | |
| 0 | 1 | 0 | 0 | 1 | 0 | |
| 0 | 1 | 0 | 0 | 0 | 0 | |
| 0 | 0 | 1 | 1 | 1 | 1 | $(1-P_A)(1-P_B) P_C P_D P_E$ |
| 0 | 0 | 1 | 1 | 0 | 1 | $(1-P_A)(1-P_B) P_C P_D (1-P_E)$ |
| 0 | 0 | 1 | 0 | 1 | 0 | |
| 0 | 0 | 1 | 0 | 0 | 0 | |
| 0 | 0 | 0 | 1 | 1 | 0 | |
| 0 | 0 | 0 | 1 | 0 | 0 | |
| 0 | 0 | 0 | 0 | 1 | 0 | |
| 0 | 0 | 0 | 0 | 0 | 0 | |

$$P_W = \sum \text{(State Probabilities)}$$

## Example 3.4

In the most reliable configuration of a fully duplex digital switching processor, shown in Figure 3-9, each of its major blocks of hardware would be duplicated.

**Question.**   What is the probability that the system will be in an operating state given that the blocks are independent?

**Solution.**   The diagram can be redrawn more simply as given in Figure 3-10. Obviously, no complicated techniques are needed to estimate the probability of the system being operational.  The condition for the system working is expressed by

$$W = (A_1 \cup A_2) \cap (B_1 \cup B_2) \cap (C_1 \cup C_2) \qquad (3.21)$$

or in terms of probability,

$$P_W = (P_{A_1} + P_{A_2} - P_{A_1} P_{A_2})(P_{B_1} + P_{B_2} - P_{B_1} P_{B_2})(P_{C_1} + P_{C_2} - P_{C_1} P_{C_2}) \ . \qquad (3.22)$$

Now, if the following six conditions hold:

$$P_{A_1} = P_{A_2} = P_A \ , \qquad (3.23)$$

$$P_{B_1} = P_{B_2} = P_B \ ,$$

$$P_{C_1} = P_{C_2} = P_C \ ,$$

then Equation (3.22) simplifies,

$$P_W = P_A(2 - P_A)P_B(2 - P_B)P_C(2 - P_C) \ . \qquad (3.24)$$

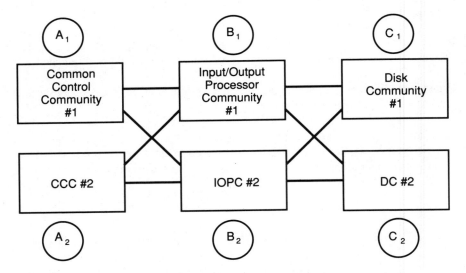

**Figure 3-9.** Configuration of a fully duplex digital switching processor.

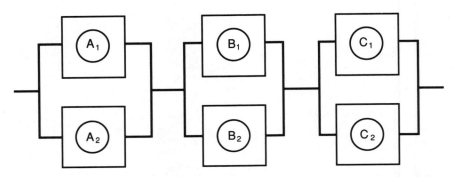

**Figure 3-10.** Reliability block diagram of the fully duplex digital switching processor.

## Summary

In this section we have calculated the probability of system operation in terms of the probabilities that each system's constituent blocks were working. And recall that reliability and availability (figures of merit for nonmaintained and maintained systems, respectively) are defined as probabilities. Thus, if a system is characterized by

$$P_W = P_A P_B P_C P_D - P_C P_E \ , \tag{3.25}$$

then the reliability and availability for that system may be immediately written down

$$R_S = R_A R_B R_C R_D - R_C R_E \ , \tag{3.26}$$

$$A_S = A_A A_B A_C A_D - A_C A_E \ . \tag{3.27}$$

The probability expression deduced from the reliability block diagram tells how to combine the availabilities* or reliabilities for the individual blocks or any other probability of interest. This means that to know the system reliability or availability we need only determine the reliability or availability for each block. The following sections explain how to obtain such information for the individual blocks.

## SYSTEM RELIABILITY ESTIMATION

Measures of equipment reliability are determined primarily from the hazard rates for the devices used in the equipment. The device hazard rate data are given in Chapter 4 and correspond to the AT&T hazard rate model for electronic devices detailed in Chapters 1 and 2. The methods described in this section are used to predict the equipment reliability from the device data, both for maintained and nonmaintained systems, during both the infant mortality and steady state portion of equipment life. Clearly, for maintained systems more information than device data is needed, which we discuss below.

It is important to keep in mind that reliability predictions are just estimates, intended to estimate the typical equipment reliability which *can* be obtained, based on the devices used. This is called *inherent reliability*. Such analyses cannot predict such things as specific, undetected device problems, equipment design flaws, defects introduced by manufacture, field abuse, and software problems. As a result, the reliability which *will* be obtained can be significantly different from the

---

* With measures of maintained system reliability, such as availability, expressions such as Equation (3.27) do *not* follow from Equation (3.25) without more assumptions. Specifically, Equation (3.27) follows from Equation (3.25) only if (1) the subsystems that do not fail continue to operate regardless of what has happened to the other subsystems, (2) the various subsystems have failure probabilities that are independent, and (3) the subsystem repair probabilities are independent.

prediction. Because of the unpredictable problems that can occur, reliability monitoring and corrective feedback are essential to ensure that the actual performance will meet stated objectives.

## Estimating the Effects of Temperature, Electrical Stress, and other Environmental Conditions

In Chapter 2, we discussed the effects of electrical stress and temperature on device hazard rates. The temperature and electrical stress effects, which are important in order to make the best predictions of system reliability, can be taken into account when using the data from Chapter 4. Ideally, the designer would determine the temperature and electrical stress that each device is subject to in the operating environment, and use this information to predict the device hazard rate. Such data are often unknown, especially at early stages of design. Consequently, the designer must use the best available estimates of temperature and electrical stress.

Reasonable estimates, especially of the temperature, can usually be made. An average temperature for all devices in a single piece of equipment may be used. Even if this temperature cannot be measured directly, it may be estimated based on similarity to other equipment. It is more difficult to make such blanket estimates of the electrical stress levels. If neither condition can be estimated, typical central office operating conditions of 40°C and 25 percent rated electrical stress can be used.* Uncertainties in the temperature and electrical stress levels used in reliability calculations should be clearly stated when discussing the resulting reliability predictions.

The effects of some factors (temperature and electrical stress) are included in device hazard rate predictions. The equipment E factor is meant to account for environmental effects, such as, temperature cycling, due to diurnal and seasonal variations, and vibration. Insufficient data exist on the effects of this factor to relate it to specific devices. The values of the environmental factor, E, are listed in Table 4-4.

## System Reliability Estimation:   Nonmaintained Systems

As defined in Chapter 1, a nonmaintained system is one that is not repaired when failure occurs. Instead, the failed system is removed and another unit put in its place. Clearly, the simplest example of such a system is a single electronic device, be it a transistor, diode, integrated circuit, etc.

What we are studying here are various measures of the *first and only failure time* that a nonmaintained system may encounter. There are no second, third, fourth, etc., failure times and there are no repair times of any sort. When we consider series systems and nonseries systems, we are only considering the structural model, *not* the type of failure/repair model. This last remark is general, for both maintained and nonmaintained systems.

---

\*   See Chapter 4 for a discussion of these reference levels.

Based on these observations, the figures of merit appropriate for a nonmaintained system are those associated with devices, which were discussed in Chapters 1 and 2.

A nonmaintained system may be handled by the methods discussed in the *System Reliability Modeling* section. We demonstrate this below.

**Series System.**    For a series system, the survival function is given by

$$S_S(t) = \prod_i S_i(t)$$

$$= \left[ e^{-\int_0^t \lambda_1(t')dt'} \right] \left[ e^{-\int_0^t \lambda_2(t')dt'} \right] \cdots$$

$$= e^{-\int_0^t \left[ \sum_i \lambda_i(t') \right] dt'} . \tag{3.28}$$

$$S_S(t) = e^{-\int_0^t \lambda_s(t')dt'} \tag{3.29}$$

with

$$\lambda_s(t) = \sum_i \lambda_i(t) . \tag{3.30}$$

These formulas and those for $F_s(t)$ and $f_s(t)$ (see Chapter 1) apply whether the $\lambda_i(t)$ are independent of time or not.

**Nonseries System.**    For a nonseries system, the survival function is not a simple product of subsystem (for example, device) survival functions. Consequently, there is no simple formula for the system hazard rate. Nevertheless, given $S_S(t)$, $\lambda_S(t)$ follows from

$$\lambda_S(t) = -\frac{d}{dt} \ln[S_S(t)] . \tag{3.31}$$

And again the other formulas, $F_S(t)$ and $f_S(t)$, follow directly, although the algebraic formulas may be rather complex. And as with nonmaintained series systems, these formulas hold, whether the $\lambda_i(t)$ are time dependent or not.

**Example 3.5.**    The following example illustrates how long-term hazard rate estimates are used in practice. Ideal use conditions are assumed for simplicity; that is, the temperature and electrical stress are at reference values and the E factor is unity.

A piece of equipment contains:

300  SSI and MSI integrated circuits,

25  linear integrated circuits,

150  low-power silicon transistors,

500  carbon composition resistors, and

450  low value ceramic capacitors.

Because the failure of any device causes a system failure, it is a series system.

**Question 1.**  Compute the long-term hazard rate.

**Solution.**  To find the system hazard rate, we sum up all component hazard rates. In a real analysis, hazard rates would be taken from the tables of Chapter 4. In this example, arbitrary (but representative) numbers are used.

| Device Type | Number Used | Hazard Rate ($\lambda_L$) | Total Hazard Rate |
|---|---|---|---|
| SSI/MSI ICs | 300 | 10 FITs | 3,000 FITs |
| Linear ICs | 25 | 30 | 750 |
| Silicon transistors | 150 | 20 | 3,000 |
| Carbon resistors | 500 | 1 | 500 |
| Ceramic capacitors | 450 | 1 | 450 |

$$\lambda_{\text{system}} = 7{,}700 \text{ FITs}$$

$$= 7.7\times10^{-6}/\text{hour}$$

**Question 2.**  If $n$ units are put in service, how many failures might we expect in a year? Assume no replacement of failed units, and that the infant mortality period is over.

**Solution.**  The expected number of failures between times $t_1$ and $t_2$ is given by multiplying the cumulative distribution function by $n$, the number of units:

$$\overline{N} = \text{expected number of failures} = n[1 - e^{-\int_{t_1}^{t_2} \lambda(t)dt}]$$

$$= n[1 - e^{-7.7\times10^{-6}(8760)}] = 0.065n \ . \quad (3.32)$$

So, for every 1,000 units we would expect 65 failures (or dropouts) per year.

Early in this chapter we stated that circuit packs are natural blocks in the sense of reliability block diagrams. This is because packs typically are series systems, used redundantly as one way to increase reliability.

It is worthwhile remarking here that circuit packs are rather special. From the system point of view, a circuit pack is nonmaintained. From the pack point of view, it is maintained. Why? When a repairman encounters trouble with a particular slot, he or she is likely to replace the pack, unless reseating the pack eliminates the problem. It is impractical to have a repairman troubleshooting circuit packs and replacing components on packs *in the field*. That is why, from the system perspective, the pack is considered nonmaintained. Now once the failed pack is removed, it goes back to the pack factory for analysis and repair. So from the pack perspective, the pack *is a maintained system*.

And even in maintained systems, nonmaintained figures of merit, usually percent dropout, are often important in studying maintenance costs. Such costs arise whenever a failure occurs even if system performance is not degraded at all, say because redundant parts are available to keep the system fully operational.

## System Reliability Estimation:  Maintained Systems

When we turn to maintained systems, the world of system reliability estimation becomes markedly more complex. In the world of maintained systems, a *sequence of failure times* must be modeled, where in the nonmaintained world, there was only one failure time, the first.[4,5]

To begin with, it is worthwhile emphasizing that, just as in the case of nonmaintained systems, we have the methodology for constructing a structural model using the technique in the *R-Out-of-N Systems* section. With a reliability block diagram in hand, our problem is reduced to solving the reliability problem for each *maintained system* block.

But what is the problem; what is it that we usually are after in a maintained system problem? What dropout is to nonmaintained systems, *availability* is to the maintained system. Availability is that figure of merit that, generally speaking, best characterizes performance of the system in terms of reliability. And there are other figures of merit of importance. The expected number of failures $\overline{N}(t)$ and its derivative, the failure rate $v(t)$ [*not* the hazard rate, $\lambda(t)$], generally are functions of time. Also the mean time between failure (MTBF) is, except for a special case, a function of time. Unfortunately, the MTBF is often used carelessly; many, if not most, equipment specifications include a *time independent* MTBF which is rarely correct. It should be mentioned that while availability is the primary measure of system reliability, dropout continues to be important in, for example, characterizing repair efforts and life cycle costs.

To understand the time dependent availability,* we will return to the failure-repair sequence introduced in Chapter 1.

Specifically, we consider the *sequence* of failure times associated with a maintained system. The time between startup (or turn on) of a system and first failure is denoted $X_1$. The time between starting and second failure is $X_2$. And the time between startup and third, fourth, and subsequent failures is denoted by $X_3, X_4$, etc.

Similarly, we consider the sequence of repair times $R_1, R_2, ...$, defined in similar fashion to the failure times.

---

* To be precise, point-wise availability.

Consider Figure 3-11, which represents the process of alternating failure and repair which is characteristic of a maintained system. In this case it is more convenient to consider the *operating time between completion of repair (or startup) and failure*, more commonly referred to as *operating times* or *up times* and defined as

$$Y_i = \begin{cases} X_i & i = 1 \\ X_i - R_{i-1} & i > 1. \end{cases} \tag{3.33}$$

We may go on to define the *times required to effect repair*, more commonly referred to as the *repair times* and defined as

$$B_i = R_i - X_i \quad i \geq 1. \tag{3.34}$$

How should we think about these *sequences of operating times* and *repair times*? First of all these sequences *alternate*; that is, after $Y_n$, $B_n$ follows, then $Y_{n+1}$, etc. But more important, what characteristic of these sequences should we use to characterize reliability?

First, we may say that in both of these sequences *each* time is fully described by a cumulative distribution function (CDF), just as *the* failure time of a nonmaintained system was so characterized. What general remarks can we make about the sequences of CDFs associated with the $Y_i$ and $W_i$?

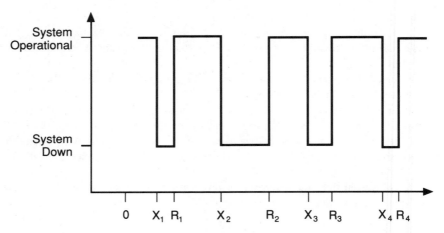

**Figure 3-11.** Failure and repair cycle for a maintained system. The $X_i$ are the times of failure and the $R_i$ are the times of repair completion.

If the maintained system we have in mind is the circuit board slot in a large electronic system, then what can we say about the failure and repair process to simplify matters? Consider a circuit pack failure. When a circuit board fails, it is replaced with one from a spare pool, which for the most part, consists of new circuit boards. It is very reasonable to assert, therefore, that the CDF characterizing a particular failure time is, in fact, the same CDF for all failure times. This is reasonable because all packs that might be in this pack slot, our maintained system, are new and, hence, the same at startup or when repair is completed.

The repair times may also be thought of as being characterized by the same type of process: when repair is effected, the same conditions constraining the repair time apply; that is, from our maintained system point of view, the pack that fails must be replaced. We may think of this as complete failure. Consequently, the repair times may also be thought of as being characterized by identical CDFs. Such a sequence, in which each element of the sequence is characterized by the same CDF, is called a *renewal process*.[6] And when there are two renewal processes that are operative in an alternating fashion, we call this an *alternating renewal process*[5,6].

The literature of renewal theory[6] is well established and, for the most part, is beyond the scope of this manual. We will, however, present the equation for the time-dependent availability and illustrate it with a simple example.

Given an alternating renewal process, with operating times characterized by Cumulative Distribution Function $F$ and repair times characterized by Cumulative Distribution Function $G$, then the instantaneous availability is given by

$$A(t) = 1 - F(t) + \int_o^t A(t-x)(F*G)'(x)dx, \tag{3.35}$$

where the * refers to convolution and where the prime indicates differentiation, i.e.,

$$(F*G)(x) = \int_o^x F(x-y)G'(y)dy \ . \tag{3.36}$$

This expression for the availability may be justified as follows: the part outside the integral of the right-hand side of Equation (3.35) represents the probability that failure has not occurred as of time $t$; recall that $1 - F$ is the survivor function. The integrand represents the probability that the system was available at time $t-x$, times the probability of one full failure/repair cycle of length of time $x$. The integral then adds up this probability for all cycle lengths $x$ between 0 and $t$.

Solving such an integral equation for the instantaneous time-dependent availability, except in simple cases, is usually performed on a high-speed digital computer, as are most modern system reliability calculations.

However, in the case when the repair and failure CDFs are given by $e^{-\mu t}$ and $e^{-\lambda t}$, respectively, then progress can be made by hand. In Appendix E, we show that in this case

$$A(t) = \frac{\mu}{\lambda+\mu} + \frac{\lambda}{\lambda+\mu} e^{-(\lambda+\mu)t} \ . \tag{3.37}$$

This is indeed the appropriate formula for the availability of a circuit board if all the components are in the steady state period of device life, and the mean operating time and the mean repair time are constant.

What about more realistic models of failure and repair? For failure we would use the AT&T hazard rate model for electronic components; the data in Chapter 4 make such an exercise possible. For repair, a number of forms, including the gamma and lognormal distributions, are frequently used.[5] And such repair rates have been determined from field studies of, for example, a Digital Signal Processing application.[7] This modeling of repair rate should take into account the more complex situations that repair crews face, such as positioning of personnel, availability of supplies, trouble priorities, etc.

One point worth noting is that the methodology we have been describing assumes that there is a repairman for each trouble call. This may not always be true. For such cases, alternatives to the block diagram approach—the Markov or semi-Markov approaches[5]—might then prove to be useful. Unless component hazard rates are strictly exponential, in order to use the data of Chapter 4 in a Markov-type model, a block diagram analysis would have to be done first. This is why, in the introductory discussions presented here, we focus on the block diagram approach.

What about other approaches? Do we need to use renewal theory in every instance? To address this question, we should consider the failure rate of complex systems during early life (*not* the hazard rate; see Chapter 1 for a review of terminology). It may look something like Figure 3-12. (In this figure, the glitches are exaggerated so as to make them visible.)

The glitches, slight increases in failure rate, are due to replacement of failed parts with new ones. These glitches would appear in a renewal analysis, albeit less dramatically. However, if one is interested in cruder estimates, then these glitches are not significant. And if we consider the replacement parts to be of the *same age* as the system being repaired, then these glitches would not appear. Such a model of replacements is called *revival* as opposed to renewal. Under revival, when a failure occurs it is repaired, but once repaired, there is no difference between this system and a system that *never failed*. Consequently, under revival, the approach used for a nonmaintained system may be used for a maintained system. Although less accurate, especially for complex systems, the revival model is a quick way to get reasonable estimates for maintained system reliability, at least for small systems.

As the last topic of this chapter, we consider the effects of electrostatic discharge (ESD) on system reliability. It is most important that circuit board and other system designers be aware of ESD issues as they relate to system reliability.

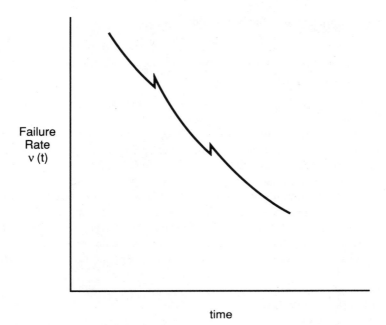

**Figure 3-12.** Sketch of failure rate illustrating the effect of renewal.

## ELECTROSTATIC DISCHARGE PREVENTION FOR THE EQUIPMENT DESIGNER

ESD can cause immediate failure of a component such as an integrated circuit, capacitor, or thin-film resistor. ESD can also reduce reliability by causing latent damage resulting in a future failure. ESD at times has reduced the manufacturing yield of components, circuit boards, and systems. Unchecked, ESD reduces profits and impairs customer satisfaction. Clearly, ESD should be prevented wherever possible. Some of the ESD considerations for equipment design and fabrication are:[8]

1. Electronic equipment must operate error-free despite the application of static discharges to circuits likely to be touched during operation or maintenance.

2. Component resistance to ESD damage may influence the selection of components such as capacitors, integrated circuits, and thin-film resistors.

3. ESD safeguards are required when fabricating and repairing components and equipment.

ESD prevention from the device-designer's viewpoint is presented in Chapter 2 of this manual. ESD prevention from the equipment-designer's viewpoint is presented in the current section.

## Designing Solid-State Circuits for Resistance to ESD

Designing circuits that are resistant to ESD is necessary to prevent damage from manufacturing and handling in the field. ESD tests now are required to be part of the qualification of a component.

## Selecting Components Resistant to ESD

Components may be inherently resistant to ESD or they may contain ESD-protective circuitry. For example, all MOS integrated circuits contain some built-in ESD protection. However, integrated circuit layout and technology differences among vendors can cause ESD damage thresholds to vary by a factor of 5 or more. If the components of a system must survive some ESD voltage, the system designer may have to select components capable of meeting this requirement. The ability of a component to resist ESD voltages can be measured in standard ways.[8] Indeed, ESD-voltage resistance must be measured and reported in the design documentation for all new AT&T electronic devices, including integrated circuits and the equipment using them (see Chapter 2).

## ESD Prevention in the Fabrication of Solid-State Components and Circuits

ESD safeguards need to be used where solid-state components and circuits are constructed and tested. ESD preventives include:[8]

- Antistatic plastic in dual in-line package (DIP) sticks should be used to hold integrated circuits.

- Solder-suckers and solder-flux removal systems should be designed to suppress static electricity.

- Wrist straps should be worn at work benches where circuit packs are fabricated, tested, and repaired.

- All such work benches should be covered with anti-static material and grounded.

- Conductive shoe straps should be worn by machine operators walking on anti-static mats.

- Circuit-pack shipping containers should be constructed of anti-static materials.

- A wrist strap is recommended when working on equipment frames. (If it is not feasible to wear a wrist strap, the equipment frame should be touched immediately before inserting or removing a circuit pack from it.).

- Humidity should be kept high enough (at *least* 20 percent relative humidity) to prevent the buildup of static electricity.

- Floors should be designed to prevent static electricity. (When it is necessary to use existing floors, they should not be covered with carpeting or standard floor-polish wax. Some new brands of floor polish seem to have overcome the ineffectiveness of the original generation of "anti-static" floor finishes. Anti-static mats should be used in critical areas.).

## REFERENCES

1. P. D. T. O'Conner, *Practical Reliability Engineering*, 2nd ed., Wiley, New York, 1985.

2. W. Feller, *An Introduction to Probability Theory and its Applications,* Volume I, 3rd ed., 1968 and Volume II, 2nd ed., 1970, Wiley, New York.

3. R. Billington and R. N. Allen, *Reliability Evaluation of Engineering Systems: Concepts and Techniques*, Plenum, New York, 1983.

4. H. E. Ascher, "Reliability Models for Repairable Systems," in *Reliability Technology—Theory & Applications*, edited by J. Moltoft and F. Jensen, Elsevier Science, Amsterdam, 1986. See also H. E. Ascher and H. Feingold, *Repairable Systems Reliability, Modeling, Inferences, Misconceptions, and Their Causes*, Marcel Dekker, New York, 1984.

5. A. Birolini, *On the Use of Stochastic Processes in Modeling Reliability Problems,* Springer-Verlag, Berlin, 1985, and references contained therein.

6. D. R. Cox, *Renewal Theory*, Chapman and Hall, London, 1962.

7. J. Poukish, Private Communication, March 1989.

8. AT&T *Electrostatic Discharge Control Handbook.* 1985. (Order Select Code 500-000), available from the AT&T Customer Information Center, 1-800-432-6600.

# 4

## DEVICE HAZARD RATES

### INTRODUCTION

Accurate reliability estimates of systems can be made when accurate hazard rates estimates of the components (devices) that constitute the system are known. Therefore, it is of extreme importance that the hazard rates estimates of the components be as accurate as possible.

In this chapter, we present the hazard rates estimates for those components (devices) used in products manufactured by AT&T. These data include infant mortality hazard rates as well as steady-state hazard rates. Also included are the AT&T hazard rate multipliers, which are used to adjust device hazard rates according to reliability classification and package material (ceramic or plastic). We also present examples of the use of this data in applications. First, we discuss the relationship between hazard rates and operating conditions. This is necessary for the reader to follow the examples of applying hazard rates that are presented in this chapter, and to go on and use these hazard rates in real applications.

To this end we present a discussion of the effects of different operating conditions, specifically changing temperature and electrical stress on device hazard rates. Part of this discussion necessarily includes some remarks on the typical operating conditions encountered by electronic telecommunication systems.

### OPERATING CONDITIONS

The hazard rates estimates given in this chapter correspond to device operation under well-controlled conditions. Temperature, electrical stress, and operating environment all affect the electronic device hazard rates. If the devices are operated at other than these well-controlled conditions, the hazard rates must be adjusted accordingly. Before discussing how to adjust hazard rates, we must examine these well-controlled conditions that will be used as our *reference conditions for the data presented later in the chapter*.

Reference conditions for AT&T equipment are termed central office conditions. Central office conditions are taken to mean that the environment is air conditioned, humidity is negligible, and the room temperature in the equipment aisles is 25°C. AT&T studies have shown this 25°C temperature to correspond to an average temperature between circuit packs of 40°C. By between circuit packs, we mean the mid-point of the imaginary line joining the center point of two adjacent circuit packs in an electronic system frame. By average temperature, we mean the average of all such positions in a typical frame. Consequently, 40°C is the temperature we refer to as *reference for electronic devices hazard rates.*

Note that this is an ambient temperature, not a junction temperature. This measure of temperature does not take into account the possibility of different thermal performance of various packaging techniques such as cooling fins and forced air cooling. Also, the existence of the environmental controlling units, such as fans and vents, has not been considered, except as it affects ambient temperature.

By using ambient rather than junction temperature, error is introduced in two ways. First, due to the nonlinearity of the Arrhenius equation,* "shifts" in temperature which exist between junction and ambient, even if constant, introduce error. Second, these "shifts" may vary, and certainly do with many modern high-power dissipating devices. That is, the differences between two ambient temperatures may be different from the differences between the corresponding junction temperature. For these high-power dissipating devices where, for example, 40°C may correspond to a junction temperature of 70°C, but an ambient temperature of 125°C may correspond to a junction temperature of 150°C, some consideration of junction temperature is important. When using these devices, circuit and circuit pack designers may use standard methodology[1] to adjust the device hazard rate. The first way of introducing error by using ambient should, however, be relatively minor, given the typical device operating temperature ranges.

The hazard rates in this chapter are given for an ambient temperature of 40°C. Implicit in this is the assumption that equipment operation causes its internal ambient temperature to rise 15°C above a 25°C room ambient. If the internal equipment temperature is above 40°C, the hazard rates will be higher than the tabulated numbers. How changes in temperature affect hazard rates is discussed in the following section.


## TEMPERATURE AND HAZARD RATES

In this chapter, we will confine our discussion of the effects of accelerated stress to the Accelerated Life Model and then apply these to the AT&T hazard rate model for electronic devices (see Chapter 2 for a discussion of these concepts). The accelerated life model gives a framework for taking into account the effects of stresses, such as temperature. And the AT&T hazard rate model for electronic devices is adequate, for our purposes, to describe those features of electronic device hazard rates that are essential if we are to be able to develop accurate system reliability estimates. (Again, see Chapter 2 for a discussion of these issues.)

---

*   See Chapter 2 for a discussion of the Arrhenius equation.

Returning to the effects of stress on the hazard rate $\lambda(t)$, we use Equation (2.2) when the use temperature is different from the reference temperature (40° C),

$$\lambda_r(t) = \frac{1}{A} \lambda_u(t/A),$$ (4.1)

where the subscripts $u$ and $r$ refer to use and reference conditions respectively, while $A$ is an acceleration factor. For our purposes, it is convenient to rewrite Equation (4.1) as

$$\lambda_u(t) = A \lambda_r(tA).$$ (4.2)

The temperature acceleration factor is given by Equation (2.9):

$$A_T = e^{\frac{E_a}{k_B} \left[ \frac{1}{T_r} - \frac{1}{T_u} \right]},$$ (4.3)

where $E_a$ is the activation energy, $k_B$ is the Boltzmann constant, $T_u$ is the ambient use temperature, and $T_r$ is the ambient *reference* temperature of 313°K (273° + 40° = 313°). Recall the AT&T hazard rate model for electronic devices:

$$\lambda^{(AT\&T)}(t) = \begin{cases} \lambda_L \left[ \dfrac{t}{t_c} \right]^{-\alpha} & 0 < t < t_c = 10^4 \text{ hours} \quad 0 < \alpha < 1 \\ \\ \lambda_L & t \geq t_c = 10^4 \text{ hours} \end{cases}$$ (4.4)

where $\lambda_L$ is the steady state or long-term hazard rate, $\alpha$ is the exponent characterizing early life reliability, and $t_c$, the crossover time, is $10^4$ hours. The superscript *AT&T* indicates that the hazard rate is of the form of the AT&T hazard rate model. The astute reader will notice that we have a different parametrization in Equation (4.4); specifically we have replaced $\lambda_1$ by its equivalent, namely,

$$\lambda_1 = \lambda_L t_c^\alpha = \lambda_L 10^{4\alpha}.$$ (4.5)

This is the form we use to present the data, and so we make this change for this entire chapter. Either form, of course, is correct.

Combining Equation (4.2) and Equation (4.4) gives

$$
\lambda_u^{(AT\&T)}(t) = A_T\,\lambda_r^{(AT\&T)}(tA_T) =
\begin{cases}
(A_T)^{1-\alpha}\,\lambda_L \left[\dfrac{t}{t_c}\right]^{-\alpha} & 0 < t < t_c \quad 0 < \alpha < 1 \\[2em]
A_T\,\lambda_L & t \geq t_c \quad .
\end{cases}
\tag{4.6}
$$

Consideration of Equation (4.6) reveals that the effect of acceleration is less, that is, the acceleration factor changes less, during the infant mortality period than during the steady-state period, if the acceleration factor is the same form for both infant mortality and steady-state (given that $0 < \alpha < 1$ and $A_T > 1$).

When the hazard rate is constant, as in the steady-state period, the hazard rate is proportional to the time acceleration factor. Therefore, the temperature acceleration factor, $A_T$, is a multiplication factor for the hazard rate. Figure 4-1 shows this multiplication factor as a function of temperature for a number of activation energy values. There is an associated table (Table 4.1) indicating the activation energy used to generate each curve. The hazard rate table (Table 4.6) indicates which curve is appropriate for each device family for estimating steady-state hazard rates. For example, the acceleration for bipolar integrated circuits is characterized by a 0.4 eV activation energy.[2] MOS integrated circuits are characterized by a 0.5 eV activation energy.[3] It should be emphasized that these acceleration factors are valid only when devices are used conservatively, that is, well within all device ratings. Some devices have maximum temperature ratings that must not be exceeded.

For the infant mortality period, an activation energy of 0.4 eV is used for all electronic devices.[4] Consequently, curve A8 is used for devices in the infant mortality period.

We may note at this point that the activation energies presented (for example, those for MOS and bipolar devices in the steady state period and for all devices in the infant mortality period) are "effective activation energies;" that is, they are based on the effects of a number of different failure mechanisms. These "activation energies" are not quite the genuine article, as they do not, generally speaking, represent the energy required for a particular reaction to proceed.[5] Furthermore, it is essential to note the difference between these "effective activation energies," and those activation energies presented in Table 2.2. These effective activation energies are used to estimate component hazard rates from those presented in Table 4.6. The activation energies in Table 2.2 are used in conjunction with accelerated life tests that are part of the device qualification process.

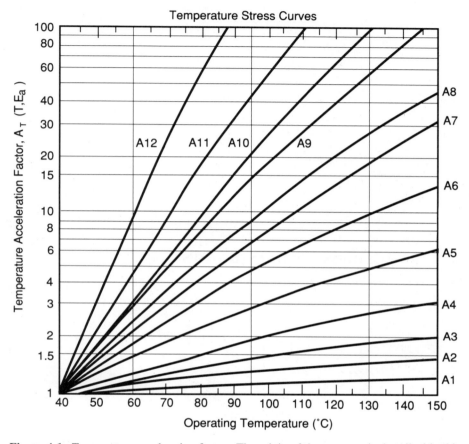

**Figure 4-1.** Temperature acceleration factor. The origin of these curves is described in this section. The activation energy associated with each curve is listed in Table 4.1.

**TABLE 4.1.** Activation Energies for Curves of Figure 4-1

| Curve | Activation Energy ($E_a$) |
|-------|---------------------------|
| A1 | 0.025 |
| A2 | 0.05 |
| A3 | 0.08 |
| A4 | 0.12 |
| A5 | 0.19 |
| A6 | 0.28 |
| A7 | 0.35 |
| A8 | 0.40 |
| A9 | 0.50 |
| A10 | 0.56 |
| A11 | 0.70 |
| A12 | 1.00 |

## ELECTRICAL STRESS AND HAZARD RATES

The equation developed in the previous section:

$$\lambda_u^{(AT\&T)}(t) = A \; \lambda_r^{(AT\&T)}(tA) = \begin{cases} A^{1-\alpha}\lambda_L \left[\dfrac{t}{t_c}\right]^{-\alpha} & 0 < t < t_c \quad 0 < \alpha < 1 \\ \\ A \; \lambda_L & t \geq t_c \end{cases} \tag{4.7}$$

applies for stresses other than temperature as well, *if we have an acceleration factor appropriate to that stress*. The form for the acceleration factor, however, is no longer as solidly grounded as we would like. For even though much work has been done, we do not have a conceptually satisfying *single* approach to describe the effect of non-thermal stresses on device reliability. However, practical considerations force the use of some model, even if its justification is purely empirical.

For electrical stress, we follow the military handbook[6] and use the following acceleration factor (for passives* only):[7]

$$A = A_E = e^{m(p_1 - p_0)}, \tag{4.8}$$

---

* Discrete semiconductor electronic components, whose operation involves the activity associated with a junction, such as diodes and transistors, are referred to as active devices. Discrete non-semiconductor electronic components, such as resistors and electrolytic capacitors, are referred to as passive devices. Monolithic microelectronic devices, or integrated circuits, are the third type of electrical component in this scheme.

where $m$ is a parameter determined from expressions in MIL-HDBK-217E,[6] $p_1$ is the percentage of maximum rated electrical stress, and $p_0$ is the reference percentage of rated electrical stress (25 percent). For resistors, $p$ represents power dissipated; for capacitors, $p$ is voltage; for relays and switches, $p$ is contact current. Figure 4-2 shows these acceleration factors for a number of parameter values, and the associated Table 4.2 indicates the parameter value used to generate each curve.

Within AT&T, the reference electrical stress rating (power, voltage, or current) is 25 percent, as this had been common practice in the Bell System before divestiture. There is no reason, however, why Equation (4.8) may not be used to estimate the *reduction* in hazard rate associated with electrical stress ratings (power, voltage, or current) *less* than 25 percent, that is, when passives are used even more conservatively than at 25 percent of maximum rated electrical stress.

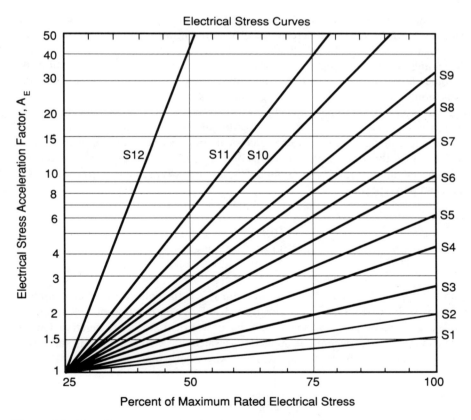

**Figure 4-2.** Electrical stress acceleration factor. The origin of these curves is described in this section. The appropriate measure of stress is: voltage for capacitors, power for resistors, and contact current for relays and switches. The parameter associated with each curve is listed in Table 4.2.

**TABLE 4.2.** Parameter Values for Curves of Figure 4-2

| Curve | Parameter Value ($m$) |
|-------|------------------------|
| S1    | 0.006 |
| S2    | 0.009 |
| S3    | 0.013 |
| S4    | 0.019 |
| S5    | 0.024 |
| S6    | 0.029 |
| S7    | 0.035 |
| S8    | 0.041 |
| S9    | 0.046 |
| S10   | 0.059 |
| S11   | 0.073 |
| S12   | 0.150 |

The acceleration factor in Equation (4.8) should not, however, be used to estimate hazard rates if the percentage of maximum rated electrical stress is to be less than 10 percent. Below that level, the hazard rate may *increase* because, depending on environmental conditions, a passive device may pick up moisture and become at-risk from a variety of failure modes, including corrosion and explosion.[8] The lower limit of 25 percent of maximum electrical rating was set in order to insure that designers stayed far away from electrical stress levels that might lead to an *increase* in hazard rates, due to humidity-related failures.[8]

For active devices there are other electrical stress acceleration factors. In MIL-HDBK-217E, three of the eleven groups of active devices discussed have electrical stress acceleration factors. For Group I,[6] transistors (Si [npn and pnp type] and Ge [npn and pnp type]),

$$A_E = \begin{cases} 0.47e^{0.03S} & S > 25 \\ 1.0 & S \le 25, \end{cases} \qquad (4.9)$$

with $S \equiv$ applied $V_{CE}$/rated $V_{CE} \times 100$, where $V_{CE}$ is the collector emitter saturation voltage. In Equation (4.9), $A_E$ varies from 1 to 9.4, as a function of $S$. Group IV, diodes (general purpose: Si and Ge),[6] have electrical stress acceleration factors given in Table 4.3. where $S \equiv$ applied $V_R$/ rated $V_R \times 100$ and $V_R$ is the diode reverse voltage. Lastly, for Group IX, microwave transistors[6]

$$A_E = 20(S - 35) \quad \text{for} \quad 40 \le S \le 55, \qquad (4.10)$$

**TABLE 4.3.** Acceleration Factor for General Purpose Diodes[6]

| S | $A_E$ |
|---|---|
| 0-60 | 1.00 |
| >60-70 | 1.07 |
| >70-80 | 1.14 |
| >80-90 | 1.28 |
| >90-100 | 1.42 |

with $S \equiv V_C/BV_{CEO} \times 100$ and where $V_C$ is the operating voltage, and $BV_{CEO}$ is the collector emitter breakdown voltage with the base shorted to the emitter. For values of $S$ less than 40 percent, no acceleration factor is needed.

Note that all of these active device acceleration factors are 1 for 25 percent of maximum electrical rating: See Equation (4.9).

As integrated circuits operate within a narrow range of voltage set by the device designer, the use of an acceleration factor is not appropriate. Regarding integrated circuits, there are no "voltage acceleration factors" in MIL-HDBK-217 except for higher voltage (12-20V) CMOS devices. However, this "voltage acceleration factor" is actually a voltage quality factor, as it serves only to penalize the circuit designer for using such higher voltage devices; there is no variation in hazard rate depending on percentage of rated voltage used. In any case, such devices are not commonly used within AT&T, and no data is available within AT&T to support the use of such a factor.[9] A similar power "acceleration factor" is in MIL-HDBK-217E for one class of active devices. Again this "acceleration factor" is actually a quality factor. There is no variation of hazard rate as a function of percent of rated power used, or even as a function of packaging characteristics, for example, package thermal impedance.

Lastly, it should be noted that these "acceleration factors" from MIL-HDBK-217 are for constant, steady-state hazard rates. Consequently, we cannot recommend their use during the infant mortality period without supporting data.

## ENVIRONMENT AND HAZARD RATES

The hazard rates of electronic devices are affected by the environmental application of the devices. For example, the hazard rate of a device operating in ground shelters (not temperature controlled) is taken to be 10 percent higher than the hazard rate listed in Table 4.6. Therefore, environmental application factors are developed to relate the hazard rates in Table 4.6 to the environment at which the device is being used. These factors are shown in Table 4.4.[10]

**TABLE 4.4.** Environmental Application Factor

| Environment | E | |
|---|---|---|
| Permanent structures, environmentally controlled | 1.0 | |
| Ground shelters, not temperature controlled | 1.1 | (Ref. [10]) |
| Manholes, poles | 1.5 | (Assumed) |
| Vehicular-mounted | 8.0 | (Ref. [10]) |

## HAZARD RATE MULTIPLIERS

The hazard rate multipliers are developed so that the steady state (or long-term) hazard rate of a device can be estimated, based on knowledge of a similar device, albeit of different* reliability classification.[11] There are hazard rate multipliers for integrated circuits (hermetic and plastic), diodes and transistors (hermetic and plastic), and all passive components shown in Table 4.5.

These multipliers relate the hazard rate of hermetically sealed Level III parts to *all* parts, that is, to plastic encapsulated Level III parts, and to both hermetic and nonhermetic Level II and Level I parts. For example, we wish to know the hazard rate of a Level II plastic integrated circuit, call it $\lambda_{II}^p$, and we know the steady-state hazard rate of a Level III hermetic integrated circuit, say $\lambda_{III}^h$. Then

$$\lambda_{II}^p = 1.3\ \lambda_{III}^h\ . \tag{4.11}$$

This is the simplest type of example of the use of an integrated circuit hazard rate multiplier: Start with a Level III *hermetic* hazard rate and estimate the hazard of some other commercial part (hermetic or plastic). Just as simple is the estimation of the hazard rate of a Level III plastic integrated circuit from a Level III hermetic hazard rate.

It should be pointed out that the multipliers may also be used to estimate the hazard rate of a more reliable part from the hazard rate of a less reliable part, even though all the multipliers presented in the table multiply the rate of the most reliable

---

\*   See Chapter 2 for a discussion of the reliability classification scheme for devices used in this manual.

part to yield the hazard rate of a less reliable part. It follows from Equation (4.11) that

$$\lambda_{III}^h = \frac{1}{1.3}\,\lambda_{II}^p \approx 0.77\lambda_{II}^p \ . \tag{4.12}$$

We note that hazard rate multipliers may be used to estimate the hazard rate of *any* type of part listed in the table, if the hazard rate of a similar part, of a different reliability classification is known. As an example, we show how to estimate the hazard rate of a Level I plastic diode, $\lambda_I^p$, from the hazard rate of a Level II plastic diode, $\lambda_{II}^p$. To do this, we must first estimate the hazard rate of a Level III hermetic diode. We do this by dividing the hazard rate we know, $\lambda_{II}^p$, by its multiplier in the table:

$$\lambda_{III}^h = \frac{1}{2.4}\lambda_{II}^p \ . \tag{4.13}$$

Then the desired hazard rate is estimated:

$$\lambda_I^p = 3.6\lambda_{III}^h = \frac{3.6}{2.4}\lambda_{II}^p \ . \tag{4.14}$$

This manipulation of hazard rates may be done for any type of device listed in the table, that is, for integrated circuits, diodes, and transistors, as well as passives.

It should be noted that these hazard rate multipliers are only engineering estimates and must be treated as such. The following two examples illustrate the use of the hazard rate multipliers in estimating $\lambda_L$.

**TABLE 4.5.** Hazard Rate Multipliers[11]

| | Integrated Circuits | | Diodes & Transistors | | |
| | Hermetic | Plastic | Hermetic | Plastic | Passive Components |
|---|---|---|---|---|---|
| Level III | 1.0 | 1.2 | 1.0 | 1.0 | 1.0 |
| Level II | 1.1 | 1.3 | 2.0 | 2.4 | 2.0 |
| Level I | 3.0 | 3.6 | 3.0 | 3.6 | 3.0 |

## Example 4.1

**Problem.**  Estimate the steady state hazard rate of plastic Level II 64K NMOS DRAM.

**Solution.**  From Table 4.6, the Level III base hazard rate is $\lambda_L = 30$ FITs.  Using a multiplication factor of 1.3 for Level II plastic (see Table 4.5), then,

$$\lambda_L = 30 \times 1.3 = 39 \text{ FITs} . \tag{4.15}$$

## Example 4.2

**Problem.**  Estimate the steady-state hazard rate of hermetic Level I microprocessor 8 Bit NMOS.

**Solution.**  The base hazard rate obtained from Table 4.6 is $\lambda_L = 100$ FITs and the multiplication factor for Level I hermetic is 3.  Therefore $\lambda_L = 300$ FITs.

## HAZARD RATE DATA

The hazard rates of devices used in AT&T manufactured products is presented in Table 4.6.  This table contains hazard rate data on both the infant mortality and steady-state periods of device life.[12,13]

It must be emphasized that these hazard rates are estimates supported by data from the sources stated in references 12 and 13.  As estimates, these hazard rates cannot be viewed as being exact data.  However, these hazard rates have been used for a number of years to predict the reliability performance of new AT&T circuit packs and systems.  Use of the hazard rates in Table 4.6 in conjunction with the procedures outlined in the two sections on procedures for system hazard rate calculations, results in a reliability prediction which is conservative when compared to actual field performance.  In most cases, the reliability prediction of a circuit pack or system has been found to be a factor of two or three greater than actual field experience.

The first page of Table 4.6 lists the major headings under which devices are classified in the remainder of the table.  The major types of information in the table are:

1. Device Class     Type of device, in outline form.

2. Package Type     H  — Hermetic package without burn-in.

   P  — Nonhermetic (usually plastic) package without burn-in.

   HB  — Hermetic package with burn-in.

   PB  — Nonhermetic (usually plastic) package with burn-in.

3. Hazard Rates

$\lambda_L$ — Steady-state (or long-term) hazard rate (in FITs*) at $\geq$ 10,000 hours at a reference ambient temperature of 40°C. For passive components, the reference electrical stress is 25 percent of maximum rating. *An asterisk indicates that the steady-state hazard rate was determined from field data.*

$\alpha$ — Infant mortality (Weibull) shape parameter.
NA — Data not available at the present time.

4. Stress Curves

These curves, Figures 4-1 and 4-2, provide multiplication factors for the long-term hazard rate, to be used when the device of interest operates at a temperature different from 40° or when the electrical stress is different from 25 percent. The electrical acceleration factors apply only to passive components, for example, resistors and capacitors.

5. (Note)

These notes offer supplemental information about a specific component and/or its hazard rate and can be found at the end of Table 4.6.

6. References

Give the sources of steady-state hazard rates for all devices and sources of infant mortality hazard rates for semiconductor devices. The reference numbers refer to the list of references at the end of this chapter.

It should be recalled that activation energy values of 0.4 eV and 0.5 eV are used for bipolar[2] and MOS[3] devices, respectively, to describe the effect of temperature on the steady state hazard rates. The activation energy used for infant mortality[4] is 0.4 eV, for both bipolar and MOS devices.


## INFANT MORTALITY HAZARD RATE DATA

The hazard rates of electronic devices during the infant mortality period are, as discussed in Chapter 2, well described by a Weibull distribution. There are two parameters of that distribution, namely $\lambda_1$, the hazard rate at one hour after "birth" (in this case production), and $\alpha$, the negative of the "shape parameter." However, in Equation (4.4) we used a different parameterization, one with $\lambda_1 = \lambda_L t_c^{\alpha}$, where $t_c$, the crossover time, is $10^4$ hours, and $\lambda_L$ is the steady-state hazard rate.

Infant mortality hazard rate data is routinely collected at AT&T whenever the electronic component populations can be identified and the time to failure of these devices can be collected. From such data the Weibull parameters mentioned above may be extracted.

The sources of such data include Operational Life Testing (OLT) of components, field tracking studies, as well as factory burn-in of systems. The operating

---

* 1 FIT is a unit of hazard rate equal to $10^{-9}$ hour$^{-1}$.

conditions of these tests are either mildly accelerated or not accelerated at all. In OLT, the conditions are more stressful to the devices than what is typically encountered in the field; however, as discussed in Chapter 2, the conditions are within the specifications of the devices being tested.

AT&T collects and publishes such data internally. It is used by systems designers, for example, and others who need to estimate system reliability realistically, in order to make decisions as to whether or not selective component burn-in or system screening, such as burn-in or temperature cycling, is necessary to meet system reliability targets. Data are available for components manufactured to Level III specifications.

Failure mode analysis (FMA) of infant mortality failures reveals the sources of failure. These typically are manufacturing defects. For example, unwanted particles in fabrication lines (factories) may cause defects in the dielectric layers of semiconductor devices. Another source of manufacturing defects is process variations. An example of this type of defect would be a weakened wire bond that is more likely to break because a wire bonding machine may be applying excessive pressure.

Failures caused by such defects cannot be said to be due to a failure mechanism that is intrinsic to the electronic device whose reliability is being judged. On the contrary, the number of infant mortality failures will vary according to the supplier of the device, as well as according to the type of device. Furthermore, the infant mortality hazard rate will vary as a function of date of manufacture. When the hazard rate *decreases with time in production*, and *approaches the intrinsic reliability of the device,* we call this reliability growth.[14,15] This is because processes are improved as the causes of problems are detected and corrected. Because of this variation, it is very important to be able to have data that shows how the Weibull shape parameter varies with device type and device technology.

Component users can ask suppliers for infant mortality data. Data from OLT is preferable in the absence of field tracking studies.* If OLT data is not available, the percent dropout from burn-in may be used to determine infant mortality hazard rates. To do this, one would need to know the time of stress and the temperature during burn-in, and assume a value of $\alpha$. Then, acceleration factors must be used to determine the hazard rates under operating conditions. See Chapter 2 for a discussion of acceleration factors and how to use them during the infant mortality period. And see the earlier sections of this chapter for other practical considerations in the use of acceleration factors.

Component users can also derive infant mortality hazard rates from their own experience, such as system burn-in and field tracking studies.

In the following two sections, we summarize the procedures used to determine both the infant mortality and the steady-state hazard rates for a simple system. Examples are used to illustrate the steps of the procedures.

---

* Field tracking studies are unlikely to be available for the latest, state-of-the-art devices.

## PROCEDURE FOR SYSTEM HAZARD RATE
## CALCULATIONS: INFANT MORTALITY

The hazard rate of a system depends on the arrangement of its components, for example, series, parallel, parallel-series, series-parallel, complex, etc. (see Chapter 3).

Steps 1 through 5 listed below are common for all systems while Step 6 is system dependent. We use a simple series system for illustrative purposes.

1.  Determine the infant mortality hazard rate exponent, $\alpha$, and the long-term hazard rate $\lambda_L$, for each device.

2.  Then express the early life hazard rate as a function of time,

$$\lambda(t) = \lambda_L \left[ \frac{t}{t_c} \right]^{-\alpha} . \tag{4.16}$$

3.  Combine each infant mortality hazard rate with the appropriate* temperature acceleration factor, $(A_T)^{1-\alpha}$, which relates hazard rates at the reference (40°C) temperature to the hazard rate at the operating temperature. The appropriate activation energy for all devices in the infant mortality period of device life is taken to be 0.4 eV. Therefore, curve A8 in Figure 4-1, or Equation (4.3) with $E_a = 0.4$ eV, gives $A_T$ for all devices in the infant mortality period.

4.  Unlike the long-term model, no electrical stress factors are used.[†]

5.  Sum up all of the individual device hazard rates to get a base system hazard rate.

6.  Multiply the base system hazard rate by the appropriate environmental $(E)$ application factor (Table 4.4).

This procedure can be summarized as

$$\lambda_{\text{total}}(t) = E \sum_{i}^{\text{All Devices}} (A_T)_i^{1-\alpha_i} (\lambda_L)_i \left[ \frac{t}{t_c} \right]^{-\alpha_i} . \tag{4.17}$$

A simple example illustrates the procedure.

**Example 4.3**

A circuit pack contains one Level III SSI TTL integrated circuit and five

---

\* See Appendix C for a derivation.

† Recall that the electrical stress factors are applicable only to constant, steady-state hazard rates.

2-megaohm Level III carbon composition resistors. The circuit pack is part of a digital system in a ground shelter which is not temperature-controlled. The circuit pack operating temperature is expected to be about 60°C and the resistors are operated at 50 percent of their rated power.

**Question.**    What is the infant mortality hazard rate at 100 hours?

**Solution.**    The infant mortality hazard rate of the integrated circuit, from Table 4.6, with $\lambda_L = 10$ FITs, $\alpha = 0.8$, is given by

$$\lambda_{\text{IC}}(t) = \lambda_L \left[ \frac{t}{10^4} \right]^{-\alpha} = 16{,}000t^{-0.8} \quad \text{(in FITs)} \; . \tag{4.18}$$

From Figure 4-1, curve A8 (always used for infant mortality) indicates that the temperature acceleration factor for operation at 60°C is $A_T = 2.4$. Therefore, $A_T^{1-\alpha}$ is equal to 1.19 and

$$\lambda_{\text{IC}}(t) \simeq 19{,}000t^{-0.8} \tag{4.19}$$

in this application.

The infant mortality hazard rate for each resistor, with $\lambda_L = 1$ FIT, $\alpha = 0.6$, is given by

$$\lambda_{\text{RES}}(t) = \lambda_L \left[ \frac{t}{10^4} \right]^{-\alpha} = 250t^{-0.6} \; . \tag{4.20}$$

Here again, $A_T = 2.4$. Now $A_T^{1-\alpha}$ is equal to 1.42, and

$$\lambda_{\text{RES}}(t) \simeq 350t^{-0.6} \tag{4.21}$$

in this application.

The base circuit pack hazard rate is

$$\lambda_{\text{IC}}(t) + 5\lambda_{\text{RES}}(t) = 19{,}000t^{-0.8} + 1750t^{-0.6} \; . \tag{4.22}$$

Multiplying by an environmental factor of 1.1 (Table 4.4), the circuit pack hazard rate is

$$\lambda_{\text{CP}}(t) \simeq 20{,}900t^{-0.8} + 1925t^{-0.6} \; . \tag{4.23}$$

At $t = 100$ hours this gives a hazard rate of 646 FITs.

## PROCEDURE FOR SYSTEM HAZARD RATE
## CALCULATIONS: STEADY-STATE (LONG-TERM)

Following the system hazard rate calculations for infant mortality, we describe the procedure for the long-term hazard rate calculations. Again, we use a series system for illustrative purposes.

1. Look up the long-term hazard rate, $\lambda_L$, for each device (Table 4.6).

2. Combine each integrated circuit long-term hazard rate with the appropriate temperature acceleration factor, $A_T$ [from Figure 4-1 or Equation (4.3)], which converts from the reference (40°C) temperature to the actual operating temperature of the device. The appropriate temperature acceleration curve to use from Figure 4-1 is specified in Table 4.6 for each device type (along with the long-term hazard rate).

3. Multiply each passive device hazard rate by the appropriate electrical stress acceleration factor, $A_E$ [from Figure 4-2 or Equation (4.8)], which converts from the assumed (25 percent of rated) stress to the actual stress level of the device. The appropriate stress curve to use from Figure 4-2 is specified in Table 4.6.

4. Sum up all of the individual device hazard rates to get a base system hazard rate.

5. Multiply the base system hazard rate by the appropriate environmental ($E$) application factor (Table 4.4).

This procedure can be summarized as

$$\lambda_{total} = E \sum_{i}^{\text{All Devices}} (A_T)_i \ (A_E)_i \ (\lambda_L)_i \ . \tag{4.24}$$

A simple example illustrates the procedure.

### Example 4.4

**Problem.** Determine the long-term hazard rate for the circuit pack given in Example 4.3.

**Solution.** Recall that ground shelter is not temperature-controlled. The circuit pack operating temperature is expected to be about 60°C and the resistors are operated at 50 percent of their rated power. What is the steady-state hazard rate of the circuit pack?

The steady-state hazard rate for the integrated circuit is given in Table 4.6 as 10 FITs. Table 4.6 also indicates that the appropriate temperature acceleration curve in Figure 4-1 is curve A8. From this curve, the temperature acceleration for operation at 60°C is $A_T = 2.4$. Therefore, the hazard rate of the integrated circuit is (10 FITs) × (2.4) = 24 FITs in this application.

The steady-state hazard rate for each resistor is 1 FIT. The temperature acceleration factor given by curve A7 is $A_T = 2.1$. The stress curve used from Figure 4-2 is curve S4, giving a multiplier of 1.6 (see Table 4.2). Therefore, the resistor hazard rate in this application is (1 FIT) $\times$ (2.1) $\times$ (1.6) = 3.4 FITs. The base circuit pack hazard rate is 24 FITs + 5 $\times$ (3.4 FITs) = 41 FITs. Multiplying by the environmental factor of 1.1, the overall steady-state (long-term) hazard rate is 45 FITs for the circuit pack.

**TABLE 4.6.** Device Hazard Rate Data

| Major Device Class Headings | Page |
| --- | --- |
| Capacitors – Fixed | 122 |
| Capacitors – Variable | 123 |
| Circuit Breaker | 124 |
| Connections | 124 |
| Connectors | 124 |
| Crystals – Quartz | 125 |
| Diodes – Silicon | 126 |
| Fuses | 126 |
| HIC Substrate Components – Thin Film | 126 |
| Inductors | 127 |

**TABLE 4.6.** Device Hazard Rate Data (cont.)

**TABLE 4.6.** Device Hazard Rate Data (cont.)

| Device Class | Expected Hazard Rates (in FITs) $\lambda_L$ | $\alpha$ | $\lambda_L$ Stress Curves | (Note) $\lambda_L$ Refs. | |
|---|---|---|---|---|---|
| **Capacitors – Fixed** | | | | | |
| A. Ceramic | | | | | |
| 1. Class I (Temp. Compensating) | | | | | |
| 1-1000 pF | 0.2 | 0.6 | A12,S10 | | 16 |
| >1000 pF | 1.0 | 0.6 | A12,S10 | | 16 |
| 2. Class II, X7R (General Purpose) | | | | | |
| <0.1 µF | 0.2 | 0.6 | A12,S10 | | 16 |
| 0.1-1 µF | 1.0 | 0.6 | A12,S10 | | 16 |
| >1 µF | 6.0 | 0.6 | A12,S10 | | 16 |
| 3. Class II, Z5U (General Purpose) | | | | | |
| <0.1 µF | 0.3 | 0.6 | A12,S10 | | 16 |
| 0.1-1 µF | 2.5 | 0.6 | A12,S10 | | 16 |
| >1 µF | 13.0 | 0.6 | A12,S10 | | 16 |
| B. Electrolytic – Aluminum | | | | | |
| 1. Chassis mounted | | | | | |
| <400 µF | 15.0 | 0.6 | A8,S5 | (1) | 7 |
| 400-12000 µF | 30.0 | 0.6 | A8,S5 | (1) | 7 |
| >12000 µF | 50.0 | 0.6 | A8,S5 | (1) | 7 |
| 2. Lead mounted | | | | | |
| <400 µF | 10.0 | 0.6 | A8,S5 | (1) | 7 |
| 400-12000 µF | 20.0 | 0.6 | A8,S5 | (1) | 7 |
| >12000 µF | 30.0 | 0.6 | A8,S5 | (1) | 7 |

**TABLE 4.6.**  Device Hazard Rate Data (cont.)

| Device Class | Expected Hazard Rates (in FITs) | | $\lambda_L$ Stress Curves | (Note) $\lambda_L$ Refs. | |
|---|---|---|---|---|---|
| | $\lambda_L$ | $\alpha$ | | | |
| **Capacitors – Fixed (cont.)** | | | | | |
| C. Electrolytic – Solid Tantalum | | | | | |
| 1. 4,8 volts | | | | | |
| <50 µF | 0.5 | 0.6 | A4,S7 | (2) | 7 |
| 50<200 µF | 1.1 | 0.6 | A4,S7 | (2) | 7 |
| 200-330 µF | 1.4 | 0.6 | A4,S7 | (2) | 7 |
| 2. 20 volts | | | | | |
| <20 µF | 2.9 | 0.6 | A4,S7 | (2) | 7 |
| 20-100 µF | 6.5 | 0.6 | A4,S7 | (2) | 7 |
| 3. 25-35 volts | | | | | |
| 1-40 µF | 4.5 | 0.6 | A4,S7 | (2) | 7 |
| 4. 60 volts | | | | | |
| 0.1-22 µF | 13.0 | 0.6 | A4,S7 | (2) | 7 |
| D. Glass | 0.6 | 0.6 | A8,S7 | | 7 |
| E. Mica | 0.05 | 0.6 | A8,S7 | | 17 |
| F. Plastic | | | | | |
| 1. Polystyrene Foil | 2.0 | 0.5 | A4,S10 | (3,4) | 7 |
| 2. Polypropylene Foil | 2.0 | 0.5 | A4,S10 | (3) | 7 |
| 3. Polyester (Mylar®) Foil | 2.0 | 0.5 | A4,S10 | (3,4) | 18 |
| 4. Metallized Polyester (Mylar®) | 2.0 | 0.5 | A4,S10 | (3,4) | 19 |
| G. Silicon Chip | 60.0 | 0.6 | A8 | | 20 |
| **Capacitors – Variable** | | | | | |
| A. Air-Piston Type | 15.0 | 0.6 | A6,S8 | | 7 |
| B. Air-Trimmer | 35.0 | 0.6 | A6,S8 | | 7 |
| C. Ceramic | 15.0 | 0.6 | A4,S10 | | 7 |

**TABLE 4.6.**  Device Hazard Rate Data (cont.)

| Device Class | Expected Hazard Rates (in FITs) $\lambda_L$ | $\alpha$ | $\lambda_L$ Stress Curves | (Note) $\lambda_L$ Refs. |
|---|---|---|---|---|
| **Circuit Breaker** | | | | |
| 1. Magnetic | 20.0 | 0.6 | | 7 |
| 2. Thermal | 38.0 | 0.6 | | 7 |
| 3. Thermal-Magnetic | 38.0 | 0.6 | | 7 |
| **Connections** | | | | |
| A. Automatic (per connection) | | | | |
| 1. Crimp | 0.25 | 0.6 | (5,6) | 7 |
| 2. Insulation Displacement | | | | |
| a. Solid Wire | 0.1 | 0.6 | (5,6) | 21 |
| b. Stranded Wire | 3.0 | 0.6 | (5,6) | 22 |
| 3. Reflow Soldering | 0.07 | 0.6 | (5,6) | 7 |
| 4. Wave–soldering (see note 7) | – | – | (7) | |
| 5. Weld | 0.05 | 0.6 | (5,6) | 7 |
| 6. Wire Wrap | 0.003 | 0.6 | (5,6) | 7 |
| 7. Interference Fit Pins | 0.1 | 0.6 | (5,6) | 23 |
| B. Manual (per connection) | | | | |
| 1. Hand Soldering (without wrap) | 2.5 | 0.6 | (6) | 7 |
| 2. Hand Soldering (with wrap) | 0.14 | 0.6 | (6) | 7 |
| **Connectors** | | | | |
| A. Coaxial | 7.0 | 0.6 | | 7 |
| B. Modular Telephone Plug and Jack | 230.0 | 0.6 | | 24 |

**TABLE 4.6.** Device Hazard Rate Data (cont.)

| Device Class | Expected Hazard Rates (in FITs) | | $\lambda_L$ Stress Curves | (Note) $\lambda_L$ Refs. |
|---|---|---|---|---|
| | $\lambda_L$ | $\alpha$ | | |
| **Connectors (cont.)** | | | | |
| C. Multicontact (per contact) | | | | |
| 1. Cable to Pinfield | | | | |
| a. Central Office Environment | 0.1 | 0.6 | (6,8) | 24,25 |
| b. Uncontrolled Environment | 0.5 | 0.6 | (6,8) | 25,26,27 |
| D. Printed Circuit Board (per contact) | | | | |
| 1. Edgeboard | | | | |
| a. Central Office Environment | 2.0 | 0.6 | (6,8) | 25 |
| b. Uncontrolled Environment | 10.0 | 0.6 | (6,8) | 25,26,27 |
| 2. Two Piece | | | | |
| a. Central Office Environment | 0.3 | 0.6 | (6,8) | 25 |
| b. Uncontrolled Environment | 1.4 | 0.6 | (6,8) | 25,26,27 |
| E. Others | | | | |
| a. Central Office Environment | 2.0 | 0.6 | | 7 |
| b. Uncontrolled Environment | 10.0 | 0.6 | | 7,25,26,27 |
| **Crystals – Quartz** | 50.0 | 0.6 | | 7 |

**TABLE 4.6.** Device Hazard Rate Data (cont.)

| Device Class | Package Type | Expected Hazard Rates (in FITs) | | $\lambda_L$ Stress Curves | (Note) $\lambda_L$ Refs. |
|---|---|---|---|---|---|
| | | $\lambda_L$ | $\alpha$ | | |
| **Diodes – Silicon** | | | | | |
| A. General Purpose | | | | | |
| ≤1 W | H | 5.0* | 0.6 | A8 | 12 |
| >1 W | H | 5.0* | 0.6 | A8 | 12 |
| | P | 6.0* | 0.6 | A8 | 12 |
| B. Microwave | P | 10.0 | 0.6 | A8 | 12 |
| C. Rectifiers | H | 5.0* | 0.6 | A8 | 12 |
| | P | 6.0* | 0.6 | A8 | 12 |
| D. Surge Protector | H | 30.0 | 0.6 | A8 | 12 |
| | P | 40.0 | 0.6 | A8 | 13 |
| E. Switching | H | 5.0* | 0.6 | A8 | 12 |
| | P | 6.0* | 0.6 | A8 | 12 |
| F. Varactors (≤ 10 W) | H | 130.0 | 0.75 | A8 | 7 |
| G. Varistors (per volt) | P | 8.0 | 0.75 | A8 | 7 |
| **Fuses** | | | | | |
| 1. Indicating | | 50.0 | 0.6 | | 7 |
| 2. Non-Indicating | | 25.0 | 0.6 | | 7 |
| **HIC Substrate Components– Thin Film** | | | | | |
| A. Film Capacitor | P | 0.64 | 0.6 | None | 28 |

---

\*   Indicates that this data is from field time to failure data.

**TABLE 4.6.** Device Hazard Rate Data (cont.)

| Device Class | Package Type | Expected Hazard Rates (in FITs) $\lambda_L$ | $\alpha$ | $\lambda_L$ Stress Curves | (Note) $\lambda_L$ Refs. |
|---|---|---|---|---|---|
| **HIC Substrate Components – Thin Film (cont.)** | | | | | |
| B. Film Resistor | P | 0.12 | 0.6 | None | 28 |
| C. Glaze Crossunder | P | 0.10 | 0.6 | None | 28 |
| **Inductors** | | | | | |
| A. Power | | 19.0 | 0.6 | A4 | 7 |
| B. RF Fixed | | 0.5 | 0.6 | A4 | 7 |
| C. RF Variable | | 1.0 | 0.6 | A4 | 7 |
| **Integrated Circuits** | | | | | |
| A. Digital | | | | | |
| 1. Bipolar ECL | | | | | |
| 1-100 Gates | P | 10 | 0.9 | A8 | 12 |
| 101-1K Gates | HB | 50 | 0.8 | A8 | 12 |
| 1001-5K Gates | HB | 50 | 0.8 | A8 | 13 |
| 2. Bipolar IIL | | | | | |
| 1-100 Gates | P | 15* | 0.9 | A8 | 12 |
| 101-500 Gates | P | 25 | 0.9 | A8 | 12 |
| 501-1000 Gates | P | 25 | 0.9 | A8 | 12 |

---

\* Indicates that this data is from field time to failure data.

**TABLE 4.6.** Device Hazard Rate Data (cont.)

| Device Class | Package Type | Expected Hazard Rates (in FITs) $\lambda_L$ | $\alpha$ | $\lambda_L$ Stress Curves | (Note) $\lambda_L$ Refs. |
|---|---|---|---|---|---|
| **Integrated Circuits** **A. Digital (cont.)** | | | | | |
| 3. Bipolar Schottky TTL | | | | | |
| 1-100 Gates | P | 10* | 0.8 | A8 | 12 |
| 101-500 Gates | P | 15* | 0.8 | A8 | 13 |
| 501-1K Gates | P | 20 | 0.8 | A8 | 13 |
| 4. Bipolar TTL | | | | | |
| 1-20 Gates | P | 10* | 0.8 | A8 | 13 |
| 21-100 Gates | P | 10* | 0.8 | A8 | 13 |
| 101-1K Gates | P | 25 | 0.8 | A8 | 13 |
| 1001-5K Gates | P | 100 | 0.8 | A8 | 13 |
| 5. CMOS | | | | | |
| 1-50 Gates | HB | 15* | 0.75 | A9 | 12,13 |
| 51-100 Gates | HB | 20 | 0.75 | A9 | 12,13 |
| 101-500 Gates | HB | 30 | 0.75 | A9 | 12,13 |
| 501-1K Gates | HB | 40 | 0.75 | A9 | 12,13 |
| 1001-10K Gates | HB | 50 | 0.6 | A9 | 12,13 |
| Custom Logic (CODEC) | PB | 100 | 0.5 | A9 | 13 |

* Indicates that this data is from field time to failure data.

**TABLE 4.6.** Device Hazard Rate Data (cont.)

| Device Class | Package Type | Expected Hazard Rates (in FITs) | | $\lambda_L$ Stress Curves | (Note) $\lambda_L$ Refs. |
|---|---|---|---|---|---|
| | | $\lambda_L$ | $\alpha$ | | |
| **Integrated Circuits** | | | | | |
| **A. Digital (cont.)** | | | | | |
| 6. NMOS | | | | | |
| 51-100 Gates | P | 30 | 0.75 | A9 | 13 |
| 101-500 Gates | HB | 30 | 0.75 | A9 | 13 |
| 501-1000 Gates | H | 40 | 0.7 | A9 | 13 |
| 1001-10K Gates | H | 50 | 0.7 | A9 | 13 |
| Custom LSI | PB | 100* | 0.5 | A9 | 13 |
| B. Interface and peripheral | | | | | |
| 1. Bipolar | | | | | |
| 20-100 Gates | HB | 75* | 0.7 | A8 | 13 |
| 101-500 Gates | HB | 50* | 0.7 | A8 | 13 |
| 2. NMOS | | | | | |
| 501-1K Gates | HB | 75 | 0.65 | A9 | 13 |
| 1001-10K Gates | HB | 125* | 0.6 | A9 | 13 |
| 3. CMOS | | | | | |
| 501-1K Gates | HB | 75 | 0.65 | A9 | 13 |
| 1001-10K Gates | HB | 100 | 0.65 | A9 | 13 |

---

* Indicates that this data is from field time to failure data.

**TABLE 4.6.** Device Hazard Rate Data (cont.)

| Device Class | Package Type | Expected Hazard Rates (in FITs) $\lambda_L$ | $\alpha$ | $\lambda_L$ Stress Curves | (Note) $\lambda_L$ *Refs.* |
|---|---|---|---|---|---|
| **Integrated Circuits (cont.)** | | | | | |
| C. Linear | | | | | |
| 1. Bipolar | | | | | |
| ≤100 Transistors | P | 50* | 0.75 | A8 | 12,13 |
| 101-300 Transistors | P | 50 | 0.75 | A8 | 12 |
| 2. MOS & MOS/bipolar | | | | | |
| ≤100 Transistors | P | 30 | 0.75 | A9 | 12,13 |
| 101-300 Transistors | P | 50 | 0.75 | A9 | 12,13 |
| 3. CMOS | | | | | |
| ≤100 Transistors | P | 30 | 0.75 | A9 | 13 |
| 101-300 Transistors | P | 50 | 0.75 | A9 | 13 |
| D. Memory – EPROM | | | | | |
| 1. NMOS | | | | | |
| 8K-64K Bits | HB | 100* | 0.6 | A9 | 13 |
| 128K Bits | HB | 200 | 0.6 | A9 | 13 |
| 256K Bits | HB | 200 | 0.6 | A9 | 13 |
| 2. CMOS | | | | | |
| 8K-64K | HB | 100 | 0.7 | A9 | 13 |

---

\* Indicates that this data is from field time to failure data.

**TABLE 4.6.** Device Hazard Rate Data (cont.)

| Device Class | Package Type | Expected Hazard Rates (in FITs) $\lambda_L$ | $\alpha$ | $\lambda_L$ Stress Curves | (Note) $\lambda_L$ Refs. |
|---|---|---|---|---|---|
| **Integrated Circuits (cont.)** | | | | | |
| E. Memory – PROM, RAM, & ROM | | | | | |
| 1. Bipolar | | | | | |
| ≤1K Bits | P | 20* | 0.7 | A8 | 13 |
| 2K Bits | P | 50 | 0.7 | A8 | 13 |
| 4K Bits | HB | 25* | 0.7 | A8 | 13 |
| 8K Bits | HB | 50 | 0.7 | A8 | 13 |
| 16K Bits | H | 100* | 0.7 | A8 | 13 |
| 64K Bits | HB | 100 | 0.7 | A5 | 13 |
| 2. CMOS | | | | | |
| ≤1K Bits | HB | 50 | 0.75 | A9 | 13 |
| 4K Bits | HB | 60* | 0.75 | A9 | 13 |
| 16K Bits | HB | 100 | 0.7 | A9 | 13 |
| 64K Bits | PB | 200 | 0.7 | A9 | 13 |
| 256K Bits | PB | 55 | 0.7 | A9 | 13 |
| 1M Bits | PB | 75 | 0.7 | A9 | 13 |
| 3. NMOS | | | | | |
| 1K Bits | HB | 25 | 0.7 | A9 | 12 |

* Indicates that this data is from field time to failure data.

**TABLE 4.6.** Device Hazard Rate Data (cont.)

| Device Class | Package Type | Expected Hazard Rates (in FITs) | | $\lambda_L$ Stress Curves | (Note) $\lambda_L$ Refs. | |
|---|---|---|---|---|---|---|
| | | $\lambda_L$ | $\alpha$ | | | |
| **Integrated Circuits** | | | | | | |
| **E. Memory – PROM, RAM, & ROM** | | | | | | |
| **3. NMOS (cont.)** | | | | | | |
| 2K Bits | HB | 25 | 0.7 | A9 | | 12,13 |
| 4K Bits | HB | 50* | 0.7 | A9 | (9) | 12,13 |
| 16K Bits | HB | 100* | 0.65 | A9 | (9) | 12,13 |
| 32K Bits | HB | 100 | 0.65 | A9 | | 13 |
| 64K Bits | HB or PB | 30* | 0.65 | A9 | (10) | 13 |
| 256K Bits | PB | 30* | 0.65 | A9 | | 13 |
| F. Microcomputers | | | | | | |
| 1. CMOS | | | | | | |
| 4 Bit | HB | 100 | 0.8 | A9 | | 12 |
| 8 Bit | HB | 100 | 0.7 | A9 | | 13 |
| 2. NMOS | | | | | | |
| 4 Bit | HB | 60 | 0.65 | A9 | | 13 |
| 8 Bit | HB | 100 | 0.75 | A9 | | 12,13 |
| G. Microprocessors | | | | | | |
| 1. Bipolar | | | | | | |
| 4 Bit | HB | 60* | 0.65 | A8 | | 13 |

*   Indicates that this data is from field time to failure data.

**TABLE 4.6.** Device Hazard Rate Data (cont.)

| Device Class | Package Type | Expected Hazard Rates (in FITs) $\lambda_L$ | $\alpha$ | $\lambda_L$ Stress Curves | (Note) $\lambda_L$ Refs. |
|---|---|---|---|---|---|
| **Integrated Circuits** **G. Microprocessors** **(cont.)** | | | | | |
| 2. CMOS | | | | | |
| 8 Bit | HB | 100 | 0.7 | A9 | 10,13 |
| 32 Bit | HB | 95 | 0.7 | A9 | 10,13 |
| 3. NMOS | | | | | |
| 8 Bit | HB | 100* | 0.6 | A9 | 13 |
| 16 Bit | HB | 100 | 0.65 | A9 | 13 |
| **Lamps** | | | | | |
| A. Incandescent | | | | | |
| 1. 6.3 Volts | | 260 | 0.6 | | 7 |
| 2. 12 Volts | | 420 | 0.6 | | 7 |
| 3. 24 Volts | | 680 | 0.6 | | 7 |
| 4. 48 Volts | | 1000 | 0.6 | | 7 |
| B. Neon | | 200 | 0.6 | | 7 |
| **Meter – Panel** | | 250 | 0.6 | | 7 |
| **Motors** | | 2000 | 0.6 | | 7 |

---

\* Indicates that this data is from field time to failure data.

**TABLE 4.6.** Device Hazard Rate Data (cont.)

| Device Class | Package Type | Expected Hazard Rates (in FITs) $\lambda_L$ | $\alpha$ | $\lambda_L$ Stress Curves | (Note) $\lambda_L$ Refs. |
|---|---|---|---|---|---|
| **Opto-electronics** | | | | | |
| A. Alphanumeric Displays (without logic) | | | | | |
| 1. LCD (Dot Matrix) | | | | | |
| a. 1 Character | P | 20 | 0.6 | NA | 7 |
| b. 8 Characters | P | 60 | 0.6 | NA | 7 |
| c. 16 Characters | P | 110 | 0.6 | NA | 7 |
| d. 32 Characters | P | 200 | 0.6 | NA | 7 |
| 2. LCD (Star Type) | | | | | |
| a. 1 Character | P | 15 | 0.6 | NA | 7 |
| b. 8 Characters | P | 45 | 0.6 | NA | 7 |
| c. 16 Characters | P | 80 | 0.6 | NA | 7 |
| d. 32 Characters | P | 150 | 0.6 | NA | 7 |
| 3. LCD (7 segment) | | | | | |
| a. 1 Character | P | 10 | 0.6 | NA | 7 |
| b. 8 Characters | P | 30 | 0.6 | NA | 7 |
| c. 16 Characters | P | 50 | 0.6 | NA | 7 |
| d. 32 Characters | P | 95 | 0.6 | NA | 7 |
| 4. LED (7 segment) | | | | | |
| a. 1 Character | P | 20 | 0.6 | A8 | 7 |
| b. 8 Characters | P | 70 | 0.6 | A8 | 7 |
| c. 16 Characters | P | 115 | 0.6 | A8 | 7 |
| d. 32 Characters | P | 220 | 0.6 | A8 | 7 |

**TABLE 4.6.** Device Hazard Rate Data (cont.)

| Device Class | Package Type | Expected Hazard Rates (in FITs) $\lambda_L$ | $\alpha$ | $\lambda_L$ Stress Curves | (Note) $\lambda_L$ Refs. |
|---|---|---|---|---|---|
| **Opto-electronics (cont.)** | | | | | |
| B. Alphanumeric Displays (with logic) | | | | | |
| 1. LCD (Dot Matrix) | | | | | |
| a. 1 Character | P | 20 | 0.6 | NA | 7 |
| b. 8 Characters | P | 85 | 0.6 | NA | 7 |
| c. 16 Characters | P | 165 | 0.6 | NA | 7 |
| d. 32 Characters | P | 320 | 0.6 | NA | 7 |
| 2. LCD (Star Type) | | | | | |
| a. 1 Character | P | 15 | 0.6 | NA | 7 |
| b. 8 Characters | P | 65 | 0.6 | NA | 7 |
| c. 16 Characters | P | 120 | 0.6 | NA | 7 |
| d. 32 Characters | P | 230 | 0.6 | NA | 7 |
| 3. LCD (7 segment) | | | | | |
| a. 1 Character | P | 10 | 0.6 | NA | 7 |
| b. 8 Characters | P | 60 | 0.6 | NA | 7 |
| c. 16 Characters | P | 110 | 0.6 | NA | 7 |
| d. 32 Characters | P | 200 | 0.6 | NA | 7 |
| 4. LED (7 segment) | | | | | |
| a. 1 Character | P | 20 | 0.6 | A8 | 7 |
| b. 8 Characters | P | 135 | 0.6 | A8 | 7 |
| c. 16 Characters | P | 265 | 0.6 | A8 | 7 |
| d. 32 Characters | P | 523 | 0.6 | A8 | 7 |
| C. Fiber Cable (1 fiber/kilometer) | P | 50 | 0.6 | | 7 |

**TABLE 4.6.** Device Hazard Rate Data (cont.)

| Device Class | Package Type | Expected Hazard Rates (in FITs) $\lambda_L$ | $\alpha$ | $\lambda_L$ Stress Curves | (Note) $\lambda_L$ Refs. | |
|---|---|---|---|---|---|---|
| **Opto-electronics (cont.)** | | | | | | |
| D. LEDs | | | | | | |
|   1. Illuminators | P | 10 | 0.6 | A8 | (11) | 12 |
|   2. Transmitters, 0.87 μm | PB | 1 | NA | A11 | (12) | 29 |
|   3. Transmitters, 1.3 μm | PB | 10 | NA | NA | (12,13) | 29 |
| E. Optical Connector (single fiber) | P | 30 | 0.6 | | | 7 |
| F. Opto-Isolators | P | 10 | 0.6 | A8 | (11) | 12 |
| **Printed Wiring Boards** | | (see Note 7) | 0.6 | None | (7) | 7,30 |
| **Relays** | | | | | | |
| A. Flat Spring – Miniature | | | | | | |
|   Code MA | | 60 | 0.6 | A4 | | 31 |
|   Code MB | | 70 | 0.6 | A4 | | 31 |
| B. Hermetically Sealed | | NA | NA | NA | | |
| C. Low Profile Miniature | | | | | | |
|   Code LR | | 50 | 0.6 | A4 | | 31 |
| D. Mercury | | 70 | 0.6 | A4,S3 | | 7 |
| E. Microminiature (Sugar Cube) | | NA | NA | NA | | |

**TABLE 4.6.**  Device Hazard Rate Data (cont.)

| Device Class | Expected Hazard Rates (in FITs) $\lambda_L$ | $\alpha$ | $\lambda_L$ Stress Curves | (Note) $\lambda_L$ Refs. |
|---|---|---|---|---|
| **Relays (cont.)** | | | | |
| F. Power/High Voltage | 140 | 0.6 | A4,S3 | 7 |
| G. Reed | 40 | 0.6 | A4,S3 | 7 |
| H. Thermal Bimetal | 70 | 0.6 | A4,S3 | 7 |
| I. Wire Spring – Miniature | | | | |
| Codes BF and BL | 50 | 0.6 | A4 | 31 |
| Codes BJ and BM | 60 | 0.6 | A4 | 31 |
| Code BG | 70 | 0.6 | A4 | 31 |
| **Resistors – Fixed** | | | | |
| A. Discrete | | | | |
| 1. Carbon Composition, Solid Slug | | | | |
| ≤1 M Ω | 0.5 | 0.6 | A7,S4 | 7 |
| >1 M Ω | 1.0 | 0.6 | A7,S4 | 7 |
| 2. Film – Metal or Carbon | | | | |
| ≤1 M Ω | 1.0 | 0.6 | A3,S3 | 7 |
| >1 M Ω | 2.5 | 0.6 | A3,S3 | 7 |
| 3. Film – Power | | | | |
| ≤1 M Ω | 14 | 0.6 | A1,S1 | 7 |
| >1 M Ω | 35 | 0.6 | A1,S1 | 7 |

**TABLE 4.6.** Device Hazard Rate Data (cont.)

| Device Class | Expected Hazard Rates (in FITs) $\lambda_L$ | $\alpha$ | $\lambda_L$ Stress Curves | (Note) $\lambda_L$ Refs. |
|---|---|---|---|---|
| **Resistors – Fixed (cont.)** | | | | |
| B. Networks (per element) | 1.3 | 0.6 | A7 | 7 |
| C. Wirewound | | | | |
| 1. Precision | | | | |
| <1 M Ω | 12 | 0.6 | A3,S3 | 7 |
| >1 M Ω | 20 | 0.6 | A3,S3 | 7 |
| 2. Power – Chassis Mount | 5 | 0.6 | A3,S5 | 7 |
| 3. Power – Lead Mount | 10 | 0.6 | A3,S5 | 7 |
| **Resistors – Variable** | | | | |
| A. Non-wirewound | | | | |
| 1. Film | | | | |
| ≤200 k Ω | 85 | 0.6 | A3,S2 | 7 |
| >200 k Ω | 120 | 0.6 | A3,S2 | 7 |
| 2. Low Precision, Carbon | | | | |
| ≤200 k Ω | 105 | 0.6 | A5,S2 | 7 |
| >200 k Ω | 155 | 0.6 | A5,S2 | 7 |
| 3. Precision | | | | |
| ≤200 k Ω | 80 | 0.6 | A5,S1 | 7 |
| >200 k Ω | 115 | 0.6 | A5,S1 | 7 |

**TABLE 4.6.** Device Hazard Rate Data (cont.)

| Device Class | Expected Hazard Rates (in FITs) $\lambda_L$ | $\alpha$ | $\lambda_L$ Stress Curves | (Note) $\lambda_L$ Refs. |
|---|---|---|---|---|
| **Resistors – Variable** | | | | |
| **A. Non-wirewound (cont.)** | | | | |
| 4. Trimmers | | | | |
| ≤200 k Ω | 18 | 0.6 | A3,S1 | 7 |
| >200 k Ω | 30 | 0.6 | A3,S1 | 7 |
| B. Wirewound | | | | |
| 1. High Power – Enclosed | | | | |
| ≤5 k Ω | 245 | 0.6 | A3,S2 | 7 |
| >5 k Ω | 350 | 0.6 | A3,S2 | 7 |
| 2. High Power – Unenclosed | | | | |
| ≤5 k Ω | 120 | 0.6 | A3,S2 | 7 |
| >5 k Ω | 175 | 0.6 | A3,S2 | 7 |
| 3. Lead Screw Actuated | 17 | 0.6 | A4,S3 | 7 |
| 4. Precision | | | | |
| ≤100 k Ω | 390 | 0.6 | A4,S1 | 7 |
| >100 k Ω | 700 | 0.6 | A4,S1 | 7 |
| 5. Semiprecision | | | | |
| ≤5 k Ω | 120 | 0.6 | A5,S3 | 7 |
| >5 k Ω | 170 | 0.6 | A5,S3 | 7 |

**TABLE 4.6.** Device Hazard Rate Data (cont.)

| Device Class | Expected Hazard Rates (in FITs) | | $\lambda_L$ Stress Curves | (Note) $\lambda_L$ Refs. |
|---|---|---|---|---|
| | $\lambda_L$ | $\alpha$ | | |
| **Switches (Panel)** (Rate per contact pair) | | | | |
| A. Pushbutton (SPST) | 3 | 0.6 | S3 | 7 |
| B. Rotary (1 per six-contact wafer) | 8 | 0.6 | S3 | 7 |
| C. Sensitive | 110 | 0.6 | S3 | 7 |
| D. Toggle (SPST) | 3 | 0.6 | S3 | 7 |
| **Switches (PWB)** (Rate per switch) | | | | |
| A. DIP (in-line) | 10 | 0.6 | S3 | 7 |
| B. Pushbutton | 10 | 0.6 | S3 | 7 |
| C. Rotary (per six-contact) | 10 | 0.6 | S3 | 7 |
| D. Thumbwheel | 10 | 0.6 | S3 | 7 |
| **Thermistors** | | | | |
| A. Bead | 20 | 0.6 | | 7 |
| B. Disk | 65 | 0.6 | | 7 |
| C. Rod | 100 | 0.6 | | 7 |
| **Transformers** | | | | |
| A. Audio | 7 | 0.6 | A4 | 7 |
| B. Power | 19 | 0.6 | A4 | 7 |
| C. Pulse, ≤5 Watts avg. | 4 | 0.6 | A4 | 7 |
| D. Radio Frequency | 30 | 0.6 | A4 | 7 |

**TABLE 4.6.** Device Hazard Rate Data (cont.)

| Device Class | Package Type | Expected Hazard Rates (in FITs) $\lambda_L$ | $\alpha$ | $\lambda_L$ Stress Curves | (Note) $\lambda_L$ Refs. |
|---|---|---|---|---|---|
| **Transistors – Silicon** | | | | | |
| A. FET | H or P | 10* | 0.6 | A9 | 12,13 |
| B. High Frequency (<1 GHz) | H | 1 | 0.6 | A8 | 12 |
| C. Microwave  (>1 GHz) | H | 1 | 0.6 | A8 | 12 |
| D. NPN | | | | | |
|   <0.6 W | P | 20* | 0.6 | A8 | 12 |
|   | H | 1 | 0.6 | A8 | 12 |
|   0.6-6 W | P | 20* | 0.6 | A8 | 12 |
|   >6 W | HB or H | 50 | 0.6 | A8 | 12 |
| E. PNP | | | | | |
|   <0.6 W | P | 20* | 0.6 | A8 | 12 |
|   0.6-6 W | P | 20* | 0.6 | A8 | 12 |
|   >6 W | HB or H | 100 | 0.6 | A8 | 12 |
| F. Thyristors | | | | | |
|   1. SCR | | | | | |
|     ≤1 amp | P | 6* | 0.6 | A8 | 12,32 |
|     >1 amp | P | 60* | 0.6 | A8 | 12,32 |
|   2. Triac | P | 25* | 0.6 | A8 | 12,32 |

---

* Indicates that this data is from field time to failure data.

## (Notes)

(1)   The hazard rate given is at 25 percent electrical stress and 40°C ambient. To assure maximum operating life, aluminum electrolytic capacitors should be operated at or near rated voltage.[8]

(2)   The following stress factors for solid tantalum capacitors

$$k = 0.23 \times 10^{\left[ 1.5 \frac{V_W}{V_R} - 0.3 \frac{R_C}{V_W} \right]}$$

where

$V_W$ = working voltage,

$V_R$ = rated voltage, and

$R_C$ = total series resistance

should be applied to the hazard rate only if $k > 1$.[33]

(3)   The infant mortality slope parameters, $\alpha = 0.5$, and $\alpha = 0.7$, for *plastic capacitors* were taken from References [12] and [19], respectively.

(4)   The hazard rates of most plastic capacitors have an appreciable humidity dependence. The hazard rate multiplying factor $H$ is used to account for humidity dependence. It is given by:[12]

$$H = e^{.046(R_1 - R_0)}$$

where

$R_1$ = percent relative humidity experienced, and

$R_0$ = reference percent relative humidity.

(5)   If a manual operation is used for connection, multiply the automatic rate by 2.

(6)   These connectors have been tested at the equivalent service temperature of 60°C continuous, which is taken to be the maximum (worst-case) ambient temperature (locations adjacent to heat generating circuit packs).

(7)   Hazard rate estimates for multilayer printed wiring boards can be calculated as follows:

$$\lambda_L = \lambda_B \left[ \left[ 2N_{smt} \right] + \left[ N_{pth} F_{cf} \right] + \left[ 2.5 N_{vpth} \right] + \left[ 15 N_{hs} \right] \right]$$

where

$\lambda_L$ = Long-term hazard rate in FITs,

$\lambda_B$ = 0.04 FITs (base hazard rate),

$N_{smt}$ = Number of surface mounted device contacts to be soldered,*

$N_{pth}$ = Number of plated-through-holes (PTHs) to be soldered,*

$F_{cf}$ = Complexity factor $(0.65) \times N_{cp}^{(0.63)}$,

        where $N_{cp}$ = Number of circuit planes.
                 If $N_{cp} < 3$ then $F_{cp} = 1.0$.

$N_{vpth}$ = Number of PTHs not soldered (layer to layer via connections),

$N_{hs}$ = Number of hand soldered connections.

The value of $\lambda_1 = \lambda_L \times t_c^{\alpha}$ for $t_c = 10{,}000$ hours, and $\alpha = 0.6$ is given by:

$$\lambda_1 = \lambda_L \times \left[10^4\right]^{\alpha} = \lambda_L \times 250$$

where

$\lambda_1$ = Infant mortality hazard rate in FITs at one hour.

(8)   The listed steady-state hazard rates for connectors should be multiplied by a factor, $K$, if the applicable resistance failure level, $R_f$, is significantly different from one ohm.  This factor may be determined as follows:

$$\text{If } 0.01 \le R_f \le 0.1 \quad K = \frac{0.25}{R_f}.$$

$$\text{If } 0.1 \le R_f \le 10 \quad K = (R_f)^{-0.4}.$$

$$\text{If } R_f \ge 10 \quad\quad K = 0.4.$$

(9)   The soft error rate is estimated to be <3000 FITs in NMOS dynamic RAMs and <1000 FITs in CMOS dynamic and static RAMs.  In general, dynamic

---

* Assumes automated soldering.

RAMs are more sensitive than static RAMs. These soft error rates are generally higher than system designers would like to experience in their designs. Error correction techniques are used to reduce the impact of these high soft error rates on the system performance.

(10)   The design objective is a soft error rate of ≤1000 FITs for dynamic RAMs.

(11)   Hazard rates for opto-electronic devices can vary substantially with operating parameters, such as, duty cycle, input and output currents. The reader is referred to a specialist if more specific information is needed. The value listed for $\alpha$ is assumed.

(12)   The long-term hazard rate listed is for unpackaged LED devices. Packaged device hazard rates are not yet available, and the infant mortality parameters for packaged devices are not yet known.

(13)   LED reliability depends upon the definition of end-of-life.

## REFERENCES

1.   See, for example, Intersociety Conference on Thermal Phenomena in the Fabrication and Operation of Electronic Components, May 11-13, 1988, Los Angeles, California and references contained therein. Cover Title: *1988 Conference on Thermal Phenomena in Electronic Components.*

2.   R. Nitsch, "Computer-Aided Prediction of Reliability," in *Reliability in Electrical and Electronic Components and Systems,* edited by E. Langer and J. Moltoft, North-Holland, Amsterdam, 1982.

3.   *Intel Reliability Monitor Program,* Intel Corporation, Santa Clara, C. Ekland-Olson, C. Shepard and R. Rivera, "MCM6664AP/66665AP Plastic Package 64K Dynamic RAM Quality and Reliability Report," Motorola, 1982.

4.   D. S. Peck, "New Concerns About Integrated Circuit Reliability," *Proceedings of the International Reliability Physics Symposium*, IEEE,1978: p. 1.

5.   H. S. Johnston, *Gas Phase Reaction Rate Theory,* Ronald Press, New York, 1966. See also R. E. Wetson and H. A. Schwartz, *Chemical Kinetics,* Prentice Hall, Englewood Cliffs, 1972.

6.   Department of Defense, *Reliability Prediction of Electronic Equipment,* MIL-HDBK-217E, U. S. Government Printing Office, Washington, D. C., 1986.

7.   The hazard rates of MIL-HDBK-217 (beginning with version C, and updated regularly, with version E being current) have been used to obtain steady-state hazard rates within the context of the AT&T hazard rate model for electronic devices. By comparing AT&T hazard rates (long-term) for composition

resistors with those from MIL-HDBK-217, it was determined that Level III*
corresponds to quality level I of MIL-HDBK-217. The early life data, in
terms of the Weibull shape parameter $\alpha$, was determined, for each device type
based on experience with OLT, factory burn-in, and field tracking.

With an $\alpha$ for each device type, and knowledge of the appropriate quality
factor to be used, the MIL-HDBK data was recast in the form commonly used
within AT&T, for those device types without sufficient field or factory data
upon which we might estimate hazard rates confidently.

Similarly, the electrical stress factors were transcribed, but in a form
appropriate for AT&T designers, that is, with no "acceleration" when derating
is 25 percent.

8. *Handbook of Components for Electronics,* edited by Charles A. Harper,
   McGraw-Hill, New York, 1977.

9. W. A. Baker, Private Communication, June 1988.

10. R. C. Winans, in *Physical Design of Electronic Systems,* Bell Telephone
    Laboratories, Prentice Hall, Englewood Cliffs, 1972.

11. The hazard rate multipliers were determined in the following way. Infant
    mortality control results and reliability life test data were obtained from
    several major integrated circuit suppliers and compared with those for AT&T
    and purchased Level III devices.* The results indicated that commercial
    plastic devices from these companies are estimated to be only slightly less
    reliable (by a factor of roughly 1.3 on the average).

    The figures of 1.1 and 1.2 for Level II hermetic and Level III plastic,
    respectively, were chosen for consistency with the consensus on the relative
    reliability of Level II hermetic (better) over Level III plastic and to preserve a
    ratio of 1.2 of plastic over hermetic for the Level II and III categories. The
    multipliers for Level I integrated circuits and all discrete components are
    based on the *Reliability Prediction Procedure for Electronic Equipment*
    (formerly the *AT&T Reliability Prediction Procedure for Electronic
    Equipment*), (TR-TSY-000332), Issue 2, Bell Communications Research,
    July 1988.

12. In 1980, data from a variety of internal AT&T sources, including the field
    tracking and factory burn-in studies, were used to develop the data tables in
    the fourth edition of the (internal to AT&T) version of this manual. This data
    analysis, like the tables in the fourth edition, pertained only to semiconductor
    devices.

13. In support of the proprietary version of this document, reliability data on
    semiconductor devices was periodically compiled in order to update the
    hazard rate tables. Six such updates occurred between 1980 and 1985. These
    updates include data analyses of new technology devices and new data
    sources, including more operational life testing (see Chapter 2), field return

---

* See Chapter 2 for a discussion of the reliability classification scheme for devices, used in this manual.

data from AT&T's 3B20 computers, and field study data of AT&T's largest electronic switching systems. Data from qualification studies of 16K, 64K, 256K, and 1M DRAM were used in these updates. Most recently, an update of the proprietary version of the data that goes into this manual was prepared in late 1987. The data in this update again is semiconductor data. See: F. Beltrano, "Estimating Integrated-Circuit Failure Rates from Field Performance," *Proceedings of the Reliability and Maintainability Symposium*, IEEE, 1988: p. 327.

14. J. T. Duane, "Learning Curve Approach to Reliability Monitoring," *IEEE Transactions on Aerospace* **2** (1964): p. 563.

15. L. H. Crow, "Reliability Analysis for Complex Repairable Systems," in *Reliability and Biometry*, edited by F. Proschan and R. J. Serfling, SIAM, Philadelphia, 1974. See also L. H. Crow, "Conference Interval Procedures for the Weibull Process with Applications to Reliability Growth," *Technometrics* **24** (1982): p. 67.

16. The hazard rates for multilayer ceramic capacitors are based on accelerated life tests conducted at AT&T Bell Laboratories in Allentown, PA. A typical mean time to failure at 105°C and 400 percent of rated voltage was found to be 120 hours.

17. The mica capacitor hazard rates are based on accelerated tests conducted between 1977 and 1979. During the course of the test period, a total of 685 devices were put on test for a 2000 hour period at 85°C, and 200 percent of rated voltage.

18. The hazard rate data for polyester capacitors is based on accelerated life test data and field failure data. These data suggest that the numbers in the hazard rate tables for polyester capacitors are somewhat conservative. For example, field data suggest that the Weibull parameter $\alpha$ may well be less than 0.5, and that the steady-state hazard rate may be less than 2.

19. The hazard rates for metalized polyester capacitors are based on accelerated testing, factory burn-in, and system test data. The system test data is time-to-replacements data. It comes from testing over 17,000 data sets (modems), each of which have 2 capacitors. By assuming that 1/2 of replacements are failures, the infant mortality hazard rate shape parameter was determined. Extrapolation to 10,000 hours provided the steady-state hazard rate value. Value is consistent with that obtained from factory burn-in.

20. This result is based on an accelerated life testing conducted at 85°C and 105°C, at DC voltage of 0, 10, 20 and 40, (max rated voltage, 15V). The testing was carried out for over 18,700 hours. A total of 123 capacitors were tested.

21. The solid wire connections were temperature cycled and temperature aged at 100°C. Estimated acceleration from the 40°C reference temperature is 2.6 during infant mortality. This is equivalent to 2497 hours of operation at 40°C. The estimated hazard rate was 0.095 FIT or $\simeq 0.1$ FIT.

22. An extensive connector field study was initiated in 1974. No actual failures were reported from any of the sites participating in the study. Therefore,

hazard rates were assigned on the basis of resistance changes of ten or more milliohms.

23. Accelerated aging of two types: (1) 90°C for 200 days and (2) temperature cycling between 5°C and 50°C with RH = 90 for 300 twelve-hour cycles, was used to assess the change of contact area with time and the change in retention forces of solder plated interference pins used in bare upper-plated through holes. This work was carried out between 1973 and 1983 at AT&T Bell Laboratories.

24. Field data on modular plugs and jacks indicate the jacks to have a hazard rate of 42 FITs while the plugs fail at a rate of 232 FITs. It was also found that three-fourths of the plug failures were caused by the cord/plug interface owing to overextending the phone cord by the users. The maximum total for a jack and plug pair should be about 80 FITs but has been maintained as a conservative estimate of 230 FITs.

25. Insertion, temperature cycling, temperature aging, and COTY (City One-Year Tests) were performed where a contact resistance of 1000 milliohms was considered a failure. The resulting hazard rate data is based on $3.46 \times 10^{13}$ contact hours. The data obtained is plotted as hazard rate versus contact resistance where the hazard rates at a contact resistance of 1000 milliohms vary from 0.6 to 1.25 FITs.

26. To assess the effects of harsh environments on an electronic switch, an electronic switching system was placed in a hut, in Lisle, for 12 months. In this uncontrolled environment, the temperature ranged between −22°F and 120°F. Relative humidities of 100 percent were not uncommon. The number of failures in such an environment were approximately 4 times that expected under controlled conditions.

27. The kinetics of corrosion of Cu, Ni, and Ag in a central office environment and in a non-air conditioned environment were studied. These studies were used to obtain acceleration factors for the one-year test of these materials.

28. A model for the hazard rate of Hybrid Integrated Circuits (HICs) was developed which treated an HIC as a small circuit pack. That is, hazard rates are assigned to each component on an HIC and combined as if these components were on a circuit pack (see examples 4.3 and 4.4). For thin film HICs, the hazard rates of the components are taken to be the same as for separately packaged devices in this manual. For thick film HICs, a model based upon the parts count method of MIL-HDBK-217 was developed. The shape parameter $\alpha$ is taken to be 0.6.

29. Steady-state hazard rates for 0.87 $\mu$ and 1.7 $\mu$ LEDs were obtained from accelerated life testing performed at AT&T-BL in Murray Hill, NJ. Tests conducted included conditions at which the device junction temperatures were estimated to be 220°C, 170°C, and 120°C.

30. The hazard rates for printed wiring boards (PWBs) in this manual are based on a comprehensive program which includes accelerated life testing, field tracking, and extensive failure mode analysis. This program is ongoing to insure the continued high reliability of AT&T PWBs.

31.   Hazard rates of relays were primarily based on field data (replacement rates only). Accelerated life test data was obtained, but this is considered to only give information about possible mechanical failures.

32.   Key Telephone Units (Model #400H) were the subject of a field study. Failure mode analysis (FMA) was performed on semiconductor devices removed from the units. From the removal data and FMA, accurate steady state hazard rates were obtained. As only dropout was recorded, however, the value of the Weibull shape parameter had to be assumed for each device studied.

33.   This stress factor was developed by AT&T Bell Laboratories personnel in Allentown, PA on the basis of over twenty years of accelerated and *unaccelerated* life testing (in the laboratory).

# 5

---

# MONITORING RELIABILITY

---

## INTRODUCTION

The goal of a reliability monitoring program is to ensure that customers' reliability requirements are being satisfied. Reliability is measured by the rates of removal or replacement of equipment during its manufacture, installation, and operation. Reliability is improved by identifying and correcting causes of excessive failure rates. In this chapter, we describe the following reliability monitoring programs:

- burn-in of metal oxide semiconductor (MOS) integrated circuits during their manufacture,

- long-term reliability tests of components just after their manufacture (life testing),

- early-life reliability audits—Operational Life Testing (OLT) of components, just after their manufacture

- system reliability tests of equipment just after its manufacture,

- field quality appraisals,

- analysis of failed equipment when returned for repair.

These programs are illustrated with examples drawn from AT&T. Figure 5-1 shows the reliability monitoring programs in temporal relation to the latter part of the product life cycle.

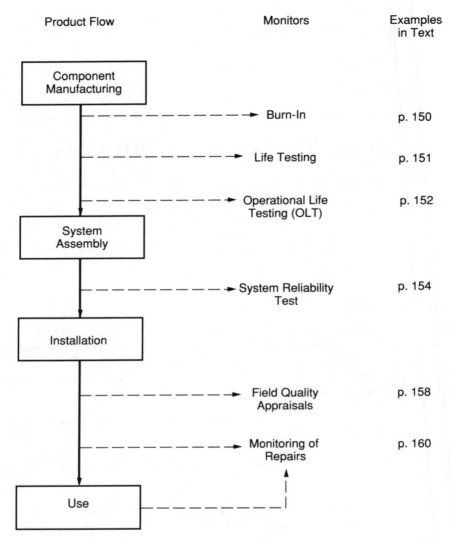

**Figure 5-1.** Reliability monitoring programs shown in temporal relation to the latter part of the product life cycle.

## BURN-IN OF MOS INTEGRATED CIRCUITS DURING THEIR MANUFACTURE

At AT&T factories, some MOS integrated circuits are burned in before being shipped from the component factory to the equipment factory. The purpose of burn-in is to cause marginal components to fail during the burn-in period and, thereby, be removed from the device population before equipment assembly. This

**TABLE 5.1.** Typical Conditions During Burn-In of MOS Integrated Circuits

| Condition | Value |
|---|---|
| Ambient Temperature | 150°C |
| Test Duration | 12 Hours |
| Bias Voltage | 25% Over Normal |
| Input Bias | Dynamic |

is accomplished by subjecting the entire population to conditions that accelerate the progress of the failure-causing mechanisms. The intent is to cause most, if not all, defective components to fail and "healthy" components to survive (see Chapter 2). An example of conditions during burn-in is shown above in Table 5.1.

At the end of this burn-in, the integrated circuits receive a final test with results monitored by the Product Engineering organization, who ensures that lots exceeding a percent defective allowed (PDA) are burned in a second or third time, as required, or the entire lot is rejected. Product burn-in with PDA can help to screen out devices that might otherwise be early-life failures in the field; it can also reject bad lots with excessive percent defective product. However, burn-in alone does not provide the best estimate of the early life reliability performance since other failure mechanisms, not accelerated by the burn-in conditions, might cause early life-failures in the field, for example, hot carriers. Alternatively, the failure mechanism that leads to failure at the more stressful conditions may not be a threat at typical use conditions. To monitor early life reliability of devices, one should employ test conditions that simulate the field use conditions; in this way, no accelerating stress assumptions are required. As described in the *Early-Life Reliability Audits — Operational Life Test* section, Operational Life Testing (OLT) is based on this notion.

## LONG-TERM RELIABILITY TESTS OF COMPONENTS

Samples of components manufactured by AT&T receive long-term reliability tests to verify that the components will perform reliably throughout their intended lifetime. These tests consist of life and environmental tests designed to detect failure modes that occur after one or more years of use. An example of these tests is shown in Table 5.2.

Reliability tests, such as those listed in Table 5.2, are used on various integrated circuits in groups of similar components. If a group displays unacceptable reliability, shipments from that group are withheld until an acceptable reliability is achieved by corrective actions, as demonstrated by subsequent reliability tests.

**TABLE 5.2.** Conditions for a Long-Term Reliability Test

| Name of Test | Sample Size | Temperature | Relative Humidity | Bias Voltage |
|---|---|---|---|---|
| High-Temp. Bias | 80 / Test Lot | 125°C to 150°C | N/A | Yes |
| Temp.-Humidity Bias | 170 / Test Lot | 85°C | 85% | Yes |
| Temp. Cycle | 57 / Test Lot | -65°C to +150°C | N/A | No |

## EARLY-LIFE RELIABILITY AUDITS—OPERATIONAL LIFE TEST

Most AT&T components are operated and tested by AT&T quality assurance personnel just after their manufacture. Electrical performance is tested and hazard rates are estimated. These hazard rate *estimates* are compared against hazard rate *standards*.* Such OLT audits were instituted to monitor infant mortality performance. The OLT equipment is capable of operating components continuously and testing each device on a scanning basis. The test conditions are mildly accelerating,† that is, designed to simulate the extremes of normal field operating conditions—temperature variations, power on/off, input vectors, for example. OLT audits have been instituted on the majority of electronic device families.[3]

### Phases of an OLT Audit

The following phases of an OLT audit (shown in Figure 5-2) are repeated weekly:[4]

1. *Sample Selection.* A sample, such as 2,000 components, is randomly chosen from a product that has passed final inspection at the device factory.

2. *Pre-Operational Test.* The components are subjected to many of the electrical tests used by final inspection. This measures the incidence of dead-on-arrivals (DOAs) and assures that the sample components are defect-free before the operating period begins.

3. *Operating Period with Testing.* During this period, which sometimes is called in-situ testing, the components are exercised dynamically for an extended duration (typically 100 hours), under the most stringent conditions

---

* There are two standards commonly used. First, the hazard rate estimates of the tables of Chapter 4 and second, the moving average[1] of the results of recent tests. This is a kind of "control chart"[2] for hazard rates.

† The temperature may be slightly higher than field conditions, but within operating specification, in order to increase the likelihood of failure.

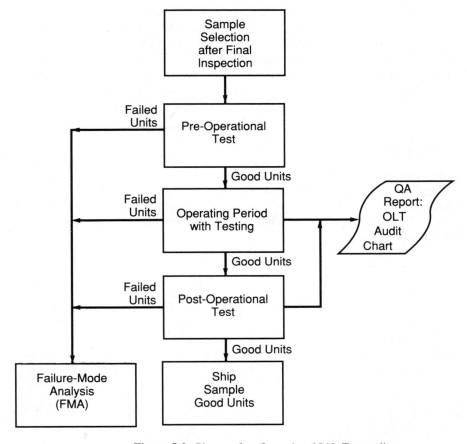

**Figure 5-2.** Phases of an Operational Life Test audit.

likely to be encountered in the field. These operating conditions are always within the components' specified limits. The components are functionally tested on a scanning basis. Intermittent failures are verified. All failures in this phase are labeled device operating failures (DOFs).

4. *Post-Operational Test.* The components are subjected to all of the electrical tests used by final inspection. Failures in this phase are also labeled DOFs.

5. *Sample Shipment.* All components passing tests are shipped as normal product since the OLT is nondestructive.

6. *Failure-Mode Analysis (FMA).* In all OLT audits, all failures are analyzed to identify their causes. This information is fed back promptly to call attention to and thereby help remedy weaknesses in either the manufacturing process or the design.

7.  *Reliability Rating Feedback.* A rating of reliability is obtained by comparing OLT hazard rates with reliability standards and periodically reporting these comparisons to management through Quality Assurance reports. The reliability standard is determined in a process capability study that takes into account the device users' early life reliability requirements as well as the manufacturer's processing capability. If device reliability is found to be sufficiently below this standard, then corrective action is taken. Corrective action may involve more testing, a no-ship order, or even stoppage of the line. This reliability rating feedback provides assurance that the user will receive a product with satisfactory early life reliability.

## SYSTEM RELIABILITY TESTS OF EQUIPMENT

Systems undergo reliability tests under conditions simulating normal use just after they are manufactured and/or installed. When conducted under well-controlled conditions, system reliability tests may provide opportunities for measuring the early-life hazard rates of components and discovering the underlying failure mechanisms.

### System Reliability Audits

System reliability is audited by assessing failure rates* during system tests. This audit estimates the system's failure rate while the system is operating during a fixed time interval. System reliability audits display similarities to OLT audits, but usually occur later in the manufacturing process at the equipment factory and/or the installation site instead of at the device factory. Any failures found are reviewed with the responsible organizations, such as the equipment assembly factory shop or the equipment installer.

**Example: Dimension[†] PBX.** The audit of Dimension PBX[‡] systems at the factory is typical. The audit has four parts, as shown in Figure 5-3. First, initial tests of the PBX equipment measure the as-received performance of the combined hardware-software system. Failures are recorded and compared against a quality standard for the installation process. During system testing and post test lasting from hour 47 to hour 167 (for 120 hours of testing time), the number of failures, if any, is noted and compared to a reliability standard derived from in-service trouble rates. Finally, workmanship is evaluated visually and is compared to standards for reliability and manufacturing quality.

**Example: 5ESS[†] switch.** The quality assurance factory system test for the 5ESS[§] switch is similar in philosophy to the Dimension PBX system tests. Instead

---

*   Failure rate, it should be recalled, is the time derivative of the expected (or average) number of failures (see Chapters 1 and 3).
†   Registered trademark of AT&T.
‡   Private Branch Exchange.
§   Electronic Switching System.

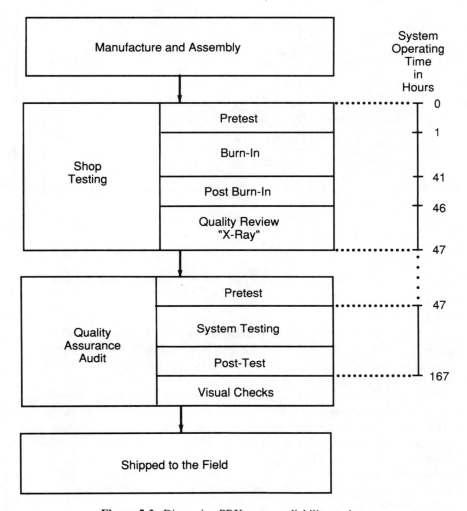

**Figure 5-3.** Dimension PBX system reliability testing.

of one continuous test, the 5ESS switch system test is divided into a 12-hour functional test and a 48-hour reliability test (see Figure 5-4). As in the Dimension PBX initial test, the 5ESS switch functional test measures the as-received performance of the switch. This room-temperature test includes operational exercises, diagnostic tests, and call-processing tests simulating normal use. Manufacturing errors, DOAs, and DOFs might be found during these tests. Failures observed during the functional test are compared to a quality objective. The functional test always precedes the reliability test because it is used as a screen for ʼailures occurring before the reliability test.

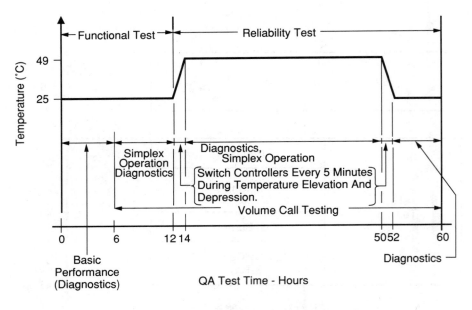

**Figure 5-4.** 5ESS switch functional test and reliability test.

The 5ESS switch reliability audit provides functional testing at 50°C. The functional testing, for the most part, consists of volume call testing. Volume call testing is performed by simulating the passage of approximately $10^3$ calls through each switch module* per hour. If a failure is encountered, diagnostic tests are used to stress and isolate defective hardware. Elevated temperature testing provides two benefits: it allows the verification of proper functionality at the upper temperature design limit and it accelerates some device failure mechanisms resulting in an "accelerated aging" effect on the switch. Hardware dropouts during the reliability test are compared to a quality objective, which is based on the design objective for the early-life failure rate of the switch. Early-life failure rates are estimated by appropriately combining the time-dependent failure contributions of each of the system components.

**Example: Transmission Systems.** In the system reliability audits, circuit packs that have passed final inspection at the AT&T factory are plugged into a test frame, where they are exercised and monitored for 24 hours. After initial failures (DOAs) are weeded out at the start of the 24-hour period, all defects occurring during this period are counted. But this should not be interpreted to mean that AT&T is satisfied with anything but zero defects. Defects may be there, but no defect level is tolerated; AT&T is continuing to drive down defect levels. All new transmission systems receive system reliability test audits.

---

\* Switches may contain as few as five to eight modules.

### System Reliability Tests Used for Infant Mortality Screening

Prior to auditing, AT&T factories use system tests to screen out infant mortality in products as diverse as AT&T's largest switching system (No. 4 ESS* switch), data sets (modems), Dimension PBX, and power supplies. Part of the system testing includes operation at elevated temperatures to simulate air conditioning failure or operation in environments without air conditioning.[†]

For example, as shown in Figure 5-5, data sets (modems) are operated in an oven at 50°C for a minimum of 36 hours. The last four hours of operation must be error-free. In the next testing stage, the operation of the data set consists of an 8-hour on and a 4-hour off power cycle at room ambient temperature. The data set must run entirely free from error for 96 hours. After passing a comprehensive final system test, the data set is ready for shipment.

For a system too large to fit into an oven, such as No. 4 ESS switch, operation occurs in an enclosed area where the air conditioning is turned off and the area heated until the desired temperature (50°C) is reached. The temperature is raised gradually and any faults that occur are repaired, one at a time. This method has been used successfully even on extremely large systems costing many millions of dollars.

---

\*   Trademark of AT&T.

†   In the event of an air conditioning system failure in the central office, the temperature in the middle of the equipment aisle may rise to 50°C.

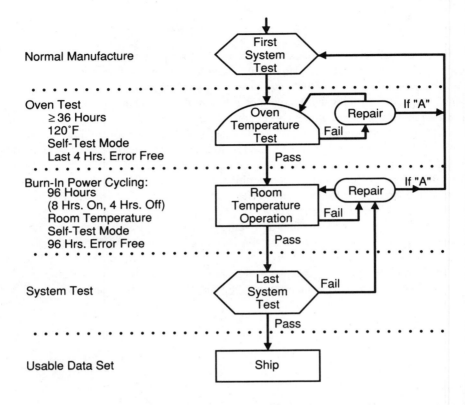

"A" = Circuit Pack, Power Supply or Backplane Replacement

**Figure 5-5.**  Data set reliability test procedure.

## FIELD QUALITY APPRAISAL

Field quality appraisal includes measuring product reliability during actual use. It can be used to verify that system reliability objectives are being met or, conversely, to point out areas needing improvement. Currently, the term "field quality appraisal" includes the study of product reliability, system availability, field support, and customer perception of the product.

Field quality appraisal has uncovered inadequacies in diagnosing failures in the field and in testing during repair, and has been particularly useful when on-site factors influence failure or removal rates. When organized to include device-level failure data, field quality appraisal can also aid in identifying and correcting problems with "bad actor" devices.

### Phases of a Field Quality Appraisal

Field quality appraisal generally is performed in the following phases:

1.  Define the objectives of the study.

2.  Design the study:

- Plan to identify the population (for example, by making an inventory) whose removals, replacements, or other events are to be monitored.

- Plan to capture these events or removals, including the collection, storage, and subsequent retrieval of the data associated with these events or removals.

- Plan to analyze failed units, using suitable test equipment and diagnosticians.

- Plan to monitor and control compliance with the procedures of the study.

- Review the study design with reliability engineers. If the study includes device failure data, also review the study with people from the appropriate device departments.

- Have a statistician review the design of the study, particularly if the study involves measuring device hazard rates that are likely to vary with time (as is the case when the hazard rates follow the Weibull distribution, discussed in Chapters 1 through 4).

- Consider assessing customer perception of the product by means of a questionnaire or structured interviewing process. Review plans with marketing.

3.  Shake down the study with a trial:

- Test the procedures of the appraisal, since difficulties in new field trials cannot be adequately anticipated. A few dry runs will prove to be helpful.

- If necessary, refine the objectives of the tracking study.

- Repeat the field trial until a successful design is obtained.

4.  Select study locations:

- Proposed study locations will be chosen from among customer locations where the equipment will be installed.

5.  Obtain concurrence and the support of the customer:

- Discuss your needs with the appropriate marketing personnel before obtaining the customer's cooperation.

6.  Provide training and documentation:

- Train the craftspersons in the specific details and importance of adequate documentation.

7.  Manage execution of the study:

- Monitor the flow of the data on-site.

- Measure (individually, if possible) the extent to which the crafts comply with the procedures.

- Make specific arrangements with the supply organization of the customer (including accounting procedures) to send removed hardware to appropriate organizations—the factory or R&D, for example—capable of determining failure causes.

8. Investigate causal relationships:

- Gain a thorough understanding of local conditions that might influence the observed data.

9. Analyze failures:

- Perform failure mode analysis of failed devices to determine the causes of failures.

10. Provide feedback to all cooperating organizations:

- Provide immediate feedback to the customer (at a variety of levels including craftspersons) about the importance of the results obtained during the study.

- Provide feedback to device and system designers so that they can improve future designs.

- Provide feedback to factory when manufacturing processes are causes of field failures.

11. Provide verification:

- Return units that tested as All Tests Passed (ATP) or No Troubles Found (NTF) to the exact position at the use location that they appeared to fail originally. This will determine whether these units *really* had failed.

12. Analyze data:

- Reliability assessment software may be available through your company's reliability engineers for analysis of data from field quality appraisals. A statistical consultant also may be helpful here.

## MONITORING FAILED EQUIPMENT WHEN RETURNED FOR REPAIR

Reliability also can be monitored by measuring the rates at which failed equipment is returned by the customer for repair. Places suitable for this monitoring include company-operated service centers, factories, and inventory accumulation points. In contrast to on-premises field quality appraisals where reliability data is collected primarily *before* failed equipment is returned for repair, data is collected primarily *after* the failed equipment is returned to a repair facility. For data to be valid, all failed units should be returned to a few repair centers (preferably only one). If failed units are sometimes thrown out or repaired in several locations, data quality may be adversely affected. The population of units in service and their operating times, as well as the operating times of the failed units, must also be known.

Typically, repair facility-based studies obtain failure data at the plug-in level, such as, circuit pack or power module. One advantage of monitoring reliability at the repair facility is the large volume of failure data that can be accumulated. Some disadvantages of such monitoring are: information about the exact location and time of failure is usually lacking unless a system is in place to insure that accurate failure times are recorded; customer perceptions of the product are not directly available through the study; additional effort may be required to obtain complete repair facility records for products that may be repaired through an external repair shop on a contract basis; and reliability problems are more expensive to correct when equipment is already in the customer's possession.

### Issues Involved in Reduction of Repair Facility Data to Provide Integrated Circuit Hazard Rate Estimate

Extracting hazard rate data from circuit pack repair data being collected by systems manufacturing areas currently is one of the most promising methods for estimating integrated circuit hazard rates when the failed equipment is returned to a repair facility. Also, this data may be obtained with little marginal cost.

Data on the manufacture, testing, and repair of circuit packs can be collected by the circuit pack factory. Integrated circuit hazard rates are computed by combining these data with population data obtained from design documents and shipping records. Note that failure mode analysis (FMA) is crucial to distinguish failures from removals. Also, care must be taken not to damage devices as they are removed from boards.

Some desirable features of measuring integrated circuit hazard rates in this manner are: a large volume of failure data is accumulated; hazard rates for devices are provided; estimates of operating time for each failed and non-failed device is available; these data can be comprehensive (hazard rates for a technology category in Chapter 4 of this manual) or specific (hazard rates for a position on a circuit pack); and, finally, since these data are not obtained from accelerated laboratory experiments, *uncertain assumptions about temperature or humidity acceleration factors have not been made.* Because studies of this type estimate hazard rates using data extracted from a factory-generated database, it is essential to ensure that entries into the database are as accurate and complete as possible.

### REFERENCES

1.  B. Hoadley, "The Quality Measurement Plan," *Bell System Technical Journal* **60**, 2 (1981): p. 215.

2.  *Statistical Quality Control Handbook*, Western Electric, New York, 1956, (Select Code 700-444) which is the classic work. It is available from the AT&T Customer Information Center, 1-800-432-6600. See also E. L. Grant and R. S. Leavenworth, *Statistical Quality Control* 6th Edition, McGraw-Hill, New York, 1988, for a more modern perspective.

3.  H. D. Helms, "Various Architectures for Measuring Early-Life Failure Rates of Semiconductor Components," *Proceedings of the International Test Conference*, IEEE, 1985: p. 540.

4.  D. F. Farnholtz, "Operational Life Testing on Semiconductor Devices," *Western Electric Engineer*, (Fall 1981): p. 3.

# 6

---

# SPECIFIC DEVICE INFORMATION

---

## INTRODUCTION

In this chapter, we describe reliability issues specific to particular classes of devices. The material presented is the result of years of experience and work by device designers and failure analysts. The chapter focuses on practical knowledge to help systems engineers avoid or reduce malfunctions and damage to devices; it includes only that information which is not readily available to designers from other sources. No attempt has been made to summarize existing information in data sheets, manufacturers' application notes, device catalogs, or design guides.

Proper device selection is critical to the reliability of any system. Devices have a wide range of reliability and can come from a variety of sources. Devices used by AT&T are classified as reliability Level I, II, or III.*

Good designs, quality control procedures, as well as quality and reliability audits ensure the quality and reliability of AT&T products. Reliability monitoring programs, such as Operational Life Testing (OLT) described in Chapter 5, indicate the reliability of AT&T products. The subsequent feedback of failure-mode analysis results also contributes to the reliability of the products. Any reliability problems that arise in system factories or on customer premises are quickly reported to the device factories where investigative work is done. These tightly linked monitoring and feedback procedures contribute to the prompt rectification of reliability problems.

Within AT&T, a central quality management and engineering (QM&E) organization provides source inspection of purchased Level III specification products at the suppliers' facilities. This organization also performs periodic surveillance on the quality system and manufacturing practices of suppliers of Level

---

\* See Chapter 2 for an explanation of the reliability classification scheme for electronic devices used in this manual.

II specified devices. Inspection of purchased Level III products is performed in accordance with the appropriate Level III specifications, which include both quality and reliability requirements.

## CAPACITORS

### Ceramic Capacitors

Ceramic capacitors are available in monolithic chip form for use in hybrid integrated circuits (HICs), dual in-line package (DIP) configurations for printed circuit board automatic insertion, and the conventional axial or radial lead types. Ceramic capacitors fall into two classes:

1. *Class I Ceramic Capacitors.* These capacitors have a dielectric that is very stable with respect to changes in temperature and are available with negative, positive, or zero temperature coefficients. They use a dielectric with a low-dielectric constant and have a high $Q$ ($Q = X_C / R$) where $X_C$ is the capacitive reactance and $R$ the series resistance, and low volumetric efficiency (large size per capacitance value).

2. *Class II Ceramic Capacitors.* These capacitors have a high-dielectric constant material that exhibits a nonlinear change in capacitance with temperature. The most common dielectric materials used in these capacitors are X7R and Z5U. The capacitors using these dielectrics have the following capacitance-temperature characteristics:

    - Type X7R—capacitance change is less than ±15 percent from −55°C to +125°C.

    - Type Z5U—capacitance change with temperature is +22 percent to −56 percent from 0°C to 85°C.

The temperature-capacitance relationship for these high-dielectric constant ceramic capacitors is generally nonlinear and the designer should always consult data sheets for temperature characteristics. If this information is not on the data sheet, designers should consult the manufacturer.

Class I ceramic capacitors have a stable capacitance beyond a 100 percent rated dc voltage, and Class II capacitors can have as much as a 15 percent decrease in capacitance at 100 percent rated dc voltage. However, this voltage capacitance effect is negligible with single disc type ceramics, owing to the thicker dielectric material used for mechanical reasons. For all ceramic capacitors, the dc-plus-ac ripple or ac peak-to-peak should not be allowed to exceed the capacitors' dc rating.

### Aluminum Electrolytic Capacitors

Aluminum electrolytic capacitors have the highest volumetric efficiency (μF · volts per unit volume) of all capacitors. This high volumetric efficiency plus low equivalent series resistance make this capacitor ideally suited for power filtering.

Aluminum electrolytic capacitors are subject to a wearout failure mechanism—electrolyte evaporation—that causes the hazard rate to increase with time. The mean-time-to-failure (MTTF) due to electrolyte evaporation is related to a number of factors. The ambient temperature and the heat generated by AC ripple currents determine the internal temperature that, combined with the condition of the electrolyte seal, determines the rate of evaporation. The rate of evaporation and the size of the capacitor (quantity of electrolyte) determine the time required for a given fraction of the electrolyte to evaporate. Under the same operating conditions, the MTTF is greater for a large power supply electrolytic capacitor than for a miniature electrolytic capacitor. The MTTF is typically between 10 and 20 years.

Inadvertent reverse and surge currents also cause aluminum electrolytic capacitors to fail. Such failures result from inadequate circuit protection.

Aluminum electrolytic capacitors should not be cleaned with halogenated hydrocarbon solvents. These solvents can penetrate the capacitor's seal and the chlorides in the solvents cause internal corrosion. This corrosion is accelerated when voltage is applied to the capacitor, or if the capacitor is subjected to elevated temperatures, and will result in a field failure.

Aluminum electrolytic capacitors are routinely burned-in to stabilize their leakage current and working voltage. This implies that Dead-On-Arrivals (DOAs) and early-life failures are reduced, which should result in a lower device hazard rate, as observed at the system level, than if no burn-in were performed. Although this is likely to be the case, no data are available.

Even with the stabilizing burn-in, shelf life can have a detrimental effect on these capacitors because their effective working voltage decreases when they are stored with no voltage applied. If rated voltage is then reapplied without proper preconditioning, breakdown can occur. Preconditioning consists of applying rated voltage at limited current for about 30 minutes. The maximum storage period for these capacitors can be obtained from the manufacturer.

*For an extended operating life and cost efficiency, aluminum electrolytic capacitors should be operated at or near their rated voltage.*

### Solid Tantalum Electrolytic Capacitors

Solid tantalum electrolytics are the only tantalum capacitors presently recommended for use in AT&T designs. Wet tantalum electrolytics are not recommended because of leakage and electrolyte evaporation problems. The volumetric efficiency of solid tantalum capacitors is high and ranks second only to aluminum electrolytics.

Solid tantalum capacitors do not experience corrosion or wearout due to electrolyte evaporation. Also, their reliability is improved by voltage derating, whereas the opposite is true for aluminum electrolytic capacitors. The predominant failure mode of solid tantalum capacitors is caused by excessive surge currents. These surge currents can cause scintillation (a momentary dielectric breakdown) and shorting. This problem can be remedied by providing a suitable series resistance in the circuit.

Such a series resistance tends to reduce the hazard rate of a solid tantalum capacitor. Reducing the ratio $V_W/V_R$, where $V_W$ is the working voltage and $V_R$ is the rated voltage, also reduces the hazard rate. The manufacturer should be consulted when operation without limiting resistance is required.

## Glass Capacitors

Although glass is one of the oldest known dielectrics, the relatively recent development of glass ribbon of one mil thickness has permitted the manufacture of glass capacitors comparable to mica capacitors. These capacitors are constructed by forming alternate layers of alkali-lead glass ribbon and high-purity aluminum foil. The interleaved stack of glass and foil is then fired to create a monolithic block. Leads are attached and the complete unit is hermetically sealed in a glass case. These capacitors have a maximum operating temperature of 200°C and a minimum operating temperature that is limited only by their encasement materials. These capacitors display a 140 ppm/°C change in capacitance as the temperature is varied. Other characteristics include high insulation resistance, low dielectric absorption, and minimal capacitance change with humidity.

## Mica Capacitors

Mica capacitors are made using natural delaminated mica or reconstituted mica. The advantages of mica are: high dielectric withstanding voltage, low dielectric loss over the audio and RF ranges, resistance to high temperatures, and stability with time and frequency. Their disadvantage is a low volumetric efficiency. The dipped mica capacitor is radial-leaded and is slightly more reliable than the molded type. Generally, mica capacitors are the most reliable of all capacitors and vary only 0.1 to 0.3 percent capacitance over a 20-year period. The biggest part of this change usually takes place during the first year of operation. Mica capacitors are normally used where precise frequency coupling, bypassing, and filtering are required.

## Plastic Capacitors

Plastic capacitors have a rolled construction and are either foil or metalized film types. The metalized films, in general, have the ability to self-heal after an overvoltage breakdown. Unlike paper capacitors, plastic capacitors are nonhygroscopic and generally do not require impregnants. However, impregnation is done to increase their voltage breakdown level that, in turn, raises the corona starting level. The present construction technique of using thinner metalized dielectric materials in plastic capacitors increases their volumetric efficiency. This makes plastic capacitors a wise choice for printed circuit board applications. They are generally used for coupling, bypass, filtering, timing, noise suppression, and power factor correction.

Polystyrene, polypropylene, and polyester (Mylar*) are the only dielectric materials used in the construction of plastic capacitors for use by AT&T. Of these materials, polystyrene is quite good as it has exceptional capacitance/frequency stability and discharges completely in a short period of time.

Both polyester (Mylar) and polystyrene capacitors are affected by humidity. As such, their long-term hazard rates (listed in Chapter 4) increase weakly with relative humidity.

---

\*    Mylar is a registered trademark of E. I. duPont de Nemoirs Incorporated.

### Silicon Chip Capacitors

Silicon chip capacitors have a metal-oxide-silicon construction using a heavily doped silicon substrate for one electrode, a silicon dioxide as a dielectric, and metallization over the silicon dioxide for a second electrode. Silicon chip capacitors are available with beam leads, having values ranging from 9 pf to 3600 pf. Their change in capacitance with temperature is about 70 ppm/°C or about 1 percent the temperature range of 30°C to 125°C. They have a low equivalent series resistance, high temperature capability, and have been designed specifically for hybrid integrated circuit (HIC) applications.

### Variable Capacitors

Variable capacitors are available with a variety of dielectric materials and a wide range of properties. Those intended for frequent adjustment usually are air-dielectric types and can be obtained with a variety of capacitance-versus-rotation characteristics.

Small, adjustable capacitors intended for use as trimmers are available in a variety of forms. The tubular types with glass or air dielectrics are preferred. The flat ceramic plate type is especially susceptible to breakage, lacks adequate protection from moisture, and sometimes "freezes," especially after a long period without movement.

In general, the capacitance stability of trimmer capacitors is poorer than that of fixed capacitors and their use should be avoided where other methods are practical.

### CONNECTIONS

Although metallic wire joining has been used for many decades, no concerted effort has been made to define reliability in terms of hazard rates. Considerable effort has been expended to study bonded joints at the device level, but any data gathered has been integrated into the overall hazard rates for the particular component under consideration. With the myriad metal joining techniques available today and the staggering number of different systems in which they are used, it is extremely difficult to arrive at an overall definition of joint reliability.

Most connection experience has been with the soldering of wires to terminals or to printed circuit boards. As might be expected, such prolonged use has led to mass soldering technologies and reliability levels with which designers have learned to feel "comfortable." When numerical control appeared, wire wrapping emerged as a reliable, mass-joining alternative to machine soldering. Many other metal-joining techniques have been developed and are used, but to a much lesser degree. The *Military Handbook—Reliability Prediction of Electronic Equipment*[1] gives some hazard rates for wire connections, which are listed in Chapter 4 of this manual. The types of connections, however, are not categorized as specifically as they might be.

## Description of Connections and Reliability Considerations

1. *Crimp*. Crimped-type connections are usually made to 26 and smaller gauge (larger diameter wires). A closed (sleeve) crimp is preferred to an open crimp because of its ability to maintain a tighter clamping force. It is preferred that crimp connections be made to stranded, tinned wire. Each crimp assembly should have at least two points where the metal sleeve impinges on the wires to assure continued metal-to-metal contact. If a crimped connection is to be subjected to movement, then a separate crimping site should be used around the insulated portion of the wire to form a strain-relief on the metal joints.

2. *Insulation Displacement*. Insulation displacement connection (IDC) (quick-connect) is a method of wire joining that uses a V-shaped wedge or slot with sharp internal edges. The sharp edges cut through the insulation of a round wire and displace some of the conductor surface, thus forming a pair of gas-tight connections. IDC designs may accommodate either solid or stranded wire, but solid wire IDC terminations are generally more reliable than stranded ones.

    Stranded wire terminations are mechanically less stable because only a few individual strands in the bundle make actual contact with the edge of the slot. The strands within the bundle are susceptible to movement. Thus, conduction through the remaining strands depends upon interstrand forces and conductivity. The overall contact resistance of the stranded wire termination is a function of how well the bundle of strands is confined at the slot. This depends on:

    - wire insulation properties,

    - twist or pitch of strands—straight lay stranded cable does not perform as well as twisted strands,

    - slot design,

    - strain relief—the terminated wire or cable should be isolated from any external mechanical forces.

    A multitude of IDC designs exists for both solid and stranded wire which are available from many commercial sources. Performance varies, depending on such factors as quality of vendor-supplied parts, wire properties, and quality of workmanship in the termination process. Consequently, the hazard rates tabulated in Chapter 4 for the insulation displacement of terminations have been constructed as conservative estimates for proven designs and should be considered as such. New designs should be evaluated individually.

3. *Solder*. Solder joints are made either on terminals or lugs, or on printed circuit boards. There are four types of solder joints on printed circuit boards:

    - wire through holes in single- or double-sided boards (crimped or not crimped),

- wire through plated-through holes,

- flat wires to pads (mechanically secured or unsupported),

- surface-mounted components.

Solder joints are evaluated visually. The weight of heavy components should not be borne by soldered joints. Soldered connections should never be made where the joint is under continuous stress. Surface-mounted components do not fall into this category because the ratio of the soldered area to the weight being carried is large. On printed circuits, crimped solder joints are preferred to keep components in place during soldering and for additional joint strength. Solder connections to plated-through-holes generally produce joints that are more reliable than those made to single- or double-sided printed circuit boards with plain holes. In a number of instances, failure to observe proper solder joint design rules (that is, use of unauthorized fluxes) has led to extensive field failures.

4.  *Spot Welds.* There are three types of spot (resistance) welds:

    - flat to flat wire,

    - flat wire to printed circuit board pads,

    - round to round wire.

    Low resistance materials such as copper or aluminum are difficult to spot-weld consistently and should be avoided, where possible. A visual inspection will not usually reveal a defect. Therefore, it is necessary to resort to destructive sampling and/or process control.

5.  *Solderless Wrap.* Since the invention of solderless wire wrap in the early 1950s, all combinations of wire type, wire gauge, and terminal design presently manufactured by AT&T have been qualified by means of standardized tests. Unauthorized terminations, such as wire wrap connections in places where soldered connections are specified, might result in field failures.

6.  *Interference Fit Pins.* Compliant section pins are used to make high-reliability connections to plated-through-holes (PTH) in backplanes and printed circuit boards. The portion of the pin that mates with the PTH is designed with a compliant section that generates a high force, gas-tight connection when inserted into the PTH. Solder plated compliant section pins, when inserted into either solder plated or bare copper PTHs, have been found to provide very reliable connections.

## Surface Mount Attachment Reliability Considerations

The basic reliability concern for Surface Mount Technology (SMT) is the sole reliance on the solder joints to provide the mechanical attachment of components to the substrate. Solder joints subjected to cyclic field thermomechanical stresses can develop fatigue cracks and eventually fail mechanically and electrically. It has been recognized that the main driving force for solder joint failures is the cyclic accumulation of plastic shear strains/fatigue damage in solder due to the difference of thermal expansion between the SM component and the circuit pack substrate.

To design for SM attachment reliability, one must reduce the amplitude of these plastic strains and the accumulation of fatigue damage by minimizing the thermal expansion mismatch. This can be achieved by the active cooperation of component and circuit pack designers. For SM assemblies using organic Printed Wiring Boards (PWBs), component designers have introduced leaded packages in an effort to accommodate the device-substrate thermal expansion mismatch. Package leads reduce the possibility of fatigue failures during the useful life of a product only if they are compliant enough to significantly lower the stress levels in the solder joints.

Following several years of testing and modeling, AT&T has arrived at the following conclusions:

- With proper design of SM assemblies and quality solder joints, SM attachment provides reliability margins comparable to Through Hole Mounting (THM) technology.

- SM is less "tolerant" than THM to design inattention.

- SM is somewhat "less robust" than THM in terms of attachment reliability in the sense that the new technology is less tolerant of solder joints defects.

With the assumption that a circuit pack is assembled with the proper level of quality, SM attachment reliability for a given application is determined essentially by design considerations. AT&T has developed design tools, called SM attachment reliability Figures of Merit (FMs),[2] that allow both the packaging engineer and the circuit pack designer to design for reliability by assuring that the fatigue caused wearout of the solder joints will not be reached during the planned active life of the circuit pack. The FMs formulation has now evolved into a simple graphical technique[3] where the designers can quickly determine the reliability of their design by plotting material and design parameters against the expected thermal environment of their application.

## CONNECTORS

### Description of Connectors

Connectors provide separable connections between conductors, such as wires and printed circuitry. These interconnections are permanently connected—by crimp, solder, or solderless wrap, for example—to each part of the connector pair. The connections are established and broken by plugging and unplugging the connector pair, respectively. The number of connect-disconnect cycles typically ranges from two or three up to a few hundred during the life of the product.

A connector pair contains anywhere from two to a few hundred contact pairs. For electronic applications, the contact surfaces are usually coated with gold or other precious metals to maintain reliability. The following list briefly describes the connector categories for which reliability information is given in Chapter 4:

1. *Coaxial.* Coaxial plugs and jacks used to terminate coaxial cable in applications requiring impedance matching connections.

2. *Modular Telephone Plug and Jack.* Multicontact plugs and jacks of the type generally used to connect telephone sets to telephone lines or handsets to telephones. Although designed for telephone applications, this type of connector is now used in a broad range of applications in which data—digital or analog—is transmitted or switched.

3. *Cable to Pinfield.* Connectors that terminate wires and mate with fields of .025-inch square pins.

4. *Printed Circuit Board*:

   - *Edgeboard.* Connectors mating with gold-plated fingers on printed circuit boards.

   - *Two-Piece.* Connectors used to connect printed circuit boards to backplanes. One part of the connector mounts on the board and the other half mounts on the backplane.

5. *Others.* The connector classification "others" in the hazard rate table given in Chapter 4 includes the following connector types: miniature ribbon, subminiature, and high voltage and power. The indicated hazard rate values are typical for the above mentioned connector types and may be used to estimate connector reliability.

## Nature of Connector Failures

The functions of a connector are to establish and maintain low-resistance connections between mating contacts and to provide very high resistance from each mating pair to all other mating pairs. The significant failure mode is high-contact resistance. The usual causes of high resistance (or opens) are:

- contact surface contaminants, such as solder flux, cover-coat material, particulates from the plastic insulator, airborne particulates, or excessive solid lubricants.

- corrosion films such as oxides or sulfides formed at the contact interface. These originate from elements in the contact finish or from substrate metals that are exposed or deposited at the interface during connector wear.

- mechanical damage that prevents sufficient contact force between contact members. This is the predominant failure mode for coaxial and modular telephone plugs and jacks.

Total resistance of a connector contact pair is typically in the range of 5 to 30 m$\Omega$, depending on connector design. Of this total, the interface resistance is usually only about 1 m$\Omega$; however, it is susceptible to increases which may cause circuit failures. Since high resistance is caused by insulating material at the very small interface area, relative movement between contacts of the mating pair can cause large changes in the contact resistance. For this reason, nonworking connectors can often be made to work, at least temporarily, by unplugging and replugging the pair ("reseating"). However, studies have shown, that while reseating causes some contaminated contacts to decrease in resistance, it causes others to increase; so, it may only move a problem from one contact to another. At best, it leaves a potential failure. Because of the intermittent nature of contact resistance failures, they are difficult to diagnose or prove. Except for situations where they occur frequently, they are often not recognized or reported.

### Factors Affecting Connector Reliability

Connector reliability is dependent on factors related to use, as well as to the design and manufacturing characteristics of the devices themselves. The more important use-related factors for separable electronic connectors are discussed below. Qualitatively, there is little question about the effects discussed; however, they are not understood in sufficient depth, to predict accurately the magnitude of reliability impact. The formula suggested for modifying hazard rates is based on limited experimental data. It is considered to be only a reasonable guideline for improving reliability estimates of printed circuit board and multicontact types. The formula does not apply to coaxial or modular telephone types since mechanical failures predominate for these.

1.  *Circuit Sensitivity.* Circuit tolerance to high resistance decreases the probability of contact failure. The tabulated hazard rates are based on an assumed failure level of 1 ohm; that is, it is assumed the contacts are functional only as long as their resistance is below 1 ohm. For circuits with significantly different sensitivities, that is, for circuits that can tolerate a *maximum* contact resistance *different* from 1 ohm, the listed hazard rates should be multiplied by the factor $K_1$, where $K_1$ is the following function of circuit failure level, denoted $R_f$ (see Figure 6-1).

$$K_1 = \begin{cases} 0.25/R_f & 0.01 \text{ ohms} \leq R_f \leq 0.1 \text{ ohms} \\ \\ R_f^{-0.4} & 0.1 \text{ ohms} \leq R_f \leq 10 \text{ ohms} \\ \\ 0.4 & 10.0 \text{ ohms} \leq R_f \end{cases} \qquad (6.1)$$

2.  *Cleanliness.* Dirt is the most important single cause of connector failure. For good performance, connectors must be protected from contamination, particularly during assembly operations, or must be cleaned after exposure. The hazard rates listed in Chapter 4 are based on the assumption that assembly shops use standard cleanliness practices. Dirt-related failures often show up during equipment installation and testing, and are the major contributor to infant mortality. They can usually be restored by cleaning. Reseating will sometimes clear a problem, but reseating without cleaning entails significant risk of only postponing or moving the problem. Dirty contacts can continue to cause problems throughout the life of the connector.

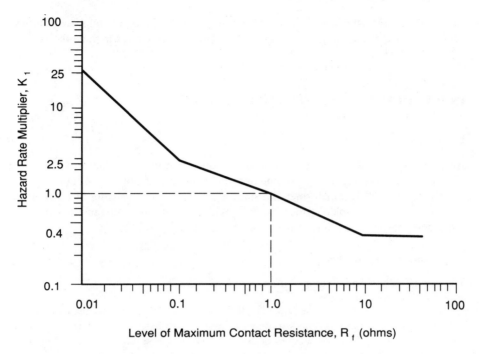

**Figure 6-1.** Multiplier for contact hazard rate, as a function of the *maximum* contact resistance for a particular circuit, that does not lead to contact failure.

3. *Environment.* To a large extent, the environment in which a connector must operate determines the hazard rate exhibited by the connector. Hazard rates are given for two environments: central office and an uncontrolled environment.

   A *central office* environment is typically air conditioned with a filtered air intake and with controlled temperature and relative humidity. It is a benign connector environment. The maximum continuous temperature is taken to be 40°C.

   An *uncontrolled environment* has no controls on temperature, humidity, airborne particulate matter, or any other environmental parameter. A typical example of an uncontrolled environment is an outdoor, unheated shelter. This environment is generally not benign and may cause deterioration of connectors, resulting in correspondingly higher hazard rates.

4. *Twin Contacts.* A contact design that uses two separate contact areas instead of one has a lower probability of failure due to the redundancy of the twin contacts.

5. *Age Mated or Unmated.* If connectors spend long periods of time unmated, they are more likely to develop contamination or corrosion on the contact surfaces than if they are mated or otherwise effectively shrouded from the

environment. This effect has been included in the hazard rates for central office and uncontrolled environments.

6.  *Insertions.* The probability of failure may be affected by the number of times a connector is plugged and unplugged. The tabulated rates include the effects of insertions.

## INDUCTORS AND TRANSFORMERS

### Definitions

An inductor, or a filter element, is used to reduce harmonic and noise currents in electronic circuits.[4] It consists of one or more associated windings, with or without a magnetic core.[5] A transformer is a static electric device consisting of a winding, or two or more coupled windings, and with or without a magnetic core for introducing mutual coupling between electric circuits.[4]

### Common Failure Modes

The hazard rate of an inductor or transformer may be:

- hazardous to people (electrically), where insulation has broken down between windings and/or core, allowing a greater than desired leakage current to flow, or where conductors have become exposed, resulting in a shock hazard,

- hazardous to equipment, where the device becomes either a potential fire hazard or a threat to the life expectancy of another component,

- functional, where the device no longer performs within its design limits,

- objectionable, where audible noise exceeds a specified level.

These failure modes may be simplified into the categories of shorted, open, or out-of-specifications.

### Conditions Affecting Long-Term Hazard Rates

Both inductors and transformers are passive magnetic devices. The satisfactory long-term performance of a magnetic device depends on the insulation system. The long-term hazard rate of an inductor or transformer is a function of voltage and temperature stresses. Over time, voltage and temperature stresses change the nature of the insulation system. When this happens, the magnetic device fails due to wearout. These devices, therefore, have a time-dependent hazard rate that is a typical "bathtub" curve (see Chapter 1).

The dissipation of power from winding and magnetic core losses in the device causes an internal temperature rise. This rise, when added to the maximum ambient temperature, becomes the operating temperature of the device. The higher the operating temperature and the higher the voltage stress, especially when corona exist, the more rapid the insulation degradation. Sufficient degradation will allow the voltage stress to break down the insulation system. Time-to-failure may be decreased with additional environmental stresses, such as shock, vibration, or humidity.

If the operating temperature exceeds the temperature rating of the insulation system's class, then the standard 20-year life, as used (for inductors and transformers) by AT&T, cannot be achieved. It becomes a function of design, therefore, to keep the operating temperature within the limits of the insulation system. To do this may require increasing the size of the device and/or using a class of insulation that has a higher temperature rating. Either alternative, of course, adds to the cost of the device.

### Events Leading to a Fail-Safe Failure Mode

Voltage breakdown normally occurs between adjacent turns within a layer of a winding or between turns of adjacent layers, resulting in a short. The magnetic field then generates a high circulating current in the shorted turn(s). The losses associated with this high current cause an increase in current at the input terminals, which leads to further power dissipation. The net effect of these losses is the formation of a hot spot at the short and more general heating. This results in additional turn-to-turn shorting in the vicinity of the first breakdown. The resulting ramping up of the current and heat in the winding(s) finally results in either the fusing open of the winding's wire, the opening of a thermal protective component within the device (if so equipped), or the opening of a fuse or circuit breaker. The desired final "open" failure must occur before the device becomes either a fire or an electrical hazard.

### Testing for Fail-Safe Operation

Magnetic devices designed to be energy-limiting or self-protecting (independent of an external fuse) are either sample-tested or 100 percent tested at the point of manufacture to insure this self-protection. Two energy-limiting types are sample-tested. In one case, the design has sufficient winding impedance to limit the current. Therefore, the device can sustain a short across the output for an indefinite period of time. In the other, a "one-shot" thermal protective component within the magnetic device will open and remain open once the protector's operating temperature is reached. Some magnetic devices have thermal protectors with an automatic reset feature, which resets itself when it cools down. These devices are 100 percent tested under overload conditions to assure proper operation. The activating temperature of the protector is chosen to be higher than the maximum operating temperature of the magnetic component, but less than a hazardous temperature.

Magnetic components that are not self-protecting depend on the fusing and testing of the circuit to assure a fail-safe failure mode.

In addition to the testing controlled by AT&T, the equipment into which magnetic components are installed is tested and audited by Underwriters Laboratories[6,7] if the equipment is intended for customer premises.

### Accelerated Stress Testing

An accelerated stress testing program has been established for self-protecting transformers. It has been determined, for example, that the life expectancy of the

AT&T telephone dial illumination transformer has a life expectancy of over 20 years.[8] This transformer is used with Princess* phones, among others, and gets the most use of any self-protecting transformer in AT&T.

## SILICON INTEGRATED CIRCUITS

To ensure the reliability of equipment, certain general practices should be followed for integrated circuits. First, exercise caution with regard to the sequence in which ground and other voltages are applied. (This is discussed in the following section.) Do not use external leads that appear to be unused as tie points, unless explicitly permitted. Leads that appear open sometimes are not.

Second, be sure that mature device codes meet contemporary standards. For example, many codes that are commonly sold were designed before damage by electrostatic discharge (ESD) was well understood. If they are not redesigned to provide protective structures, they may be unusually vulnerable to damage in handling. (See Chapter 3 for a discussion of ESD.) As another example, sometimes a new class of devices may be susceptible to latch-up (see the section *Complementary Metal-Oxide Semiconductor,* below). Later codes may be designed not to latch up, but the early codes are often not redesigned.

Third, be cautious of soft errors in memory, that is, random, single-bit errors caused by residual radioactivity of device packages. This topic has recently become a major concern to large systems' reliability.

### Voltage-Sequence Sensitivity

For integrated circuit reliability, designers recommend that the ground connection be made before the supply voltage connections. For many integrated circuits, when voltages are applied to the device pins in an improper sequence, the device may operate incorrectly or even be damaged. This problem can occur when a device is plugged into a powered board or a board is connected to operating equipment, as in routine maintenance. The voltage sequences depend on the order in which connector pins make good contact. Connector design can affect the contact sequence.

Obviously, it is best to shut off voltages during plug-in. A reliable method of shutting off voltages during plug-in is to provide an interrupt switch and verify that the board design containing sequence-sensitive integrated circuits will function properly if exposed to the range of voltage sequences experienced when plugging into operating equipment.

### Complementary Metal-Oxide Semiconductor

Susceptibility to latch-up can be a major problem with complementary metal-oxide semiconductor (CMOS) integrated-circuit codes, especially in very-large-scale-integration (VLSI) designs. Basically, any situation that can turn on a semiconductor-controller rectifier (SCR)-like parasitic structure within the device,

---

*   Registered trademark of AT&T.

might result in two adjacent transitors, typically, latching CMOS devices. The latch is removable by shutting off the power supply. But, it is possible that a latch-up can damage an integrated circuit. Classically, latch-up occurs when system boards are plugged into powered equipment.

AT&T Bell Laboratories integrated circuits have been carefully designed to avoid latch-up. However, commercial products are often susceptible. The qualification of an integrated circuit requested by a Notification-To-Use (NTU) checks for latch-up susceptibility. General evaluation of a manufacturer also takes this into account. Major manufacturers usually refer to latch-up either in data sheets or in application notes. The caution may simply state that no input or output is permitted to exceed $V_{cc}$ by a diode drop.

In a commercial product, latch-up is apt to occur in one of the following basic circumstances:

- Power is applied to the integrated circuit and tens of milliamps (either sign) are externally forced into an input or out of an output.

- Power is applied to the integrated circuit and an input and the $V_{cc}$ lead (supply voltage with respect to ground) are tied to separate supplies with nominally equal voltages. If a transient either causes the input voltage to increase or $V_{cc}$ to decrease by more than a diode drop, the input or output current can be sufficient to cause latch-up.

### Digital Bipolar

When using positive-logic integrated circuits, avoid the incidence of negative voltage of a magnitude greater than or equal to 0.7 volt on an input or output. Such voltages can cause the circuit to come up in a wrong state.

Digital bipolar integrated circuits are susceptible to sequencing problems. When an integrated circuit is plugged into a powered board, it is impossible to know the sequence of states as the chip is powered in this ill-defined way. For example, excessive current may be sunk by a terminal in the initial state. Inputs and outputs momentarily in indeterminate states (between a LOW and a HIGH) may be especially vulnerable. Similarly, there is some risk in plugging a board into operating equipment. The input or output current can be sufficient to cause latching.

### Memory—Soft Errors

Modern VLSI random access memory (RAM) or charge-coupled-device (CCD) integrated circuits are vulnerable to upset by a *single*, heavily ionized particle. Primarily, these are alpha particles issuing from minute levels of radioactive impurities in device package or metallization system materials used in the chips. In systems containing large numbers of these memory chips, such random single-bit errors can cause significant problems in stored data.

### Nature of Soft Failures

Errors are called *hard failures* if they are permanent in nature. This type of failure is often caused by a defective integrated circuit. The term *soft failure* refers to a temporary failure. It is often a random single-bit failure that is not related to a physical defect. A soft failure of a bit does not increase (or decrease) the probability that the bit will fail again.

Soft errors suddenly became prominent when large numbers of new-generation VLSI memory integrated circuits appeared.[9] These circuits are dynamic and static RAMs and CCDs. A typical system soft-error rate requirement is that of a device hazard rate of less than 1,000 FITs. This rate does not change with time, because the radioactive impurities are compounds of uranium and thorium, which have effectively infinite half-lives.

In a typical memory cell, data is stored as a charge on an MOS capacitor. In 1978, memory cell geometries became small enough that the charge collected from the ionization track within the silicon of a single alpha particle was sufficient to charge an uncharged cell. Suppose that in a memory cell of a dynamic random access memory (DRAM), a ZERO is represented by a stored charge in the range of a few hundred thousand electrons ($5\times10^{-14}$ coulomb) to a few million electrons ($5\times10^{-13}$ coulomb) and a ONE is represented by no stored charge. Then, the collection of electrons can charge an uncharged cell to a charged state. Therefore, a change from ONE to ZERO will occur. It should be noted that the physical assignment of ONEs and ZEROs is arbitrary.

The *critical charge,* denoted by $Q_{crit}$, is the amount of collected charge that will *just* cause a soft error. $Q_{crit}$ varies greatly with device layout and technology. A very low value of $Q_{crit}$ is 50,000 electrons for a particular modern CCD device. In a commercial 256K or 1 Megabit DRAM, $Q_{crit}$ ranges from $0.5\times10^6$ electrons to $0.8\times10^6$ electrons.

Soft errors can also occur due to charge collection by the floating nodes of bit-sense lines and of sense amplifiers of static and dynamic RAMs. Therefore, the susceptibility to soft errors depends on the *cycle time, $t_c$*. For short cycle times, $t_c<10\mu s$, the bit lines and sense amplifiers are the most likely sites of soft errors. For long cycle times, $t_c>10\mu s$, the memory cells themselves (memory cell "upset") are the most likely site of soft errors.

## Alpha Emission in VLSI Memories

An alpha particle that is emitted from an atom close to the inside surface of the package and has an unobstructed path (no die coating) to the active surface of the silicon chip will cause an error. Therefore, both the package materials and geometry affect the severity of the alpha particle problem.

All common package types contain alpha-emitting materials. The molding compounds used for plastic packages contain alumina or silica fillers. These materials are refined from natural ore materials that contain a few parts per million of radioactive impurities such as thorium and uranium, which emit alpha particles. In hermetic packages, if the lid is ceramic, it is made from ore materials that contain impurities such as thorium and uranium. The lid can also be metal, usually gold-plated kovar, and the "solder glasses" used to seal these packages can contain zirconium. Both are strong alpha sources. The range of flux at the chip surface typically is 0.01 to 1 per $cm^2$ per hour from lids and 0.1 to 5 per $cm^2$ per hour from solder glasses. These are high levels of flux for our purposes and can be unacceptable for given chip designs.

Material improvements, yielding a factor of ten reduction in flux at the chip surface, may be realized eventually. For plastic packages, a lower limit on the order of 0.001 to 0.01 per $cm^2$ per hour may be possible. This is about the present limit of measurability. However, for some users even this level of alpha flux will be too high. The levels may thus be high from the point of view of reliability, though very low in magnitude.

The use of CMOS technology has permitted a great reduction in soft error hazard rates. High-C cell and trench capacitor designs have also contributed to an improvement in the soft-error hazard rates. Measurements of soft-error hazard rates of 1 Megabit CMOS DRAMs with High-C cell have yielded less than 1,000 FITs.

An important idea for flux reduction is to coat the chip with a film that intercepts alphas. Clearly, its properties must include the following:

- the coating must be benign electrically and mechanically at all temperatures required of the chip,

- the coating material must not emit any alpha flux,

- the range of alphas in the film material must be less than the thicknesses of the film.

Integrated circuit suppliers have made substantial progress along these lines. The coating materials used are Polyimide and Room Temperature Vulcanizing (RTV) rubber. Measurements of the alpha particle activity of RTV rubber and the actual error rate of alpha-particle sensitivity for AT&T 256K DRAM with this coating indicate that a hazard rate of ≤1,000 FITs, with a cycle time of 10μs, can be achieved.[10] The metallization system in the chip, such as Titanium-Tungsten (TiW) can also contain some radioactive impurities that emit alpha particles.'

**Estimation of Error Rate for a Device**

To estimate the error rate for a particular device, specific information is needed about the chip design, processing, package geometry, and package materials.

One method of estimating the soft-error hazard rate is to irradiate an exposed chip with a known alpha flux from an alpha source while functionally exercising the device for a period of time and counting the errors (accelerated testing). The soft-error hazard rate $\lambda_s$ in FITs is given by

$$\lambda_s = \frac{R_{\alpha b} \times E \times 10^9}{t \times R_{\alpha s}}$$

where

$E$ = the total number of errors counted
$t$ = the test time in minutes
$R_{\alpha s}$ = the sources alpha flux in alpha per $cm^2$ per minute
$R_{\alpha b}$ = the background alpha flux density in alpha
     per $cm^2$ per hour

The other method for estimating soft-error hazard rate involves a direct measurement of the operating hazard rate of an operating system containing many devices (system testing). If a system with 1,000 RAMs can tolerate one system error per six weeks (a high rate for some systems), this implies an error rate per RAM of 1,000 FITs. To verify that a device code has a soft error rate of less than 1,000 FITs requires millions of device hours of continuous testing, simulating system operation. Errors of other origin have to be excluded.

## Actions Available to System Designers

A system designer should ask for information on the soft-error characteristics of the memory codes being considered for a system. The most useful information would be the average rate of soft errors per chip and identification of those chip segments most sensitive to alphas. Other influences on error rate are device process variations and the effects of operating conditions, such as cycle time and power supply voltage.

## Methods of Error Correction in Systems

Common acronyms in error correction are error correction code (ECC) and error detection and correction (EDAC). Generally, large systems already have such circuitry to deal with other sources of soft errors stemming from various forms of system noise.

In EDAC, one reserves some bits for reconstruction of the data following an error. In a dynamic RAM, reconstruction is done when refreshing the data. Relatively fewer extra bits are needed for error correction as the word length increases.[11]

A commercial example of EDAC is a family of memory systems having "built-in-intelligence."[12] A 16-bit microprocessor provides tolerance of both soft and hard memory faults. "A 4-Mbyte system will have a mean-time-between-interruptions (MTBI) of more than 5,000 hours, compared to an MTBI of less than 3,000 hours for a system with error correction but no intelligence, and an MTBI of less than 500 hours for systems without error correction." It should be noted that EDAC was used in the No. 1 Electronic Switching System (ESS) first installed in 1965.

A comprehensive treatment of system solution to soft errors was published in 1980.[13] The method described deals with soft errors from alphas and their interaction with hard errors. Use of ECC is combined with a strategy of system maintenance. This effective method involves virtually no additional cost. It is generally compatible with existing memory designs. The errors it deals with do not respond to the usual simple error-correcting, double-error detecting codes.

## Expectations for the Future

Advances in device design will lead to changes in the soft-error situation. Smaller device geometries will lead to smaller values of $Q_{crit}$ and changes in collection efficiency of sensitive chip circuitry. Certainly, there will be lower values of alpha flux in the next generation of packages. Nevertheless, the excessive error rate will probably necessitate EDAC. Perhaps EDAC circuitry will be included on the memory chips themselves.

At even lower levels of intensity than alpha particles, there are ionizing particles resulting from cosmic rays. In the future, as alpha-particle fluxes are reduced, soft errors arising from these secondary cosmic-ray particles may become significant.

### Electromigration

High temperature and high-current density can accelerate electromigration of metallization stripes on integrated circuits. The large current density creates an "electron wind" that causes metal ions to migrate and vacancies to occur in the opposite direction. This results in hillocks of metal at one end of the line and voids at the other end until an open develops. Electromigration-related failures can be due to defects (such as metal line constrictions and thin metal step coverage), poor design or metal deposition process.[14] Device qualification may uncover problems due to poor design or process. It is important, however, that the devices be used within the current and temperature limits of the device specifications.

### Hot Carrier Effects

Degradation of electrical characteristics of MOS devices can happen as a result of hot carrier injection from the silicon into the gate oxide. Hot carriers are generated under high voltage conditions that can cause a large hot carrier current in the silicon. Both hot electron and hole injection degradation are known to occur, resulting in a change of the threshold voltage[15,16] that can lead to device failure. These effects are more pronounced at low temperatures (room temperature and below); high temperature can anneal out the defects. This is important to keep in mind since accelerated aging is usually done at high temperatures and, therefore, this failure mechanism would go unnoticed under those conditions. Properly designed and processed devices do not exhibit hot carrier instabilities. Qualification procedures for Level III and Level II devices are designed to detect problem codes with hot carrier instabilities.

### OPTO-ELECTRONICS

### Laser Diodes in Transmitters
### for Optical Communication

This section refers to both the short-wavelength (0.82 micrometer) and the long-wavelength (1.3 through 1.5 micrometer) lasers.

In general, long-term performance of a laser diode is degraded by high temperatures. To prevent degradation, avoid long exposure to temperatures approaching the maximum allowed operating temperature and do not locate the transmitter in the hotter regions of the equipment.

Shelf life should be indefinitely long, provided that the specified maximum temperature is observed. Excessive temperature, combined with environmental contaminants might, for example, damage the plastic of the pigtail.

Laser diodes can be damaged by currents or voltages that significantly exceed specified maxima. Be sure that these limits are not exceeded by transients, either forward or reverse. For example, it is not advisable to discharge a capacitor through a laser diode. When connecting a laser diode to a constant-current source, turn the source to zero beforehand. As with any small semiconductor device, adhere to approved practices to avoid ESD. (See Chapter 3 for a discussion of ESD.)

Two other precautions to take when using laser diodes are:

- avoid unnecessary flexing of the device pigtail to prevent damage to the optical fiber,

- avoid humidity-temperature combinations to prevent condensation on the device, particularly if the package is non-hermetic.

### Short-Wavelength PIN Diodes
### for Optical Communications

For these devices, used at 0.87 micrometer, general approved ESD practices are necessary (see Chapter 3). Other precautions are:

- do not plug the device into operating equipment,

- observe the specified device ratings, especially breakdown voltage, forward current, and power dissipation.

### Long-Wavelength PIN Photo-Diodes as Laser Monitors
### and Optical Receivers

These devices, used at 1.3 micrometer, can be damaged by current or voltage transients. As with almost all semiconductor devices, it is important to abide by approved ESD practices (see Chapter 3).

These devices should *never* be exposed to forward bias. This precaution includes transients. Therefore, do not plug the device into powered circuitry. Turn the power off first. Also, it is advisable to by-pass the supply voltage with a capacitor.

The devices are routinely burned-in at large reverse voltage and high temperature to eliminate early failures. Generally members of this class fail as infants. They fail "open" catastrophically. One of the following bonds comes apart: platform to chip base, wire to chip top, or wire to package post. Long-term end of life (drop of intensity to half the original value) seldom occurs in equipment.

### Light-Emitting Diodes in Transmitters
### for Optical Communication

In practice, "light-wave" light-emitting diodes (LEDs) are coupled to optical fibers. Infant mortalities in 0.87μm LEDs are the result of dark-line defects (DLDs), generally due to dislocations induced in the chip during manufacture. Devices prone to DLD failure are largely weeded out by a room temperature burn-in. The median life for burned-in 0.87μm devices generally exceeds $10^6$ hours.

The 1.3μm LEDs are not subject to DLD formation. However, they do require burn-in to screen out unstable devices. Median life then generally exceeds $10^6$ hours.

These LEDs are vulnerable to damage by reverse bias and uncontrolled transients. Two precautions to take when using these LEDs are:

- Prevent accidental plug-in with leads reversed.

- Avoid plugging into a powered board. Consider using sockets which are shorted while the device is being plugged in.

### Surface Acoustic Wave Filters

Some general precautions in the use of AT&T surface acoustic wave (SAW) filters are given here.

Since the package may be vacuum sealed with glass eyelets, undue mechanical or thermal stresses of the pins might cause glass cracks, thus resulting in pressure change and performance variation. Therefore, perform device insertion and soldering with care.

A temperature range is specified for operation in a given system. Adhere to this range or center frequency values might shift excessively.

Although the devices are quite tolerant to storage temperatures, it should be noted that storage at temperatures above 100°C for years would cause irreversible performance drift.

## PRINTED CIRCUITS

Historically, printed circuits manufactured by AT&T have been very reliable. The major reliability concern has been premature wearout rather than infant mortality failures. This result is consistent with high reliability, long-life applications and is implemented through the use of conservative design rules and careful material selection and process controls.

With the entry of AT&T into new and broader markets, printed circuits have been classified by intended end product use. *Consumer products* (Class I) includes noncritical applications that shall be reliable and cost effective. However, extended life is not a primary objective. *General industrial* (Class II) includes high-performance commercial and industrial products for which extended life is required but for which uninterrupted service is not critical. Examples include high-performance computers. *High-reliability* (Class III) includes applications, such as, undersea cable, satellites, and life support systems for which uninterrupted service is essential. The distinction between Class II and Class III is a matter of repairability and life-threatening issues and is much less than the differences with Class I.

The reliability emphasis for each of these classes may be quite different. Wearout will remain an important concern but infant mortality failures will require increasing attention, particularly for the newer, high-density interconnection technologies. These new technologies use new, high-performance material systems and advanced processing.

### Pre-Wearout Failures

Two types of failure occur in the pre-wearout period. *Extrinsic* failures are randomly occurring failures caused by external effects. Examples include: fault conditions causing overvoltage and/or overcurrent, exposure to corrosive atmospheres, moisture condensation on unprotected circuits and contamination or mechanical damage caused by handling during repair. *Intrinsic* failures are caused by conditions within the printed circuit and are generally related to defects in the raw materials or flaws introduced during printed circuit fabrication, coating, or assembly. Examples include: incomplete removal of residual processing chemicals, foreign fibers incorporated in the substrate or covercoat, and clearance defects between isolated conductor paths. Avoiding early intrinsic failures depends on the proper selection of materials and processes, and on the maintenance of effective controls, or both.

Isolated clearance defects on double-sided rigid printed circuits have been studied extensively. Researchers found that as the clearance was reduced below 2 mils the probability of early failures increased rapidly. The failures observed were primarily the result of poor etching which left copper debris in the defect space. Clearance defects in multilayer boards are under investigation. Preliminary results indicate that for clearances below about 2 mils the probability of early failure increases rapidly as the clearance decreases.

Clearance defects are likely to become a more significant problem as circuit densities increase and design spacings decrease. High voltage screening may be a method for eliminating clearance defects.

## Wearout Failures

Wearout can occur at any of several types of risk sites in a printed circuit. Typical risk sites include: the region between adjacent PTHs, between PTHs and adjacent circuit paths, and between PTHs and power or ground planes in MLBs. Wearout phenomena continue to be the subject of several studies, the purpose of which is to assure that wearout failures do not occur within the intended circuit life. The studies are carried out using accelerated stress tests at elevated temperatures and humidities. The failure modes of the risk sites are identified, and the dependence of the lifetime on environmental factors is established. Projections are then made to obtain the hazard rate of the risk sites at operating conditions.

Wearout failures have been observed in covercoated circuits. The failures were caused by copper or copper complex migration through the coating or along the coating/substrate interface to form dendritic structures. These growths caused a catastrophic failure of insulation resistance.

In fiber reinforced epoxy substrates exposed to high humidities, early wearout may result from the growth of conductive anodic filaments (CAF) along the resin/fiber interfaces. This phenomena has been extensively studied.[17]

It is clear that CAF is not a reliability problem for circuits operating at central office (CO) conditions. For double-sided rigid (DSR) circuits operating in high relative humidities, hazard rates can be estimated. If the estimated hazard rate for a circuit is too high, the circuit can either be redesigned to eliminate the CAF risk sites or the circuit can be made from a material which is resistant to CAF.

## Factors Affecting Printed Circuit Reliability

1.  *Environment* – The pre-wearout hazard rate of printed circuits will be increased when the circuits are exposed to corrosive atmospheres or atmospheres in which condensed moisture may form on unprotected circuit paths. Both pre-wearout and wearout failures are generally accelerated by increased temperature and relative humidity.

2.  *Operating Voltage* – In all materials studied, increased voltage levels tend to shorten the time to failure, $t_f$. Voltage dependence $t_f$ varies from failure mode to failure mode; however, in no case has this dependence been observed to be stronger than $t_f \sim V^{-1}$ and, in some cases, it is considerably weaker.

3. *Wiring Density and Conductor Geometry* – Studies show that for a constant operating voltage a reduced conductor spacing tends to shorten printed circuit life. In particular, glass fiber reinforced substrates show this behavior. Some conductor geometries are more susceptible to failure than others, particularly for epoxy-glass circuits operated in high humidity environments or at high operating voltages. The regions between a closely spaced PTH and a surface conductor, a power or ground plane, or another PTH are particularly susceptible as is the region between closely spaced internal layers in a MLB.

4. *Contamination and Handling* – Contamination of printed circuits due to handling or poor process control can affect reliability. It has been found that ionic contamination levels above $1\mu g$ / $cm^2$ (equivalent NaCl) will reduce circuit life. Levels above $10\mu g$ / $cm^2$ are considered unacceptable. The application of protective coatings to boards of acceptable cleanliness can preserve that condition and improve reliability. The use of water soluble flux (WSF) generally lowers the insulation resistance of printed circuits. However, studies have shown that with proper cleaning procedures WSF residues do not reduce printed circuit reliability. Foreign material, especially in the form of fibers, can lead to the early failure of printed circuits. Foreign material inclusion can occur during manufacture of substrate materials, during covercoat application, or during the lamination of MLBs. Circuit designers should also consider the mechanical effects of handling printed circuits during maintenance and repair. For example, flexible circuits that have undergone repair may exhibit increased hazard rates from broken conductors as a result of excessive bending.

5. *Protection* – Designers should consider providing appropriate overvoltage/overcurrent protection against conditions such as power crosses and lightning strikes.

6. *Substrate Materials* – New substrate materials are constantly being evaluated for use in printed circuits. Many of the new materials are intended for use in lower cost applications (typically Class I) where epoxy glass (FR-4) material is not required. Some of these new materials are currently available, while others are being evaluated. Although complete reliability data are not available, some general statements can be made. From a reliability point of view, the substrate properties of interest are thermal and hydrolytic stability and resistance to electrochemical corrosion. These properties are related to the polymer dielectric matrix and type of reinforcement used. For resins, the thermal stability (and cost) of printed circuit substrates generally increases as one goes from polyester to epoxy to bismaleimide-triazine (BT) to polyimide. Two resin systems—polyester and BT—when appropriately processed, have been found to be significantly more resistant to CAF than the others. These resins should be used in applications in which closely spaced PTHs are used in high relative humidity environments.

7. *Types of Printed Circuits* – Printed circuits may be classified in several ways, for example, by the process used to make the conductor pattern (additive, subtractive, discrete wiring), by the type of substrate material used (flexible, rigid), or by the number of conductor layers (single-sided, double-sided,

multilayer). The reliability of a circuit varies depending on the type. However, the reliability of different circuits made using the same technology can vary considerably because the number and types of risk sites vary from design to design.

8. *Types of Covercoat* – A covercoat is a permanent coating applied to a printed circuit board or assembly. Its purpose is to protect against the deleterious effects of condensed or spilled liquids, airborne particles, and handling-related contaminants, and to provide electrical isolation between components and circuit conductors. It should be recognized, however, that covercoats are not hermetic seals. After continuous exposure, gases and water vapor will eventually penetrate. Nevertheless, the delay produced by the coating often improves a circuit's ability to survive harsh cyclical environmental conditions. Covercoats can be divided into two major categories: solder masks and conformal coatings. A solder mask is applied after the wiring paths have been formed, but prior to the assembly operations of component insertion and attachment. It is typically applied in a pattern that covers all metallization, except for those terminal pads that must remain bare to accept solder, mate with connectors, or be accessible to test probes. Coated on the wiring side, component side, or both sides of the board, the solder mask prevents molten solder from bridging between conductor paths during assembly and, then, remains as further protection during the circuit's operating life. Solder masks can be applied by either screen printing or photoprinting and cured thermally or with ultraviolet (UV) light. A conformal coating is applied after components have been permanently attached to the board. Like the solder mask, it may be applied to either or both sides of the assembly. When a solder mask is used, the conformal coat is applied over it and protects metallization that has not been previously coated, for example, solder fillets and component leads. Conformal coatings are often applied by spraying or dipping and are UV or thermally cured. Currently, solder masks are required on circuits with conductor spacings less than 0.020 inches.

Circuit designers should be aware of the factors that affect reliability and should, wherever possible, specify materials suitable for the operating conditions expected and specify circuit operating parameters that will ensure the reliability. Designers requiring information about specific applications should contact the appropriate consultants in interconnection technology.

## RELAYS

Most relays are electrically operated switches, which have metallic contacts and an electromagnetic coil, with terminals for connections. Conventional relays are operated by energizing the coil to move the contact springs, closing normally open or "make" contacts and opening normally closed or "break" contacts. When the coil is de-energized to release the relay, the contacts return to their normal states. In latching or bi-stable relays, a coil current pulse switches the relay into one state, where it remains until switched back by a different pulse.

A closed contact provides a low-resistance electrical connection between its terminals. Opening the contact breaks the connection. An open relay contact is a pair of contact surfaces separated by a gap. To close it, one or both surfaces are moved until they touch. The surfaces of the contacts usually are made of precious metal to minimize oxidization.

Clean, nonoxidized surfaces are important for low-resistance connections, especially in low-voltage circuits below one or two volts. To help guard against contact contamination and to provide other features, there is a variety of contact and relay types, each having its advantages and limitations.

The type of relay that should be used for a printed circuit application depends upon criteria such as: number of contacts required, number of operations expected during service life, electrical load switched, area available to mount the relay, relay height allowed by the spacing between boards, mounting orientation, cost, and environment. In an unfavorable environment, a sealed-contact relay usually is recommended.

## Sealed Contact

Most sealed-contact relays have contacts hermetically sealed in glass envelopes. Sealed-contact relay types include reed relays and mercury relays.

1.  *Reed Relays.* Reed relays are sometimes called dry reeds. They have reed-like contact springs sealed in a nonoxidizing atmosphere in a glass tubular envelope. One to five of these glass-sealed reed contacts, also called *reed switches,* are placed inside a coil to form a relay. Reed relays are used when the following conditions are met:

    - only a few contacts are required,

    - contact life is not required to exceed $2 \times 10^5$ operations at nominal switched resistive loads of less than 50 volts and 100 milliamps dc,

    - a mechanical life of $10^7$ operations is adequate at much smaller loads,

    - there is no capacitive or other inrush current in the load circuit to cause contact sticking or welding,

    - contact chatter is acceptable,

    - fractional-ohm instability of contact resistance is acceptable,

    - the wearout mechanism of steadily increasing contact resistance (up to about 30 ohms) is acceptable.

    Dry reed relays should not be used where currents of more than two or three amps could flow through a closed contact, because the current's magnetic field might open the contact.

2.  *Mercury Relays.* Mercury relays have mercury-wetted reed switches in which a small amount of liquid mercury inside the hydrogen-pressurized glass

envelope provides the reservoir for a mercury film that wets the reed contact surfaces by capillarity. Mercury relays are used where one or two contacts are required and where somewhat higher cost is justified by the following particular attributes:

- capability of up to $10^9$ operations at any load within ratings,

- ability to handle capacitive inrush loads,

- absence of contact bounce or chatter,

- low and stable contact resistance throughout life,

- ability to switch loads of up to 2 or 3 amperes,

- ability to withstand 1000 volts ac across open contacts or from coil to contact.

Mercury relays must be mounted within 30° of vertical except for the special types. These types have a smaller amount of mercury and, consequently, much less current switching capability. Mercury relays should not be used where currents as large as 10 amps could flow through a closed contact, because the current's magnetic field might open the contact.


## Sealed Relays

In a sealed relay, the entire relay is sealed into a can or cover which protects the contacts from the environment. The cover does not protect the contacts from any organic materials of the relay or the manufacturing process, such as plastic parts and lubricants. Therefore, precautions must be taken against traces of organic vapors that could emanate from these materials and form films on the contacts. These films, especially when pyrolyzed by operation under certain electrical loads, can cause increased contact resistance. Loads in the 5 to 30 volt range are the most critical. Sealed relay types include hermetically sealed and plastic sealed.

1. *Hermetically Sealed.* Hermetically sealed relays are enclosed in metal cans with glass-insulated terminals. Vacuum-baking before sealing in an inert atmosphere helps to minimize organic vapors. These relays provide two transfer contacts. Because of their cost, they should be considered primarily for use where space is extremely tight, or where the contact path must carry very high frequency signals (>100 MHz) or fast pulses (<10 nsec).

2. *Plastic Sealed.* Plastic sealed relays have plastic covers closed with an epoxy or other sealant. This enclosure can exclude flux and cleaning solutions used during circuit pack production. Evaluations of plastic sealed relays have been made, and some but not all manufacturers' product has been found to offer satisfactory service over a variety of electrical loads and operating environments.

### Exposed Contact Relays

*Exposed* means not sealed. Exposed contacts, like sealed relay contacts, are subjected to organic vapors from relay materials and process residues, but natural ventilation helps dissipate these vapors. In addition, exposed relay contacts are subjected to ambient vapors and particles. To help avoid particle contamination, these relays have nonremovable dust covers or enclosures (except miniature wire-spring relays that have removable covers to allow field adjustment and cleaning). When exposed contact relays are soldered to circuit boards, solder flux and cleaning solvent residues must not be left on the contacts.

Generally, exposed contact relays are vulnerable to silicone oil films that creep onto them from adjacent surfaces and can cause very high and unstable contact resistances for many loads. Since 1978, AT&T relays for printed circuit applications have been treated with a barrier compound to protect their contacts from silicone oil contamination. Other Level III (non AT&T) relays are now similarly protected. Older, untreated relays can be protected with a barrier coating applied in the field or service center. Other silicone-contaminated relays generally must be replaced.

There are many types of exposed contact relays. Exposed contact relays are used when the following conditions are met:

- the environment is favorable,

- as many as twelve make, break, and/or transfer contacts are required,

- the expected number of operations is moderate, up to $2 \times 10^8$ mechanical operations for the miniature wire spring type, and up to $10^7$ mechanical operations for other types,

- the erodible volume of contact material will provide sufficient electrical life as contrasted to mechanical life (electrical contact life may be limited by erosion due to electrical arcing),

- any capacitive or other inrush current is insufficient to weld the contacts or reduce the contact life significantly,

- some contact chatter is acceptable,

- some increase in contact resistance during life is acceptable.

### Preferred Materials Used in Level III Relays

In general, Level III relays use materials preferred for telephone system applications. For example, most relays with nylon bobbins use a nylon material that must pass lot acceptance tests to guard against chemical corrosivity and electrical conductivity. Other nylon materials are not used, as they may cause coil failures under conditions of combined temperature, humidity, and electrical bias.

Flame retardant plastics with an oxygen index of 28 or more are used for all external relay surfaces. Plastic cover materials lower in oxygen index are more readily flammable and are not used.

Phosphor-bronze and copper-nickel-tin spring materials are used, but not "nickel-silver" (copper-zinc-nickel alloys). Nickel-silver is susceptible to stress corrosion cracking and failure in environments with substantial nitrogen-oxide air pollution.

For most applications, the contacts used are a 60 percent palladium-40 percent silver alloy with a thin gold surface layer. This alloy resists both tarnishing and arc erosion, and the gold surface minimizes formation of "brown powder" (frictionally polymerized organics). Silver and high-silver-alloy contacts are not used in telephone applications, to avoid tarnish. Gold-plated or gold-flashed silver is not used because the tenacious tarnish emerging from pores, scratches, or edges can creep over the gold surface.

### Nature of Relay Failures

Relay failure modes include either slow (drifting) or abrupt changes in any operating characteristic. These failure modes may involve contact resistance, contact sticking, changes in timing or contact sequence, operate or release sensitivity changes, decreased insulation resistance, and voltage breakdown. Causes of failure include the following:

1. *Process Residues.* Some examples are: electroplating residues on dry reed contacts have contributed to early resistance failures; solder flux from circuit pack manufacturing has caused resistance failures in exposed contact relays carrying low-level signals; residues from contaminated cleaning materials have caused resistance failures on exposed contact relays; and oxidized metallic particles from faulty welding electrodes that are used to attach contact surfaces to springs have resulted in contact resistance failures.

2. *Welding.* Many instances of sticking or welding of dry reed contacts have been caused by current inrush due to cable capacitance or other circuit capacitance. "Cold" (currentless) welding may occur if the gold contact surfaces of the reeds are too soft.

3. *Electrical Erosion.* Electrical erosion of the contacts caused by arcing is the classic cause of electrical wearout when switched load voltages and currents exceed about 12 volts and 30 mA, especially if the load is inductive or capacitive, or includes motors or incandescent lamps. Contact protection devices should be connected across such loads. Mercury relay contacts have been used to switch excessive loads. After many operations, the contact surfaces changed such that the mercury bridge would not rupture and the contact would not open.

4. *Mechanical Wear.* Mechanical wear at bearing surfaces, springs, actuating cards, or contacts is another wearout mechanism. Premature wear usually is caused by problems in relay manufacture or by poor design.

5. *Carbonized Organics.* Carbonized organics, or "black powder," can result from insufficient venting of exposed contact relays. Organic films on the contacts are converted by minor arcing ("molten bridge" conditions) into resistive or nonconducting black debris.

6. *Latent Defects from Manufacture*. Springs have failed in service due to overstressing in manufacture. Welds improperly made have later broken. Plastic parts improperly molded have eventually failed. Another recurrent problem has been fatigue and breakage of coil lead wires that had no slack or that were nicked when being stripped.

7. *Leakage of Seals*. Seals have been damaged on mercury relays allowing the mercury to become contaminated and lose its fluid characteristics, or sometimes to leak from the relay. Cracked seals on dry reeds have allowed contaminants to enter. Broken seals lower the breakdown voltage of sealed contacts that were pressurized during manufacture to increase the breakdown voltage.

## Factors Affecting Relay Reliability

The most important factor affecting relay reliability is the proper application of the relay. Even the finest of relays can fail if misapplied. Other factors are the following:

1. *Environment*. Extremes of ambient temperature, humidity, vibration, or shock, and the presence of contaminants like silicones, organic fumes, or atmospheric pollution.

2. *Stress*. Operation under stress caused by operation-dependent conditions, such as coil heating.

3. *Contact Load*. Neither maximum nor minimum load is necessarily the most severe. Tests have shown that intermediate loads can be worst when contaminants are present.

4. *Contact Material Selection*. Standard contact materials are compromises, balancing contact resistance stability, erosion tendencies, sticking, and other factors.

5. *Age*. Age includes both number of operations and duration of environmental exposure.

6. *Circuit Sensitivity*. Circuit sensitivity to changes in resistance, timing, or chatter of contacts, and effects of relay drive conditions on these parameters.

7. *Manufacturing*. Manufacturing process control and cleanliness in both relay manufacture and equipment assembly.

8. *Design*. Design problems such as improper choices of materials or inadequate allowance for stresses.

## Information Sources

The many factors affecting relay reliability are complex. Extensive knowledge of the relay and the application conditions is required to achieve the desired reliability. Quantitative estimates of the effect of these factors on hazard rates are difficult to make because of the difficulty in isolating each effect. Quantitative data on relay field hazard rates also are difficult to obtain.

Relay selection assistance can be found in the *Engineer's Relay Handbook*.[18] See also *Physical Design of Electronic Systems*[19] which describes the physics of electrical contacts. Users of relays are urged to obtain the advice of a relay applications consultant.

## RESISTORS

AT&T now purchases resistors from outside suppliers. Such resistors are subject to a set of engineering end-point requirements written into a specification for the resistor being purchased. The specification does not cover the manufacture of the resistor in detail and, therefore, more than one supplier may furnish the part. A multiple-sourced resistor can be manufactured differently by each supplier and, although each meets the end-point requirements, the reliability of each supplier's product is likely to be different in the same application.

Resistor failures can be characterized into catastrophic and drift. A *catastrophic failure* is an open or shorted resistor that causes the circuit to immediately cease functioning normally. A *drift failure* is a change in resistance value, over a period of time, beyond an acceptable circuit performance level (circuit end-of-life tolerance). Proper selection of a resistor helps minimize both categories of failures and is important to achieving good reliability.

Improper selection of resistors may be difficult to correct if the equipment mechanical design has limited the space allotted for mounting the resistor. More seriously, wrong selections may result in fires. A resistor is a heat dissipating device and many are capable of operating with surface temperatures exceeding 400°C. Careful selection of a resistor can avert fires caused by resistor overheating.

### Carbon Composition

Carbon composition resistors have a history of being the most reliable of all types when correctly applied. However, they also have a record of being one of the most misapplied. Only when *all* of their operating characteristics are accounted for will high reliability be achieved in the application.

Power ratings assume mounting the resistor in free air with adequate heat sinking to remove up to 80 percent of the generated heat out through the leads. Printed circuit board applications are apt to violate both of these criteria. Carbon composition resistors are correctly applied on printed circuit boards by derating to at least 50 percent of their specified power rating. Also, for any application, the effects due to humidity may be minimized by operating the resistors at more than 20 percent of their specified power ratings. Carbon composition resistors are permanently damaged by temperatures above 105°C, either from ambient temperature or ambient temperature plus the resistor's operating temperature rise. New resistors starting their operation at temperatures near the damaging value have been known to catch on fire after 8 years of use.

One manufacturer supplies carbon composition product as a generic thick carbon film type. This type has poorer reliability than the solid slug type. The usual failure mode for the film type is a catastrophic open when the resistor is subjected to a surge condition. For this reason, the film type is not included in the high reliability series of Level III specifications.

## Metal Film

Some metal film resistors are classified as thick or thin film types. The terms do not refer to physical thickness but rather to methods of manufacture. A thick film is painted, screened, or dipped onto a substrate and fired; whereas, a thin film is evaporated or sputtered in a vacuum onto a substrate. Other metal film resistors do not classify as either thick or thin, but are generally referred to and distinguished by their generic styles, for example, tin oxide or bulk metal foil.

Metal film resistors, in particular thin film, are more susceptible to manufacturing imperfections than are carbon composition or wirewound types. They are also more susceptible to damage by power overloads and by fast rise time voltage surges. Nonhomogeneous (imperfect) films develop hot spots that cause permanent increases in resistance. Overloads increase the rate of these changes or cause burnout. Voltage surges that do not allow sufficient time for the resistance structure to act as a heat sink (typically less than 1 millisecond) may instantaneously open even perfect films.

Excluding the bulk metal foil type, the other film resistors may be furnished under the same specification without distinction. Although they meet the end-point requirements, there may be differences in their capabilities for such characteristics as tracking (constancy of resistance ratio of two or more resistors), stability, and reliability. Problems related to these characteristics should be discussed with a resistor specialist.

The jacket of a metal film resistor dissipates more heat than the jacket of a carbon composition resistor. Metal film resistors are correctly applied at 20 to 80 percent of their specified power ratings for normal reliability. Derating to 50 percent may increase the reliability capability. Operation at low power (less than 20 percent of rated power) in a high-humidity environment usually decreases the reliability capability.

## Wirewound

Wirewound resistors have good capability for reliability, comparable to that of carbon composition resistors. They are the most rugged of all resistor types and have high capability for withstanding power overloads. Wirewound resistors can dissipate ten times their rated power for 5 seconds without being harmed. Repetitive applications within 15 minutes reduces this capability. General-use wirewounds, from 2 to 10 watts, are designed to have a surface temperature rise of 275°C at rated power; 50 percent derating lowers this to only about 200°C.

Wirewound resistors are correctly applied at powers up to 100 percent of their power ratings. Due consideration must be given to the physical mounting conditions for proper circuit protection.

Of all resistor types, wirewounds present the greatest hazards to the operation of a circuit. An overload of only two times rated power will bring their temperature to about 450°C. Greater overloads can cause temperatures in excess of 700°C before the resistor ceases operation. It is good engineering practice to mount wirewound resistors so that they are not in contact with printed circuit boards or other components when sustained overloads are possible.

## THIN FILM HYBRID INTEGRATED CIRCUITS

The models and methods described in Chapter 3 are used for predicting the reliability of systems that are composed of packaged devices. The methods also can be extended to predict the reliability of hybrid integrated circuits (HIC). As its name implies, a HIC is made using a hybrid technology that combines standard (but nonpackaged) devices with thin film components on a ceramic substrate.

The HIC technology uses metal conductor paths, glaze crossunders, film capacitors, and film resistors all laid out on the substrate. Devices are then appliqued to the substrate. These devices are typically silicon devices (including silicon chip capacitors) or ceramic chip capacitors. The silicon devices are attached using beam-lead bonding or wire bonding and the ceramic chip capacitors are soldered on. Finally, plug-in pins are attached to the ceramic and the assembly is coated with RTV silicone rubber.

### Hazard Rate Calculation

The approach used to calculate hazard rates of HICs is the same one used to calculate the hazard rate of a series system; that is, the hazard rate of the HIC is the sum of the hazard rates of the individual devices on the HIC (see Chapter 3). The long-term ($t \geq t_c$ hours) hazard rate is given by

$$\lambda_{HIC} = \overset{\substack{\text{All} \\ \text{Substrate} \\ \text{Devices}}}{\underset{i}{\sum}} (\lambda_L)_i + \overset{\substack{\text{All} \\ \text{Appliqued} \\ \text{Devices}}}{\underset{i}{\sum}} (A_T)_i (A_E)_i (\lambda_L)_i \tag{6.2}$$

and the infant mortality ($t < t_c$ hours) hazard rate is given by

$$\lambda_{HIC}(t) = \overset{\substack{\text{All} \\ \text{Substrate} \\ \text{Devices}}}{\underset{i}{\sum}} \left[ (\lambda_L)_i t_c^{\alpha_i} \right] t^{-\alpha_i} + \overset{\substack{\text{All} \\ \text{Appliqued} \\ \text{Devices}}}{\underset{i}{\sum}} \left[ (A_T)^{1-\alpha_i} (\lambda_L)_i t_c^{\alpha_i} \right] t^{-\alpha_i} , \tag{6.3}$$

where it should be recalled that $t_c = 10^4$ hours (see Chapters 1 and 4).

The first term of each equation accounts for the hazard rates of the substrate components. These include film capacitors, film resistors, and glaze crossunders. The hazard rate parameters for these components are listed in Chapter 4.

The second term reflects the contribution of the devices appliqued to the substrate. These include integrated circuit chips, capacitors, diodes, and the attached connector. A standard DIP can consist of a beam-leaded chip bonded to a ceramic substrate with thin-film metal conductor paths on it, all covered with RTV. Since this is virtually identical to the HIC technology, these packaged device hazard rates are assumed to include the hazard rate contributions of the HIC ceramic substrate, metallization, and device pins, since these elements are common to both HICs and DIPs.

A second assumption in this procedure is that the devices have the same hazard rates in HICs as when packaged individually. Engineers at various locations of AT&T have accumulated data that show similar hazard rates for integrated circuit chips when used on HICs as in the standard DIP package. This result is expected because the normal processing of HICs includes careful cleaning of integrated circuit chips prior to RTV encapsulation.

### Effects of Temperature and Electrical Stress

As expressed in Equations (6.2) and (6.3), no stress factors are applied to the hazard rates of the substrate components. Since HICs are custom-designed for each application, the hazard rates for substrate components quoted in Chapter 4 are assumed to be correct at the conditions of temperature and electrical stress for which they are designed.

The effects of temperature and electrical stress on the hazard rates of all appliqued devices are treated in essentially the same way as they are for separately packaged devices, as described in Chapter 2. The one difference is the determination of the "effective ambient temperature." The effect of temperature on a device hazard rate depends on the temperature rise, $\Delta T$, of the chip above the nominal use chip temperature. The nominal use chip temperature is the temperature of an equivalent packaged chip operating at the reference ambient of 40°C. This actual use chip temperature depends on the type of device. A packaged low-power TTL device will have a chip temperature of only about 2°C above ambient, while the chip temperature of a packaged memory device can be 10°C above ambient. The quantity $\Delta T$ is the difference between the chip (or HIC substrate) temperature and the nominal use chip temperature. The effective ambient temperature for any device, therefore, is $(40 + \Delta T)$ °C. The acceleration factor is approximately equal to that for an equivalent packaged device operating in this effective ambient temperature.

## THICK FILM HYBRID INTEGRATED CIRCUITS

Thick film integrated circuits are also built on a ceramic substrate. However, the metallization on the thick film HIC is deposited by a screen printing method rather than vapor deposition of titanium, palladium and gold as is the case of thin film HICs. The conductor materials for thick film are either gold, palladium-silver alloys or palladium-platinum-silver alloys. The thick film HIC also contains passive film components such as film capacitors and film resistors. They also may contain appliqued discrete devices, thermocompression bonded beam-lead devices, and wire-bonded integrated circuits. Finally, the entire substrate is coated with RTV.

Many AT&T manufacturing locations have experienced similar hazard rates with thick film and thin film HICs. Therefore, the formalism of hazard rate calculations for thin film HICs, described in the *Thin Film Hybrid Integrated Circuit* section, can also be used for thick-film passive components such as the film capacitors and resistors listed in Chapter 4.

### REFERENCES

1.  Department of Defense, *Reliability Prediction of Electronic Equipment*, MIL-HDBK-217E, U. S. Goverment Printing Office, Washington, D.C., 1986.

2.   J. P. Clech, W. Engelmaier, R. W. Kotlowitz, J. A. Augis, "Surface Mount Solder Attachment Reliability Figures of Merit - 'Design for Reliability' Tools," *Proceedings of the SMART V (Surface Mount Advanced Related Technologies) Conference*, January 9-12, 1989, New Orleans, Louisiana, technical paper SMT V-48.

3.   J. P. Clech, M. J. Tervalon, J. A. Augis, "Reliability Evaluation of 25 and 50 mil pitch Surface Mounted Plastic Leaded Packages", to be published in the *Proceedings of the International Electronic Packaging Society Conference*, Sept. 11-14, 1989, San Diego, California.

4.   Institute of Electrical and Electronic Engineers, *Terminology for Power and Distribution Transformers* (ANSI/IEEE C57.12.80 - 1978), IEEE, New York, 1978.

5.   Institute of Electrical and Electronic Engineers, *Recommended Practice for Testing Insulation Resistance of Rotating Machinery* (ANSI/IEEE STD 43 - 1978), IEEE, New York, 1978.

6.   Underwriters Laboratories, *UL Safety Standard for Specialty Transformers* (UL 506), UL, Melville, N.Y., 1979.

7.   Underwriters Laboratories, *UL Safety Standard for Power Supplies* (UL 1012), UL, Melville, N.Y., 1979.

8.   Based on accelerated tests performed at AT&T facilities in Allentown, PA, by R. A. Frantz in 1979. In this study, plug-in telephone power supplies were subject to destructive life testing at 150°C and 165°C. At each temperature, about 60 devices were stressed, and operated, to failure. Mean times to failure of 2797 hours and 727 hours, respectively, were observed. The data was analyzed in accordance with IEEE Standard 101, "IEEE Guide for the Statistical Analysis of Thermal Life Test Data." The test results were compared with the results of similar testing for an older power supply system with a history of field service that indicated a service life of 20 years can be expected under typical use conditions. A comparison suggests that the newer (1979) power supplies would have a smaller hazard rate at typical use conditions.

9.   T. C. May and M. H. Woods, "A New Physical Mechanism for Soft Errors in Dynamic Memories," *Proceedings of the International Reliability Physics Symposium*, IEEE, 1978: p. 33.

10.   M. L. White, J. W. Serpiello, R. M. Striny, D. Rosenweig, "The Use of Silicon RTV Rubber for Alpha Particle Protection On Silicon Integrated Circuits," *Proceedings of the International Reliability Physics Symposium*, IEEE, 1981: p. 43.

11.   T. C. May, "Soft Errors in VLSI, Present and Future," *Proceedings of the Electronic Components Conference*, 1979: p. 247.

12.   "General Purpose Memory System from Intel Is Smart," *Electronic Engineering Times*, March 2, 1981: p. 18.

13.   D. C. Bossen and H. Y. Hsiao, "A System Solution to the Memory Soft Error Problem," *IBM Journal of Research and Development* **24** (1980): p. 390.

14. S. Vaidya, D. B. Fraser, A. K. Sinha, "Electromigration Resistance of Fine-Line Al for VLSI Applications," *Proceedings of the International Reliability Physics Symposium,* IEEE, 1980: p. 165.

15. S. M. Sze, "Physics of Semiconductor Devices," 2nd ed., Wiley, New York, 1981.

16. R. C. Sun, J. T. Clemens, J. T. Nelson, "Effects of Silicon Nitride Encapsulation on MOS Device Stability," *Proceedings of the International Reliability Physics Symposium* , IEEE, 1980: p. 244.

17. M. J. LuValle and J. P. Mitchell, "The Design and Interpretation of Accelerated Life Tests for Printed Circuit Products," *Proceedings of the International Electronic Packaging Conference,* IEEE, 1987: p. 444; M. J. LuValle, T. L. Welsher, J. P. Mitchell, "A New Approach to the Extrapolation of Accelerated Life Test Data," *Proceedings of the Fifth International Conference on Reliability and Maintainability,* European Space Agency, 1986: p. 630, and reference contained therein.

18. *Engineers Relay Handbook*, 3rd ed., National Association of Relay Manufacturers, Elkhart, IN., 1980.

19. H. N. Wagar, in *Physical Design of Electronic Systems*, Bell Telephone Laboratories, Prentice Hall, Englewood Cliffs, 1972.

# APPENDIX A

The probability of failure, at use conditions, occurring at times before or equal to time $t$ is given by the cumulative distribution function, $F_u(t)$. Equation (2.1) allows us to state that this failure probability is equal to the cumulative distribution function at accelerating stress conditions, but now at time $\dfrac{t}{A}$, that is

$$F_u(t) = F_s(t/A) \; , \tag{A.1}$$

where the subscript $S$ denotes accelerating stress conditions. A similar relation involving the probability of failure density function, $f(t)$, follows from Equation (A.1). We rearrange and differentiate:

$$f_u(t) \equiv \frac{d}{dt} F_u(t) = \frac{d}{dt} F_s(t/A) = \frac{(1/A)}{(1/A)} \frac{d}{dt} F_s(t/A) = \frac{1}{A} \frac{d}{d(t/A)} F_s(t/A)$$

$$= \frac{1}{A} f_s(t/A) \quad . \tag{A.2}$$

Given equation (A.1), a similar relationship must hold for the survivor (or reliability) function, that is,

$$S_u(t) = S_s(t/A) \quad . \tag{A.3}$$

Now recall the definition of the hazard rate,

$$\lambda(t) = \frac{f(t)}{S(t)} \quad , \tag{A.4}$$

and use equations (A.2) and (A.3) to write

$$\lambda_u(t) = \frac{1}{A} \lambda_s(t/A) \quad , \tag{A.5}$$

which is Equation (2.2). Recall that as mentioned in Chapter 2, Equation (A.5) holds for any distribution, and for any sets of conditions for which the basic assumption, embodied in Equation (2.1), holds.

# APPENDIX B

Consider a simple reaction that leads to or causes failure. For example,

$$A + B \rightarrow C \qquad \qquad (B.1)$$

where the disappearance of $A$ leads to failure. For convenience, failure is defined to have occurred when the concentration of $A$ drops to some threshold concentration, below which failure occurs. So the failure time is defined to be that time at which

$$[A] = [A_f] \ , \qquad \qquad (B.2)$$

where $[A]$ is the concentration of $A$, and $[A_f]$ is that concentration of $A$ associated with failure. The simplest differential rate expression that may describe an elementary reaction such as Equation (B.1) is the first order equation,[1]

$$\frac{d[A]}{dt} = -k\,[A] \ , \qquad \qquad (B.3)$$

where $k$ is the rate constant of the reaction. The rate constant is independent of time.

Integrating Equation (B.3) yields

$$[A] = [A_0]e^{-kt} \ , \qquad \qquad (B.4)$$

where $[A_0]$ is the initial concentration of $A$. Now set the right-hand side equal to that expression for the concentration of $A$ that defines the failure time,

Equation (B.2).

$$[A_f] = [A_0]e^{-kt_f} \; .$$

(B.5)

Solving for the failure time yields,

$$t_f = \frac{1}{k} \ln\left\{\frac{[A_0]}{[A_f]}\right\} \; .$$

(B.6)

In this simple case we have shown the failure time to be inversely proportional to the rate constant of the reaction that leads to failure.

We can go on to consider more complex reaction mechanisms, for example, a more general form for a single elementary reaction,

$$\frac{d[A]}{dt} = -k\, g([A]) \; ,$$

(B.7)

where $g([A])$ is some function of the concentration of $A$. If $1/g([A])$ is integrable, we find the concentration of $A$ to be described implicitly by

$$G([A]) - G([A_0]) = -t\,k$$

(B.8)

where $G([A])$ is the integral of $1/g([A])$. The failure time is then given by

$$t_f = \frac{1}{k}\left\{G([A_0]) - G([A_f])\right\} \; .$$

(B.9)

Again, the failure time is inversely proportional to the rate constant of the reaction that leads to failure, that is,

$$t_f = \frac{D}{k} \; ,$$

(B.10)

where $D$ is constant. These two examples have two important points in common, aside from the integrability of the differential equation governing the concentration of $A$. In both cases a single reaction dominates the approach to and onset of failure. And in both cases, there is *no explicit time dependence* in the differential equation; that is, the rate equation is *autonomous* in time.

Clearly for more complicated reaction mechanisms, Equation (B.7) and, therefore, Equation (B.9) need not hold. On the other hand, if one reaction dominates the others (that is, if one reaction is slower than all other reactions in a sequential reaction, or faster in a parallel reaction mechanism), then it is the *rate determining step*, and a differential form such as Equation (B.7) may be a reasonable approximation. For example, consider the reaction

$$A \rightarrow B \rightarrow C \ ,$$

(B.11)

where the failure time may be defined in terms of the concentration of C.* We consider first order kinetic processes for both reactions in Equation (B.11). We also take the initial concentration of $B$ and $C$ to be zero, that is, $[B_0] = [C_0] = 0$. In this case, the expression that determines the failure time is a transcendental equation involving the rate constant characterizing $A \rightarrow B$, $k_1$, and the rate constant characterizing $B \rightarrow C$, $k_2$. But if

$$k_1 \gg k_2 \ ,$$

(B.12)

then the transcendental equation for the failure time simplifies and the failure time is then given by

$$t_f = \frac{1}{k_2} \ln \left\{ \frac{[A_0]}{[A_0] - [C_f]} \right\} \ .$$

(B.13)

Again, we have the inverse relationship between the rate constant and the failure time. If no reaction is *rate determining* over the entire environmental regime under consideration,[1] then more sophisticated approaches[2] may be needed.

We should also point out the generality of the structure of equations such as (B.3) or (B.7). Specifically, the time should not appear explicitly in equations such as (B.3) or (B.7), etc. If the time were to appear explicitly, this equation would not be autonomous in the time variable. Then such an equation would be describing a process that would change depending on when the process begins, rather than on just the constituents and the physical laws governing their interaction. This would be contrary to our intuition that if this rate expression describes a particular reaction, not a mixture of reactions, then *when* the reaction begins should not affect the dynamics; that is, we expect the rate equation, like the classical dynamical equations, to be autonomous and, hence, have solutions that are homogeneous in time.[3]

## REFERENCES

1.  R. E. Weston and H. A. Schwarz, *Chemical Kinetics*, Prentice Hall, Englewood Cliffs, 1972.

---

\*   For example, $t_f$ is that time at which $[C]$ exceeds $[C_f]$.

2. M. J. LuValle, T. L. Welsher, J. P. Mitchell, "A New Approach to the Extrapolation of Accelerated Life Test Data," in *Proceedings of the Fifth International Conference on Reliability and Maintainability,* European Space Agency, 1986. See also: M. J. LuValle, T. L. Welsher, S. W. Swoboda, "Acceleration Transforms and Statistical Kinetic Models," *J. Stat. Phys.* **52** (1988): p. 311 and references contained therein.

3. V. I. Arnold, *Mathematical Methods of Classical Mechanics,* Springer Verlag, Berlin, 1978.

# APPENDIX C

Given

$$t_u = A \ t_s \ , \tag{C.1}$$

where $t_u$ is the failure time at use conditions, $t_s$ is the failure time at accelerating stress conditions, and $A$ is the acceleration factor, then, as shown in Appendix A,

$$\lambda_u(t) = \frac{1}{A} \ \lambda_s(t/A) \ , \tag{C.2}$$

where $\lambda_u(t)$ is the hazard rate at use conditions, and $\lambda_s(t)$ is the hazard rate under the more stressful conditions.

Until now, no mention has been made of the type of accelerating stress, the form of the acceleration factor, or of any particular distribution of failure times. This expression is completely general, given the assumption that the failure times at two different sets of conditions are strictly proportional to each other.

If $\lambda(t)$ is Weibull, that is,

$$\lambda(t) = \lambda_1 \ t^{-\alpha} \ , \tag{C.3}$$

where $\lambda_1$ is the hazard rate at 1 hour, and $\alpha$ is the Weibull shape parameter, then

$$\lambda_s(t/A) = \lambda_1(t/A)^{-\alpha} = A\lambda_u(t) \ . \tag{C.4}$$

So that the hazard rate for the accelerated (more stressful) condition at time $t$ is equal to $A$ times the hazard rate at use conditions at time $t'$, that is

$$\lambda_s(t) = A\lambda_u(t') \ , \tag{C.5}$$

where

$$t' = At. \tag{C.6}$$

Since

$$\lambda_u(t') = \lambda_1(t')^{-\alpha}, \tag{C.7}$$

using Equation (C.6) to substitute for $t'$, we write

$$\lambda_s(t) = A\lambda_1(At)^{-\alpha} = A^{1-\alpha}\lambda_1 t^{-\alpha}, \tag{C.8}$$

or

$$\lambda_s(t) = A^{1-\alpha}\lambda_u(t). \tag{C.9}$$

which is the desired expression for relating a Weibull hazard rate at use conditions to a Weibull hazard rate at more stressful conditions.

# APPENDIX D

The Cumulative Distribution Function (CDF), $F(t)$, represents the probability that the failure time, $X$, is less than or equal to time, $t$. It is related to the hazard rate, $\lambda(t)$, by

$$\text{Prob } (X \leq t) = F(t) = 1 - e^{-\int_0^t \lambda(t')dt'} = 1 - e^{-H(t)} \ , \tag{D.1}$$

which defines $H(t)$. We now expand Equation (D.1)

$$\text{Prob } (X \leq t) = 1 - [1 - H(t) + \tfrac{1}{2}H^2(t) - \tfrac{1}{6}H^3(t) + \cdots ] \ ,$$

$$= H(t) - \tfrac{1}{2}H^2(t) + \cdots \ ,$$

$$= H(t)[1 - \tfrac{1}{2}H(t) + \cdots ] \ , \tag{D.2}$$

so that when

$$\tfrac{1}{2}H(t) \ll 1 \ , \tag{D.3}$$

we may approximate the CDF by

$$F(t) = H(t) = \int_0^t \lambda(t')dt' \ . \tag{D.4}$$

# APPENDIX E

The instantaneous availability of a maintained (repairable) system is given by

$$A(t) = S(t) + \int_0^t v_r(t')S(t - t')\,dt' \quad , \tag{E.1}$$

where $S(t)$ is the survivor function, and $v_r$ is the *repair* rate: See Chapters 1 and 3 for definitions and discussion of these terms. The survivor function, $S(t)$, the probability of survival up to time $t$, is equal to $1 - F(t)$.

As discussed in the text, the right-hand side of Equation (E.1) is the sum of probabilities that[1]

- the system survives to time $t$, and

- there is a repair in the interval $(t', t' + dt')$, for some $t' < t$, and that the new part introduced by the repair survives to time $t$.

This equation may be solved for certain cases by using the Laplace Transform. The Laplace Transform of a function $f(u)$ is defined to be[2]

$$L[f(u)] = f^*(s) = \int_0^\infty e^{-su} f(u)\,du \quad . \tag{E.2}$$

The Laplace Transform of Equation (E.1) is then given by

$$A^*(s) = S^*(s) + S^*(s)v_r^*(s) \quad , \tag{E.3}$$

where we used the convolution theorem.[2]

Using the definition of $S(t)$,

$$S^*(t) = [1+F(t)]^* = [1 - f^*(s)]/s \quad , \tag{E.4}$$

where we have used the relation, $L[1] = 1/s$, and noted that if $F(t) = \int f(t)dt$, then $F^* = \dfrac{1}{s} f^*$. Now Equation (E.3) may be rewritten

$$A^* = (1+v_r^*)(1 - f^*)/s \quad , \tag{E.5}$$

where we have dropped writing the dependence on $s$ explicitly, and will continue to do so, unless we need to for clarity or emphasis. We will now develop a relation for an ordinary renewal process.[1] For the moment we are no longer considering an *alternating* renewal process. Now recall that the renewal density (or repair rate, see Chapter 1) is given by

$$v_r = \frac{\partial N_{\bar{r}}}{\partial t} = \sum_{n=1}^{\infty} k_n \quad , \tag{E.6}$$

where the $k_n = \dfrac{\partial K_n}{\partial t}$ is defined to be the probability distribution function of the renewal (repair) times, $X_1 + X_2 + ... + X_n$, that is,

$$k_n(t) = \int_{-\infty}^{+\infty} ... \int g(u_1) g(u_2 - u_1)...g_n(t - u_{n-1})du_1 \, du_2 \, ...du_{n-1} \quad . \tag{E.7}$$

From Equation (E.7), we obtain, after taking Laplace transforms and using the convolution theorem,

$$k_n^*(s) = [g^*(s)]^n \quad , \tag{E.8}$$

which may be inserted in Equation (E.6)

$$v_r^* = \sum_{n=1}^{\infty} [g^*]^n = \frac{g^*}{1 - g^*} \quad . \tag{E.9}$$

Now we no longer consider the failure time to be negligible and reconsider the alternating renewal process. The probability distribution function for $X_i + Y_i$ is given by the convolution of $f$ and $g$, and the Laplace transform of this probability distribution function is given by $f^* g^*$. The repair rate at time $t$ is then given by Equation (E.9), but with $g^*$ replaced by $f^* g^*$, that is,

$$v_r^* = \frac{f^* g^*}{1 - f^* g^*} \quad , \tag{E.10}$$

so that the Laplace transform of the availability is given by

$$A^*(s) = \frac{1}{s}\left[1 + \frac{f^*(s)g^*(s)}{1 - f^*(s)g^*(s)}\right](1 - f^*(s)) \quad , \tag{E.11}$$

or

$$A^*(s) = \frac{1}{s}\frac{[1 - f^*(s)]}{[1 - f^*(s)g^*(s)]} \quad . \tag{E.12}$$

This expression is general for an alternating process representing failure and repairs. This is the Laplace transform to invert once the failure and repair processes are specified. If the failure and repair processes are exponential, then

$$f(t) = \lambda e^{-\lambda t} \qquad g(t) = \mu e^{-\mu t} \quad , \tag{E.13}$$

and so

$$f^*(s) = \frac{\lambda}{\lambda + s} \qquad g^*(s) = \frac{\mu}{\mu + s} \quad , \tag{E.14}$$

which may be inserted into Equation (E.12) to write

$$A^*(s) = \frac{1}{s}\frac{(1 - \dfrac{\lambda}{\lambda + s})}{(1 - \dfrac{\lambda}{\lambda + s}\dfrac{\mu}{\mu + s})} = \frac{s + \mu}{s(s + \mu + \lambda)} \quad . \tag{E.15}$$

Now we do a partial fraction expansion of the right hand side of Equation (E.15) to write

$$A^*(s) = \frac{\mu}{\mu+\lambda}\frac{1}{s} + \frac{\lambda}{\mu+\lambda}\frac{1}{s+\mu+\lambda} \quad , \qquad (E.16)$$

which is readily inverted.

$$A(t) = \frac{\mu}{\mu+\lambda} + \frac{\lambda}{\mu+\lambda}e^{-(\mu+\lambda)t} \quad , \qquad (E.17)$$

which is the well-known formula[3] for instantaneous availability for exponential failure and repair processes. Note that Equation (E.17) is the origin of the well-known formula for the steady-state (or the long-term) availability, namely

$$A = \lim_{t\to\infty}A(t) = \frac{\mu}{\mu+\lambda} \quad . \qquad (E.18)$$

## REFERENCES

1.  D. R. Cox, *Renewal Theory*, Methuen, London, 1962.
2.  C. M. Bender and S. A. Orszag, *Advanced Mathematical Methods for Scientists and Engineers*, McGraw-Hill, New York, 1978.
3.  P. D. T. O'Connor, *Practical Reliability Engineering*, 2nd ed., Wiley, New York, 1985.

# GLOSSARY

This glossary is provided to define some of the terms and acronyms used in the manual. It is important to note that some of the terms may have somewhat different meanings in other fields or in common everyday use.

## Acronyms

| | |
|---|---|
| ASIC | application specific integrated circuit |
| CAF | conductive anodic filaments |
| CCD | charge coupled device |
| CMOS | complementary metal oxide semiconductor |
| CO | central office |
| DIP | dual in-line package |
| DRAM | dynamic random access memory |
| ECC | error correction code |
| EDAC | error detection and correction |
| EEPROM | electrically erasable programmable read only memory |
| EOL | end of life |
| EOS | electrical overstress |
| EPROM | electrically programmable read only memory |
| ESD | electrostatic discharge |
| ESS | electronic switching system |

| FIT  | failure in time, a unit for hazard rate |
|------|------------------------------------------|
| FMA  | failure mode analysis |
| HIC  | hybrid integrated circuit |
| IC   | integrated circuit |
| IM   | infant mortality |
| LED  | light emitting diode |
| MOS  | metal oxide semiconductor |
| MOT  | mean operating time |
| MRT  | mean repair time |
| MTBF | mean time between failure |
| MTTF | mean time to failure |
| MTTR | mean time to repair |
| NMOS | n-type MOS |
| NTU  | notification to use |
| OLT  | operational life test |
| PBX  | private branch exchange |
| PDA  | percent defective allowed |
| PMOS | p-type MOS |
| PTH  | plated through holes |
| PWB  | printed wiring board |
| RAM  | random access memory |
| RH   | relative humidity |
| ROM  | read only memory |
| RTV  | room temperature volcanizing (rubber) |
| SAW  | surface acoustic wave |
| SCR  | semiconductor controlled rectifier |
| SMT  | surface mount technology |
| QA   | quality assurance |
| QC   | quality control |
| VLSI | very large scale of integration |

# Terms

active component
: A discrete component whose operation involves the activity of a semiconductor junction.

availability
: The probability that a system is in an operable state when called upon to perform.

burn-in
: The operation of a device (often under accelerated conditions of temperature, voltage, or load) to stabilize its characteristics; it is typically used as a method to screen devices.

circuit pack
: An assembled printed circuit board with components; in telecommunications systems, this typically refers to a board that may be installed easily, by plugging it into a frame (or backplane).

component
: Any electrical part (integrated circuit, diode, resistor, etc.) with distinct electrical characteristics, and with means (for example, terminals or leads) of connecting it to other components to form a circuit. This term is used interchangeably with "device."

device
: Any electrical part (integrated circuit, diode, resistor, etc.) with distinct electrical characteristics, and with means (for example, terminals or leads) of connecting it to other components to form a circuit. This term is used interchangeably with "component."

device code
: The equipment supplier's or vendor's part number for a particular device.

device family
: A group of devices made by the same manufacturer, fabricated using the same basic process flow, having similar complexity and packaging.

discrete semiconductor
: A packaged, electronic component consisting of a single active element (for example, a resistor, transistor or diode).

electronic component
: A component which is able to amplify or control voltages or currents without mechanical or other non-electrical commands, or which is able to switch currents or voltages without mechanical switches (for example, integrated circuits, transistors, and other solid-state devices).

extrinsic failure

This is a failure caused by some external event. Such failures are often referred to as random or chance events. Examples include lighting strikes and accidental mishandling in field use.

failure analysis

The examination of a failed device to determine its failure mode, the failure mechanism, and the cause.

failure mechanism

The detailed physical or chemical processes that produces failure. An example of a failure mechanism is the migration of nonradiative defects into the active region of a laser caused by recombination-assisted diffusion.

failure mode

The observed consequences (manifestation) of the failure mechanism. An example of a failure mode is an open in the metalization line of an integrated circuit.

failure mode analysis

A process used to diagnose an unexpected failure in order to determine the failure mechanism and suggest corrective action.

failure rate

In this manual, the failure rate is the time derivative of the cumulative expected number of failures for a particular system; it is a measure of maintained system reliability. Often it is used interchangebly with hazard rate; this has been a source of much confusion in the reliability literature for some time.

hazard rate

The conditional (upon survival) probability (of failure) function. Electronic device reliability is usually described in terms of a particular hazard rate model, and particular parameter values, given that model.

hermetic

Airtight.

incoming inspection

The inspections and tests performed on a lot to ensure that it meets purchase specifications.

integrated circuit

A packaged device consisting of a single (monolithic) substrate, on which an interconnected array of active and passive elements are integrated, capable of performing at least one electronic function.

intrinsic failure

This is a failure due to some defect in material, design or manufacturing process, or a wearout of material used, in a device or system. Intrinsic failures are preordained; this should be contrasted with extrinsic, random failures.

life test
: A test designed to estimate a device's life time, hazard rate, and failure mechanism(s).

lot
: A group of devices, made by the same manufacturer, with the same device code and packaging; a lot is usually received as a single shipment.

lot acceptance test
: The inspections and tests performed by the supplier on a lot to ensure that it meets purchase specifications and any additional criteria for use; such tests are part of the lot-to-lot controls.

mean operating time
: The average time that a system is operating, or up. This quantity is generally a function of time.

mean repair time
: The average time that is taken to repair a system, or the average time that a system is down. This quantity is generally a function of time.

mean time between failure
: The mean cycle (one failure and one one repair) time of a maintained system. This quantity is generally a function of time.

mean time to failure
: The average time that a system functions before first failure. It is also referred to as the mean time to first failure. For nonmaintained systems, it is the average survival time.

mean time to repair
: Another term for the mean repair time.

non-hermetic
: Not airtight (for example, a plastic-encapsulated integrated circuit).

passive component
: A component that is not "active" in its function (for example, a resistor, capacitor, or inductor). That is, there is no semiconductor junction active in the device.

qualification
: The entire process by which a device is examined and tested, before its use in a product, to assess its ability to meet quality and reliability requirements.

reliability
: The ability of a component to operate under stated conditions for a stated period of time.

reliability monitor
: A test (or set of tests) used to monitor component reliability over time; as compared to a reliability audit, it is typically performed at specified time intervals rather than on a lot-by-lot basis for every device code.

screening
: The process of inspecting and/or testing devices to remove those that are unsatisfactory or that are

likely to exhibit early failure; it is used in lot-to-lot control to reduce the variations in certain characteristics (possibly including reliability) between lots.

service life
The time an electronic component or system is expected to perform in actual field use.

system
A combination of complete assemblies, components, parts, and accessories connected to perform a specific operational function.

wearout failure
In contrast to the ordinary usage, where wearout refers to the using up of some quality or material, wearout in reliability refers to an ever increasing hazard rate, either toward the end of *service life* (the usage in this manual), or strictly speaking, for all time as time tends to infinity.

# INDEX

## J

## L

## M